PAPA COKE

Sixty-five Years Selling Coca-Cola

By SANDERS ROWLAND
with BOB TERRELL

Bright Mountain Books
Asheville, North Carolina

Printed in the United States of America

Library of Congress Cataloging-in-Publication Data

Rowland, Sanders, 1906–
    Papa Coke: sixty-five years selling Coca-Cola.

    1. Rowland, Sanders, 1906– . 2. Sales personnel—
United States—Biography. 3. Coca-Cola Company.
I. Terrell, Bob.   II. Title.
HF5439.32.R69A36   1986   338.7'66362'0924 [B]   86-9526
ISBN 0-914875-14-0

TO MIMI
with whom I have shared the ultimate adventure

BOOKS BY BOB TERRELL

J. D. Sumner—Gospel Music Is My Life

Fun Is Where You Find It!

Holy Land: A Journey Into Time

A Touch of Terrell

Billy Graham in Hungary

Grandpa's Town

Woody (with Barbara Shelton)

Old Gold

The Peace That Passeth Understanding
  (with Connie Hopper)

Disorder in the Court! (with Marcellus Buchanan)

Billy Graham in the Soviet Union

Keep 'em Laughing

Contents

'I had the good fortune of working under men who taught me sound business practices; but more than that, they taught me fairness.'

CHAPTER 1

'They Sweat a Lot!'

SELLING COCA-COLAS IN BOSTON in 1929 was not the job I would have chosen if I had not wanted to work for a living. It was not an easy job. First, I was a Southerner with the slowest Southern drawl ya'll ever heard. The depression was deepening toward Black Tuesday, and money was scarce. Coca-Cola was still not the easiest product to sell in virgin territory because a lot of people thought it contained cocaine. That's why Coca-Colas were called "dopes."

I was taken to Boston by William (Pig-Iron Bill) Brownlee, vice president in charge of Coca-Cola's company-owned plants in New England. My job was to find new customers for Coca-Cola and to boost the sale of Coca-Cola coolers in Boston.

I had specified routes that I worked. I called on my customers once a week. My books showed several hundred customers, and my daily sales were six or eight cases.

My routes took me out toward the edge of the Boston territory. It bordered one of the routes of the Lowell, Massachusetts, franchise. I knew those routes were vigorously protected by the franchise agreement, and I stayed out of the other fellow's territory. I expected him to stay out of mine.

Between the territories in this area was a strip of land like a No-Man's Land. There were too few prospective places in it to make it worthwhile.

One day I came to the point where I thought my route ended. It was about midday, and I hadn't sold a thing. From the edge of my territory I could see down the road a one-pump gas station with two bays and a little office on one side. It was just a square building on an unlevel lot, one story in front, two stories in back.

7

I drove to the station and climbed down from the truck to talk to the proprietor. Selling him wasn't on my mind as much as finding out exactly where I was to determine that I was still in my own territory and not in Lowell's.

The owner came out of the station, and looking at my truck, he said to me, "I see you brought my machine."

To this day, I don't know exactly what he meant by that, but I was not one to look a gift horse in the mouth—not with coolers selling as slowly as they were in Boston.

"Yes, sir," I said, "right there she is," and I pointed to the cooler on my truck.

"Fine," he said, "bring it in."

As I unloaded it, I hoped he hadn't ordered a cooler from anyone else. He seemed to be sure the cooler was destined for him.

I got the cooler off the truck and said, "It will sell more if we put it outside."

"I want it inside," he said very amicably; so I put it inside.

I asked where the nearest ice house was and went for ice.

When I got back and began to unload a few cases of Coca-Colas, he said, "I'll take twenty-five cases."

I'm sure surprise was written all over my face when I looked at him to make sure he wasn't joking. There was nothing for what seemed to be miles. The nearest business was a long distance away, and I had to look hard to find the nearest house.

I had never sold that many cases before. Six or eight were the most anyone ever bought.

I filled the cooler, chipped in the ice, and stacked the remaining cases where he showed me.

I handed him a bill for $32.50 for the drinks and $15 for the cooler. He fished a roll of bills out of his pocket and counted off ninety-five dollars.

"I believe that's right," he said. "I've got another place on Post Road in Waltham—number ten-twenty Post Road. Take another machine up there and twenty-five cases. I'm paying you for both right now."

I must have gulped. I only had twenty-five cases left on the truck, and I carried only one cooler. "May I use your telephone?" I asked, and he showed me to it.

I called the office and got Clarence Herr, my boss, on the line. He was general manager of the Boston Coca-Cola Company. "I'm out of Coca-Cola," I blurted, "and I need some more."

"What?" His surprise was genuine. This was an unusual request from any of his salesmen.

"I've got a new customer for twenty-five cases and a cooler," I said, "and he wants another twenty-five cases and another cooler delivered to his place on Post Road. He wants it delivered today. Now!"

"Don't come in," Herr said. "I'll meet you out there with the cooler and the Coca-Colas."

I drove to the meeting place and soon Herr drove up in a truck loaded with a cooler and forty cases. We found the station and unloaded and set up. I looked around when we had finished and saw a few houses, some other businesses, and a lot of activity in the neighborhood.

"There's some business around here," I said, "but there was nothing near that first place. That fellow won't sell twenty-five cases in twenty-five weeks."

"Why did you sell him so many?" Herr asked. Overselling was bad business, and we knew it. We were trained not to oversell.

"I tried to sell him five cases to get started," I said, "but he insisted on twenty-five. I'm gonna have to pick up some full cases when I go back there next week."

However, when I worked that route the next week, that isolated gas station had twenty-two cases of empties stacked beside the cooler. I couldn't believe it! But the man told me to replace them, and I sold him twenty-two more cases.

At his place on Post Road in Waltham, I found twenty empty cases and replaced them.

The following week, I put twenty-one cases in each of the stations. I worried about that man. I didn't know how he was selling so much. There was no obvious traffic, at least not at that first station. I never saw a car parked there.

Those sales made me the top salesman in the Boston plant, and everybody suddenly wanted those distant routes; but since I had developed the business, Herr told me to keep it.

After a few weeks, I got to know the owner of those stations better. His name was Marshall. He was still buying as many Coca-Colas as he bought that first trip.

When my curiosity overcame my better judgment, I asked him one day, "Mr. Marshall, will you tell me how you're selling so many Coca-Colas? There isn't that much business around here?"

A twinkle appeared in his eye. "Sometimes there is," he said.

I looked at the wide open spaces around his station. "Mr. Marshall, twenty cases is four hundred and eighty bottles. You couldn't get that many customers in a week."

He gauged me accurately. "I'm going to level with you, Coca-Cola," he said. He called me Coca-Cola. "I'm not selling them; I'm giving them away."

"You're giving them away!"

"Tell you what. Give me your word you won't tell what I'm going to show you, and I'll show you how I use Coca-Colas."

"I promise," I said. "I sure would like to know."

He led me into one of the bays and opened a trapdoor in the floor. He went down a flight of steps. He closed the trapdoor above us and switched on the lights. In that underground room was the most complete gambling layout I had ever seen. Chuck-aluck, black jack tables, roulette wheels, crap tables, poker tables.

"I get a lot of people here," he said.

I couldn't say a word.

"They sweat a lot," he said.

I still couldn't find my tongue.

"So I give 'em Coca-Cola."

CHAPTER 2

Toughest Sale

THAT BOSTON JOB was offered to me because of a sale I made in Memphis, Tennessee, in 1928. Not that Boston was a better territory than Memphis; it wasn't. But good salesmen were needed in territories where Coca-Cola had not secured a major foothold, and in New England Coca-Cola was far from being a household word.

Some in the Coca-Cola Company seemed to think the sale I made in Memphis branded me as an outstanding protege of salesmanship. I don't know, but I do know how hard I worked to get it.

By many standards I was still a kid, fresh out of Georgia Tech, trying to catch the world by the tail, but older and wiser I thought, than most who were twenty-two. I had been a child laborer on the payroll of the Coca-Cola Company since the age of thirteen.

There I was in Memphis, assigned to the Fountain Department of the Coca-Cola Company, trained primarily to be a repair and service man, but knowing deep down that the way to get ahead in the Coca-Cola Company and in the world was to sell. I was determined to be the best salesman who ever came out of Atlanta.

I had come to Memphis to replace a fellow named Roosevelt Day, Coca-Cola's fountain department representative for that area of Tennessee including Nashville and all towns west. For a week, Roosevelt Day drove me around Memphis, introduced me to all of his customers, and familiarized me with the territory.

Almost every day we passed a huge drive-in on Union Street.

Fortune's it was called, and Fortune's made such good ice cream that it sold for fifteen cents when everybody else's went for a dime.

Near the end of the week, when we passed Fortune's, I asked Roosevelt, "Why don't we go in? You've introduced me to customers for a week, and we've passed the biggest customer of all every day."

"Oh, no," he said. "I'm not going to take you in there to meet that son of a bitch. His name is Bill Winters, and he won't talk to Coca-Cola people."

"Why won't he?"

"He's a terrible fellow," Roosevelt said. "He'll insult you and call you names. He's better left alone."

I thought about Bill Winters for several days and couldn't understand why we should not try to sell him. At that time we were pushing Coca-Cola glasses, those beautiful cone-shaped glasses that are still Coca-Cola's trademark.

They were excellently made by Libby's. We were trained to sell them by demonstration. We would show them to a customer and drop one on the floor in such a way that it wouldn't break. We were trained exactly how to drop the glasses to prevent breakage, and I never broke one. I sold a lot of them, too.

I had a little black demonstration box that contained a cutaway glass, showing its no-nick, no-chip rim, and showing how thick the glass was. I kept my box with me at all times and used it to demonstrate when the opportunity arose.

The first opportunity I had to visit Fortune's was an afternoon a few days after Roosevelt Day left town. I asked the soda fountain boy when Mr. Winters would be in and he said, "Oh, he's downstairs making chocolate syrup."

I said, "Can I go down and see him?" and he replied, "Go on down."

Bill Winters had an apron on and was stirring chocolate in a large vat. Nothing at Fortune's was small. The drive-in was so large that Winters employed sixty car boys to wait on cars at the curb, and they stayed busy.

I spoke right up. "Mister Winters?"

He kept on stirring. "Yes?"

"I'm Sanders Rowland, the new Coca-Cola man. . . ."

That's as far as I got. Winters stopped stirring and froze me with a stare. "I see," he said, "that you brought your little black box and you want to sell me some glasses."

Before I could answer, he snapped, "Well, I don't want any glasses, and I'm busy, and you can get the hell out of here!"

I left. Roosevelt Day had been right. Bill Winters was like a bear-dog, gruff, unrelenting. He had driven off every salesman who had made an attempt to sell him, and I was the latest.

But I had determination. It would be a feather in my cap if I sold him.

Winters sold Coca-Cola. He was no fool—not with a business that big. He was the biggest customer of Coca-Cola in Memphis, but he resisted all efforts to sell him Coca-Cola glasses.

But in that basement I had seen the guts of his operation. Those sixty car boys would take the trays off cars, slide them down a chute to the dishwashing area, and in the process break a lot of glasses. What a customer Fortune's would be if I could only sell Bill Winters!

I became more determined than ever. I began to consider all the angles I knew. I plotted all day and into the nights. I didn't have much else to do in the evenings. I had a two-dollar room in the Tennessee Hotel across the street from the Peabody Hotel. The Peabody was the finest hotel in Memphis. It had ducks in the lobby. I couldn't afford the Peabody. So I was like a lot of others who couldn't; I would eat at my hotel and go over to the Peabody to pick my teeth.

Late in the evening, I made a habit of going to Fortune's and spending some time. I would speak to the cashier, who was Bill Winters's wife, then I would speak to the sodajerk and have a Coca-Cola.

Fortune's closed at eleven o'clock. I would get there about a quarter to eleven and would be there when the place closed. Winters always came from his office to get his wife, and they went home in a taxi.

Each evening I sat on a stool; and when he passed, I said, "Evening, Mr. Winters," and he wouldn't even look my way. He paid no attention to me but walked right on by.

After a week of this, he stopped when I spoke one evening and said, "You're the Coca-Cola man, aren't you?"

I said, "Yes, sir," and he walked on.

Soon after that I went to Nashville for two weeks. My work

alternated, two weeks in Memphis, two in Nashville. When I came back to Memphis, I went to Fortune's that first evening and every succeeding evening. I made it a habit to leave when he did, and I said, "Good night, Mr. Winters," and he didn't say a word to me.

When I returned from my next two weeks in Nashville, I had to go out and work the western end of the state, Union City, Dyersburg, and some other towns. The Coca-Cola bottler in Dyersburg was Dick Grogan, a bachelor who made his own whiskey—this was Prohibition, remember. He lived in an apartment upstairs at the bottling plant and had a little still in which he made the whiskey.

He insisted that I spend the night with him; and he offered me a drink, but I politely refused.

When I returned to Memphis, I spent two more weeks sitting on that stool at Fortune's. Near the end of that period on a stormy night, I overheard Mrs. Winters say their taxi had been delayed because of an automobile accident.

I walked to her and said, "Mrs. Winters, I'm Sanders Rowland, the Coca-Cola man. I have a car here and since your taxi has been delayed, I'll be happy to drive you and Mr. Winters home."

Winters heard my offer. He said, "Like hell you will. We don't have anything to do with Coca-Cola people." I never found out what his problem was with Coca-Cola people.

"Bill," his wife spoke up, "this young man has offered to drive us home. It's raining, I'm tired, and they don't know when they can get a taxi to us. I want to go home."

He relented. "All right," he said. She was pleasant enough, but Winters didn't say a word on the way home. She thanked me for the ride, and they got out and went in the house.

The next night at the drive-in, she thanked me for taking them home; and I said, "When I'm in town I'm out here every night. Let me take you home every night."

She laughed. "Bill wouldn't approve of that," she said.

"Talk to him," I said. "I haven't got anything else to do. I'm living at the Tennessee Hotel by myself, and I would be happy to take you home every night."

Evidently she talked to him because the next night she said, "Bill said you can take us home," and for two weeks I drove her and her silent husband home each night.

I noticed one habit Winters had. Every night before closing time he took a glass of ice, mixed Coca-Cola and bourbon in it, and drank it.

On my next trip to Dyersburg I begged a bottle of Dick Grogan's bourbon. I told him I had a tough customer I wanted to give it to.

The next time I took the Winters home, I said to him, "Mr. Winters, I have a friend in Dyersburg who makes his own bourbon. Is that what you drink?"

"Yes," he said.

"I have a bottle of it here, and I would like for you to try it if you're willing to."

That's the first time I ever saw him smile. "Yes," he said. "I'm willing to."

The next night, the Winterses invited me into their apartment. He opened the conversation. "Are you selling any of those Coca-Cola glasses?"

"No," I said. "I'm not having much success."

"Have you called on Wes Gunther at the Plantation Drive-In?"

"Yes, but I didn't sell him any glasses."

"Well, let me tell you how to sell Wes Gunther," Winters said, and he explained the strategy he would use. The next day I went to see Gunther and sold him six dozen glasses. If he liked them, he promised to buy ten barrels of glasses—and there were thirty-six dozen glasses to the barrel. Ten barrels would be four thousand, three hundred, twenty glasses.

The next night I told Winters of my success with Wes Gunther, and he puffed up with pride. Taking the Winterses home that evening, we talked a bit about the sale to Gunther, and Winters suddenly asked, "Do you sell to Mrs. Saylor at the soda fountain downtown?"

"No," I said.

"I'll tell you how to sell her," he said, and again he outlined the sales strategy he would use. The following day I sold Mrs. Saylor six dozen glasses.

That night I told Winters about the sale and thanked him. I was feeling great. "The Coca-Cola Company is having a contest," I told him. "All the salesmen are in it to see who can sell the most glasses."

He pondered that a moment and asked, "How much would a

carload of glasses be?" I almost drove off the road. A carload was
sixty barrels, almost twenty-six thousand glasses.

When I recovered my voice I said, "The best price we've got is
for ten barrels."

"Oh, hell," he said, "I buy by the carload. You get me a carload price."

I went into the apartment with them, and we talked about the
deal some more. I saw he was serious; so when I left the apartment at two a.m., I drove to Western Union and sent a telegram
to my boss, Ross Creekmore, the district manager. He was in
Charlotte, North Carolina. He had come through the ranks and
had been with the Coca-Cola Company forever. I worded the telegram this way: "Fortune, Inc., interested in carload of glasses.
Do we have special price for carload? Please call me in the morning, nine o'clock."

When Creekmore got the telegram the next morning, he was
with D. Sales Harrison, Coca-Cola's vice president in charge of
the South for the Fountain Department. Creekmore said to
Harrison, "Look here, that kid, Sanders Rowland, has gone to
Memphis and started drinking. Look at this telegram wanting a
price on a carload of glasses for Fortune's. Fortune's won't even
talk to a Coca-Cola man."

"Well, well, well . . ." Harrison mused, reading the wire.

"Roos Day got pitched out of Fortune's," Creekmore said,
"and Bill Winters even threw me out once."

Harrison laughed. "Well, do we have a special price?" he
asked.

"I think the kid's drunk," Creekmore said.

"One way to find out," Harrison said. "Let's call him."

Creekmore put the call through. The first thing he said to me
was, "Buddy, are you all right?"

"Yes, sir," I said. "Did you get my telegram?"

"Did you actually mean it?" he asked.

"Absolutely," I said. "Give me a carload price, and I'll sell a
carload."

"We don't have a price for a carload," he said.

"Well, if you can get one, I can make the sale."

Ross Creekmore and D. Sales Harrison secured a carload price
for glasses and brought the information to Memphis. The three of
us went to Fortune's, and Bill Winters couldn't have been nicer.
He bought the carload to Creekmore's amazement.

Three months later I sold another carload to Winters, and those two carloads plus the ten barrels each to Wes Gunther and Mrs. Saylor helped me lead the nation's four hundred salesmen and win the glasses-selling contest.

The challenge of selling a tough nut like Bill Winters also was such an adrenalin-flowing experience that I knew salesmanship would be my life's work. As I sat on that stool night after night, I wasn't looking for that particular opportunity when the taxi didn't show up. I was just hoping he would talk to me in time. I thought if I stayed there long enough and was nice to his wife, he might eventually break down.

Too, it was my good fortune, I suppose, that I discovered how well he liked bourbon; and I had a ready source. I brought him quite a few bottles of Dick Grogan's homemade bourbon; and during the year I was in Memphis, Bill Winters became one of my best friends. He introduced me to a lot of nice girls, customers at his drive-in, and they invited me to parties. All in all, I had a ball in Memphis.

The Memphis bottler, Uncle Jim Pidgeon, was a story in himself. He said he spent his first night in Memphis sleeping on a park bench with a newspaper for cover; he was that broke. He came to Memphis as a young man, got a job sweeping out a saloon, and finally became bartender. The owner of the bar died, and his widow let Uncle Jim run the bar. He made enough money to buy the Coca-Cola franchise for Memphis and some of Mississippi.

He also owned the Memphis Baseball Club in the Southern Association. I came into the plant about noon one summer day to pick up some advertising materials, and Uncle Jim said, "Let's go to the ball game." When I stepped up to the window at the ball park to buy the tickets, he stopped me.

"I'll take care of this," he said. "I've got more money than you have."

"I thought I would let Coca-Cola pay for it," I said.

"Well, you just save their money," he said. "This is my treat."

Of course, since he owned the team and the ball park, we didn't have to pay. As he furnished hot dogs and Coca-Colas, we became better acquainted that afternoon.

He knew how to hold onto his money. Coca-Colas were a nickel apiece in 1928; and when Uncle Jim bought two from a vending boy, he gave him a quarter and said, "Keep the change."

The boy evidently didn't hear him and handed Uncle Jim the change. Uncle Jim pocketed it and said, "If he doesn't want it, I do." He didn't tell the boy twice.

The most amazing thing about Uncle Jim was the way he ran his Coca-Cola business. At a time when Ford Motor Company paid its mechanics five dollars a day, Uncle Jim paid his mechanics five dollars an hour—and he had the best in Western Tennessee.

He wanted production; so he struck an agreement with his mechanics. He would pay them five-dollars an hour while the machines ran, and subtract ten dollars an hour from their pay for all the time the machines were down.

His machines ran ninety-eight percent of the time. I never saw one down in the daytime. The mechanics worked on them at night and kept them in excellent running order.

Uncle Jim paid his route men $140 a week and furnished them with $160 uniforms at a time when no one paid wages like that. As a consequence, everybody in Memphis wanted to work for Coca-Cola, and no one then employed by Uncle Jim dared quit his job. The uniforms were whipcord riding pants, leather boots, short jackets, white shirts, and bow ties. They were snappy—anyone could tell a Coca-Cola man at a distance.

Uncle Jim came to the plant every morning at seven o'clock when the loaded Coca-Cola trucks rolled out to begin their route service. He stood to the side watching the trucks roll by, shouting, "Give 'em hell, boy—give 'em hell!"

He hired Negro help to load and unload the trucks, three or four men per truck. In the afternoons when the trucks came back, the helpers swarmed over them, unloading empties and reloading with filled crates. Then the uniformed route men walked to the cashier's window and turned in their cash. Everything was done in cash—no credit, no checks, nothing but cash. That's the only way Coca-Cola bottlers operated in the early days.

CHAPTER 3

Early Days

MY FATHER WORKED fourteen years for the Coca-Cola Company. He was employed there when I was born in Decatur, Georgia, December 3, 1906. He was Henry Sanders Rowland. He had gone to work in 1896 for Asa Candler, who founded the Coca-Cola Company ten years before that. Because of his job with Coca-Cola, my father met my mother, Agnes Knox Carmichael, in Jackson, Georgia. He went there to call on her cousin's drug store to sell Coca-Cola and met mother sitting there eating ice cream. He began courting her that night; and they were later married and had six children, five girls and me. One of the girls died in infancy; so I grew up with my mother and four sisters around the house.

Actually, there were more than that around our house most of the time. I remember when my mother's brother, Uncle George, had a stroke and lived with us for a while in Decatur. Both of my grandmothers also lived with us for several years—so there were five kids, an uncle, two grandmothers, and our parents crowded into the same house. I slept on a cot in the back hall, and my sisters slept together in one room.

My mother was a college graduate, and she kept an orderly house, even with that many people around. My father's father was an educated man, a school teacher who was headmaster of Donald Frazier Academy in Decatur. He had been a sergeant in the Confederate Army and worked with the Veterans Services. He died when my father was ten and my father was able to complete only the fifth grade. The only other education he received was in Spencerian School where he learned to write beautiful letters. Being a smart man who had a knack for mathematics, he

19

became an accountant. He worked as an accountant for the Coca-Cola Company.

My parents were good to me, but I didn't have the normal childhood that most others enjoyed. I had little time to play: I had to work. Sometimes the neighborhood kids would gather, and we would play ball on one of our lots. But we had a neighbor woman who would run out and confiscate the ball every time we hit it in her yard, and she wouldn't give it back. My father would have to go get it when he came home from work. That cut a lot of our ball games in half.

Occasionally, I got to go to the moving picture shows, but not often. I didn't have much time to play because I had extensive chores. Too, I went to work part-time for the Coca-Cola Company when I was thirteen, and after that I didn't think much about playing.

Our house was on Sycamore Street in Decatur, right across the street from the Methodist Church. My father owned five lots, three on Barry and two on Sycamore. Our home was an old frame house built before the War Between the States, and the kitchen was separate from the house. We had a Negro cook who brought the food from the kitchen to the house under an umbrella.

The nine-room house was one story tall. A hall ran down the center of the house with four rooms on one side and five on the other. It was heated by seven fireplaces. One of my chores in the winter was to keep the fires going. I brought in coal for all the fireplaces—each fireplace had its own scuttle. I had to lay the fires, light them, and keep them going to insure warmth throughout the house. The ceilings were high, the rooms were large, and this was no small job for a boy.

My father had a garden, a cow, and chickens; and I did the garden work. I had to get down and pull weeds and hoe the garden. Because I hated cutting grass and working in the flowers and garden, I promised myself that when I got to a position where I could afford to pay someone to do the garden and yard work, I would never do it again. I am happy to say that I realized that position in later years.

We had so many chickens—usually fifty or sixty—that I had to clean out the chicken house every day, which was a job I didn't like either. I spread the chicken manure on the garden, which measured about sixty by a hundred feet; it certainly made things grow. I also had to tend the cow and clean up after her. My father did the milking.

My sisters were kept busy, too. They gathered the eggs—usually two or three dozen a day, sometimes more. They had other chores to do around the house. We all worked; we didn't have time to play. And at night we did our homework for school.

We did have indoor plumbing and a bathroom. Sometime before I can remember, my parents, or someone, had converted one of the bedrooms into a bathroom. It was large and a bit drafty. But with all the people in the house, we could have used another bathroom or two.

I have no complaints about my childhood. Circumstances made it what it was, and if I had not been accustomed to working then, I might not have received the opportunities I did in later life.

My father promised my mother to build her a new house, a more modern one in which we could all be more comfortable. He decided to move our house to the lower lot on Barry Street and build the new one on the corner of Barry and Sycamore.

I remember the summer day when a huge crew of workmen descended on our house. They loosened it from its foundation and brought in several big, long logs for rollers. With a strong mule pulling, several men guiding, and several others moving the rollers, they rolled the house down the way and put it on a new foundation on the lower lot.

Unfortunately, Father never got to build the new house.

He quit the Coca-Cola Company in 1910 after fourteen years. He was not too well paid, and automobiles were coming along by that time. He saw a better future in the automotive field. He was hired by a new company, the Firestone Tire and Rubber Company, as Southeastern Regional Manager at three times the salary Asa Candler paid him at Coca-Cola, and he felt he could not turn the new job down.

He worked a while for Firestone and did well. But my father was an opportunist, and when a man named Roundtree convinced him there was big money to be made in motion pictures, he left Firestone and put everything he had into this new business. One of their partners was Tommy Atkins, who made the first animated cartoons—the same thing Disney parlayed into an immense fortune.

My father's company made the first animated cartoons for moving pictures, and the future looked bright—until a fire destroyed their studio. Everything my father had in the business world went up in the smoke of the fire.

Undaunted, he went back to Firestone and became a dealer. His shop was just across Peachtree Street from the Governor's Mansion in Atlanta. His partner was named Reese, and their company was "Reese and Rowland." They had a fleet of little service trucks and part of their business was going out and repairing flat tires. Everybody who had an automobile in those days had a lot of punctures because tires weren't so good.

Unfortunately, my father had not picked his partner well. Reese left his wife, ran off with their secretary, and left my father to pay all the bills. He did, but he lost the business in the process.

He went back to the desk and became an auditor for the S. A. (Diamond) Lynch Enterprises. Diamond Lynch owned a lot of moving picture theaters, including some in Atlanta, and my father worked steadily there for some time. When Lynch decided to move his headquarters to New York, he wanted to take Father along; but Father had five children and was rooted in Georgia. Father refused the offer and left the company. He went to work for a public accountant in Atlanta and was working there when he became ill with cancer.

It fell my lot and my sister Mary's to support the family. Mary was teaching school and making $75 a month. I was making $12.25 a week at the Coca-Cola plant, and together we made our family's way. Our father worked when he could, but in his condition he was unable to do much.

My original idea was to be a lawyer, but this was only a boyhood dream because of my occasional association with my Grandfather Carmichael, my mother's father. He was a lawyer and judge in Jackson, Georgia. In the summer when I was a youngster, we visited my grandparents for a while. My grandfather took me to the courthouse about ten in the morning, and I stayed with him till noon. I was deeply impressed by the lawyers who argued cases before my grandfather. I like how they talked and how they strutted around the courtroom, trying to convince the judge that their clients were right. I decided that I was going to be a lawyer, but I was never really serious about it.

I earned money before I went to work for Coca-Cola. I had a newspaper route, carrying *The Atlanta Constitution*, and I worked up a good business selling *The Saturday Evening Post*. I had to get up at five o'clock and meet the five-thirty trolley from Atlanta, which brought my bundle of newspapers. My mother got up and filled me with hot oatmeal before I left to work my paper route. She wasn't too strong—she had diabetes—but she wouldn't let me get up alone. I think she worked herself to death, taking care of everybody in our house, especially with my father ill. She died at the age of forty-seven in 1927.

I wasn't satisfied with just delivering the newspaper and Saturday Evening Post in our neighborhood; therefore, I expanded into Atlanta. On the afternoon of the day the Saturday Evening Post came out, I rode the streetcar to Atlanta for only a nickel. I picked up a bundle of Saturday Evening Posts at the distributor's place, and then I called on the Coca-Cola Company offices, the Gulf Refining Company, and the film exchanges on Marietta Street. That was about all I could work in the time I had, and I usually made about two dollars profit for the afternoon's work once a week.

That's how I met Harrison Jones, sales manager and vice president of the Coca-Cola Company. The Coca-Cola offices were on the seventeenth floor, the top floor, of the Candler Building. The syrup plant was on Magnolia Street, and I occasionally went over there and sold magazines. Harrison Jones was always nice to me. He was a big man in the Coca-Cola Company, but he always found time to speak and say a few words to me. I think he liked me because I was always working when he saw me, trying to turn a dollar, or a dime.

Before I entered high school in 1920, I looked for a part-time job, and my mother, knowing I had been working that area of Atlanta for some time, suggested I apply at the Coca-Cola Company and the Gulf Oil Company. I made the applications and Harrison Jones hired me at eight dollars a week as an errand boy and mail carrier. I went to work on May 30, 1920.

My first boss at Coca-Cola was a woman, Margaret Landers, who was in charge of the file room and the mail. She weighed all the outgoing mail, stamped it, and sent it to the Post Office by a Negro boy who worked with us. I helped her weigh and stamp the mail. The same boy who took the mail to the Post Office brought the incoming mail back. Miss Landers sorted it out on her desk, and I delivered it to the offices.

In Decatur we went to school on Saturday and had Sunday and Monday off. I don't know why. I've never heard of such a system anywhere else, but it was good for me. Monday was a heavy day at the Coca-Cola Company for checks coming in, and I helped in the cashier's office. So, working in the mail room, the file room, and the cashier's office, I learned the ropes fairly well.

Through high school I worked all day Monday and on Wednesday afternoon of school weeks, but during summer vacation Coca-Cola let me work full time.

My duties lay primarily in the mail and file rooms with Miss Landers. But in the summer of 1920, my first year on the job, they gave me another, most pleasant duty.

The company was building a new, modern plant on North Avenue across from the Georgia Tech campus, meanwhile, we were still downtown in 1920. I worked in the Candler office building, and the syrup plant was on Magnolia.

Orders for Coca-Cola syrup came into the offices in the Candler building, and every morning and every afternoon I gathered these orders and took them to the syrup plant. With the orders in an envelope, I crossed the street in front of the Candler building, took the street car for a nickel and asked for a transfer. At Five Points I transferred to the Marietta Street car, got off at Magnolia Street, and walked a block and a half to the Coca-Cola Syrup Plant. They took the orders I brought and shipped the syrup the same day. My trip took about an hour, and doing it twice a day I got to know the people who worked in the syrup plant very well.

In 1921 everything moved into the new building on North Avenue. We had a great deal of room and rattled around a lot. There were about seventy-five people who worked in the administrative offices, while approximately fifty worked in the syrup plant, maybe twenty-five whites and twenty-five blacks.

Coca-Cola only had two vice presidents at that time. Harrison Jones was vice president in charge of sales, and a man named Cash was vice president for advertising.

I also learned a good lesson in honesty that I have never forgotten. Miss Margaret had a girl named Louise Neal helping her in the file room, and a young man named Gatewood Workman and I worked for her in the mail room. Gatewood was the nephew of a company official and was a regular guy. We got along well. We didn't have to spend too much time distributing files and mail and had plenty of time to sit around and talk.

One day Gatewood saw an ad with a coupon in a magazine that offered a pound of chocolates for two dollars in stamps and the coupon.

"Sanders," Gatewood said, "why don't we send two dollars worth of stamps and get a pound of chocolates? We got all the stamps we need right here in the mail room."

I knew it was wrong, but I went along anyway. I was fourteen; he was thirteen, and of course we both loved chocolates. Gatewood filled out the coupon in his name, and we put two dollars worth of company stamps in the envelope and mailed it.

Since the chocolate company was in Atlanta, we thought we would get the candy by mail; but because it was a local operation the candy company had its outlets deliver the candy.

A few afternoons later, all of us—Miss Margaret, Louise Neal, Gatewood and I—were sitting in the file room when Dr. Cox from the drugstore down the street came in. He asked, "Is Gatewood Workman here?"

Miss Margaret said, "He's right over there."

Dr. Cox came over to where Gatewood and I were sitting, and said, "Mr. Gatewood Workman, here's your chocolates that you sent the two dollars worth of stamps for."

Miss Margaret turned snow white. She caught on right away what we had done, and I was embarrassed. I'm sure Gatewood was, too.

I said to Miss Margaret, "It was Gatewood's idea, but I agreed to go along with him," and when she was slow in replying, I added, "I am responsible as much as he is for using the stamps; and if anything happens to Gatewood, it should happen to me, too."

She finally found her voice. "You boys come in here with me," and she took us in the supply room; closed the door; and if ever a woman gave two young men a lesson in honesty, she gave it to us. She said if we continued to do things like that our lives would be ruined and we would end up in prison—and she insisted that we always remember this and never steal anything again.

The only thing she did was give us that tongue-lashing and take the candy away from us—but I remembered the incident the rest of my life.

I discovered one summer how costly mischief can be. The son of the grammar school principal and two other boys and I were playing in the school yard and found a window open to the basement of the school. We crawled in and thought we would have some fun. We strewed toilet paper up and down the halls and wrote on the blackboards with chalk and on the walls of some of the classrooms with a dark substance—I don't remember what it was—but that was all the physical damage we did.

When the principal discovered our mischief, he questioned his son, who evidently broke down and told him what we had done and who had done it. The chief of police came to see my parents and told them they would have to take me before the school board. The board assessed each of our four families two hundred dollars, which I thought extravagant. All we had caused them to do was repaint a couple of classrooms. It is possible that we were blamed for someone else's mischief, but my parents had to pay two hundred dollars for my wrong-doing. Believe me—that les son and the one I learned about the chocolates have kept me on the straight and narrow since.

I worked hard for the Coca-Cola Company—as hard as a teenaged boy could work, and I kept up with my studies and chores at home. In 1924 when I was graduated from high school, I made my mother proud.

Graduation night, with my mother and father sitting there, was one of the proudest moments of my life. The principal announced that thirteen girls and one boy were to be graduated with honors. I figured the boy would be Wallace Austin, who had beaten me in several debates and who I thought had always been a teacher's pet; but instead, Wallace was given a scholarship, and I was graduated with honors.

That closed one chapter of my life, for soon after that I went on the Coca-Cola Company's payroll full time.

CHAPTER 4

Pemberton's Tonic

WHEN I FINISHED HIGH SCHOOL in 1924, I knew I would make Coca-Cola my life's work. There was no question about it. My mother always told me the biggest mistake my father had made was leaving the Coca-Cola Company. "Coca-Cola is a good company," she told me repeatedly. "You stay with it."

About that time some interesting things were happening at the Coca-Cola Company.

Asa Candler, an Atlanta druggist, started the Coca-Cola Company back in 1886. Dr. J. B. Pemberton had invented a concoction he called "Pemberton's Tonic." It had secret ingredients that he revealed to no one except Asa Candler, who mixed the tonic and sold it at his drug store at Five Points in Atlanta.

When Pemberton died and Candler continued to get calls for Pemberton's Tonic, Candler bought the formula from Pemberton's widow, who was about thirty years younger than Pemberton.

My father knew the story well. He worked for Candler, remember, from 1896 till 1910.

Candler changed the name of the tonic as soon as he bought the formula. His bookkeeper and secretary-treasurer, Frank M. Robinson, originated the name of Coca-Cola. It was he, also, who wrote the words in the beautiful Spencerian hand that are still the trademark of Coca-Cola.

As my father told the story, Robinson said to Candler, "Let's change the name."

When Candler agreed, Robinson came up with "Coca-Cola" from the coca leaf and cola nuts in the formula. Coca is a tropical shrub whose leaves are the source of cocaine, and at the start

27

many people would not drink Coca-Cola because they thought it contained cocaine. That is why, even into the 1930s, many in the South still called soft drinks "dopes."

Only those who know the formula, or knew the first formula, know whether Coca-Cola contained cocaine, but I suspect that it did not. It did contain alcohol, however, because it was invented to be a tonic, not a refreshing soft drink.

The first Pure Food and Drug Administrator of the United States, Dr. Wiley, made the company take the alcohol out of Coca-Cola. My father was subpoenaed to appear in the case after Dr. Wiley seized some barrels and kegs of Coca-Cola in interstate shipments and had them analyzed. He found them to contain alcohol.

I do not know if Asa Candler and Robinson changed the original formula when they bought it.

Business that first year wasn't anything to write home about, but I suppose it was good for a small drug-store operation. Candler sold forty-seven gallons of Coca-Cola at the Five Points Drug Store and spent forty-seven dollars advertising it.

My father used to tell me that he was in the office and overheard the transaction the day Asa Candler sold the bottling rights to Thomas and Whitehead of Chattanooga. Candler signed over the rights on a one-sheet contract that gave Thomas and Whitehead bottling rights in the United States with exceptions. For these rights, Thomas paid Candler one dollar.

Candler dealt in Coca-Cola syrup in his drug store. He apparently did not want to become involved in mass bottling because in those days bottling places were back-alley dumps. Few bottling plants had proper means of sterilization of bottles.

Anyway, Asa Candler became a wealthy man with Coca-Cola and never forgot Pemberton's widow. He paid her two hundred dollars a month for the rest of her life. I don't know whether that was in the purchase contract, or whether it was one of Asa Candler's whims; but I do know that in 1920 when I worked in the cashier's office in Atlanta, I drew the monthly checks for Mrs. Pemberton—and that was thirty-four years after. A fellow named Bobby Brawn was in charge of the check register in 1920. He gave me a list of checks to type, and Mrs. Pemberton's name was on the list for two hundred dollars every month.

Candler built the Coca-Cola Company into a national giant. He owned it for thirty-three years, selling it for twenty-five million dollars in 1919 to three men: W. C. Bradley, Ernest Woodruff, and Eugene Stetson.

Stetson was a vice president of Manufacturers Trust in New York. He was from Macon, Georgia. Bradley was from Columbus, Georgia. He owned the W. C. Bradley Company and the Eagle and Phoenix Mills Company in Columbus. He was a Georgia corporate giant. Woodruff was Atlantic Steel Company, Trust Company of Georgia, and Atlantic Ice and Coal Company of Atlanta.

Candler sold the company because of his advanced age, I suppose, but also because he had made a bad investment of great magnitude. When America went into the First World War in 1917, sugar was selling for fifty cents a pound. Candler bought all he could lay hand on for forty-five cents a pound, which seemed to be a good investment, one that would keep Coca-Cola operating, he hoped, for the duration.

However, the duration was less than he had speculated. When the war ended in November of 1918, Candler had his warehouses filled with forty-five-cent sugar which was selling on the post-war market for five cents a pound.

Rather than continue to fight such battles at his age, he decided to sell out.

Not any of the three men who bought the company knew anything about the soft-drink business: therefore, when Asa Candler volunteered his son, Charles Howard Candler, to be president of Coca-Cola, the new owners accepted the offer.

The younger Candler was a fine gentleman, in my estimation, but was less than the dynamic individual needed to put the Coca-Cola Company back on its feet.

Four years later, in 1923, Robert Winship Woodruff, the thirty-four-year-old son of Ernest Woodruff, became the Coca-Cola Company's third president.

Woodruff was president of White Motor Company. He attended the University of Georgia for a year, didn't like it, and his father put him in a steel mill firing the boiler. That, Woodruff thought, was worse than college; so he quit and took a job selling White trucks in Atlanta. He suited that job well, and soon was so prominent in the company that Walter White, who had founded the firm, moved Woodruff into the presidency in 1922.

A year later, Ernest Woodruff and his two Coca-Cola partners talked Robert Woodruff into taking the presidency of their company, which was in a bad way, actually on the verge of going broke.

Woodruff wore two hats for a while, continuing as president of White Motor Company. He was a busy man who stayed on the move. He had a fancy automobile, a Wills St. Clair, and a chauffeur named Lawrence Calhoun. The St. Clair was a big car, and Woodruff got in the back seat and went to sleep and Calhoun drove him to Cleveland, or Miami, or wherever he needed to go on business. When he finished his business, he returned to the back seat of the car and Lawrence drove him back to Atlanta.

The Coca-Cola Company was in a new office building on North Avenue across from Georgia Tech in Atlanta. It was a spacious three-story building which housed all the business offices. The third floor of the building was not occupied at that time, but Woodruff built a fourth story and included in it a private dining room, a private office, a public office, a massage room, a barber's chair, and a comfortable area where he could sleep when he wanted to.

He had a private elevator installed in the garage that went only to his quarters. It would not stop anywhere else. When he came in the mornings, he parked in the garage; rode his elevator up to his offices; and no one saw him that he didn't want to see. He was a very private person—but he knew what he was doing, and he jerked the Coca-Cola Company back onto its feet in no time.

At that time I was going to Georgia Tech and working full time for Coca-Cola, but I didn't know if Woodruff knew I existed. I remember quite well the first time I saw him.

I was in charge of the janitorial staff in 1924. On my staff were six Negro men and one Negro woman. My responsibility was to see that they kept the building clean. Each night when they finished their work, they would contact me to inspect the building to make sure everything had been done.

One of the men, Tom Freeman, was assigned to the fourth floor. That was his only responsibility. In the hall near the door to Woodruff's quarters we kept an "Icy-O" cooler. There were no mechanical coolers then. This one had a handle that we turned to open each section, into which we put ice to cool the drinks.

One evening when I made the inspection rounds, I noticed that water was pooled on the floor beneath the cooler. It had been that way the previous night.

"Tom, I told you to wipe that water up last night and see if it's back here today," I said, "and it still is. Did you wipe it up last night?"

"No, sir, I didn't," Tom was a truthful person. "I forgot it."

"Damn it," I said, "I told you to do that and I want you to do it now. If the cooler leaks, let's find out and get it repaired."

Someone tapped me on the shoulder and said, "That's right, Sanders, give 'em hell if they don't do want you tell them to."

It was Woodruff. He was with someone else, passing through to his quarters and overheard what I said. I was flabbergasted that he caught me fussing at Tom—and even more amazed that he knew my name.

Under Woodruff's leadership, Coca-Cola expanded into a giant company. When he came in 1923, Coca-Cola was sold only in the United States, Canada, and Cuba.

Bottled drinks, sold only in six and one-half ounce size, made up less than twenty-five percent of the business. The fountain business—and syrup for the fountains—commanded Coca-Cola then.

CHAPTER 5

College Years

THE ATLANTA CONSTITUTION ran an ad one morning in which the Capital City Tobacco Company advertised for a driver, offering fifteen dollars a week. That was $2.75 more than I was making, and we needed the money at home. Without telling anyone at Coca-Cola, I applied to Ed Malone, head of the tobacco company, and got the job. Then I went back to Coca-Cola and found Harrison Jones in his office.

"Mr. Jones, I want to give my notice," I said. "I'm quitting."

"Quitting?" he said. "Aren't you going to college?"

"No, sir, I've got to work," I said. "You know my father has cancer, and I've found another job that pays fifteen dollars a week."

"Where is this job?"

"It's at Capital City Tobacco Company, driving a truck."

"Wait a minute," he said, heaving his huge frame out of his chair. He went to the next office and asked Frank Boykin, the secretary and treasurer, to come into his office.

"Frank," he said when we were all seated, "this damned little kid is talking about not going to college, and he's going to quit and go to work for Ed Malone at Capital City Tobacco Company."

Boykin frowned at me, executive fashion.

"We just had a talk at the Rotary today about keeping kids in school, didn't we?" Jones asked.

"Yes, we did, Harrison," Boykin said.

Jones looked me straight in the eye. "You're going to college," he said flatly. "you're not going to work for Ed Malone. We'll pay you fifteen dollars a week. Now, while I call Ed Malone and tell him you're not coming, you go down and see Horace Garner; and he'll tell you how to go to school. He just finished college himself. He went to night school, and he's going to law school now. He can tell you how to do it."

I hadn't really wanted to leave Coca-Cola, and I learned something from Harrison Jones that day: I learned that to solve a problem you must go to the source, or to the proper people. In no time at all he had solved all my problems.

I knew Horace Garner over in the old plant, and he talked to me for a long time that day, explaining how I could work and go to college at once. During the four years I was in college at Georgia Tech, Horace and I talked often.

Harrison Jones was a big man, maybe six-feet-seven or -eight and two hundred seventy pounds. I took my class schedule to him at the start of each Georgia Tech semester, and he would set up a work schedule I could live with.

I went to Georgia Tech four years; summers, days, and sometimes night school. I studied business all the way—business law, accounting, advertising. I chose the subjects I thought would be helpful to me in a career of selling Coca-Cola.

I learned many practical things, both in school and out. One of the most practical things I learned was in the field of advertising. Advertising should neither be false nor vague. It should be straight to the point and should fully explain the product.

During the time I was at Georgia Tech, there were nine boys in the home office who were designated by Harrison Jones as tour guides for the plant; and I was one of them. When the receptionist had a group to be taken through the plant, she called one of the guides who met the group in the lobby and conducted a guided tour through the syrup factory and the rest of the plant.

One winter day she called me for a group of teachers. They were sharp people, mostly women. I took them first to the advertising department and showed them the latest in Coca-Cola advertising. One of the slogans that year, which was printed on our billboards and on the metal advertising signs we put on the sides of stores and in drugstores, was, "Thirst Knows No Season." I stressed that point through my spiel: "Thirst Knows No Season."

Later in the tour we came to the barrel factory, and there were several empty work benches. I explained that in the summer when we sold more Coca-Cola all of the benches were occupied by workers who had to turn out a lot more barrels than we did in winter.

One of the teachers spoke up, "Mr. Rowland, when we were upstairs in the advertising department you impressed on us that 'Thirst Knows No Season;' so how can you explain the empty work benches?"

I couldn't. And I'm sure I stood there red-faced, stammering and muttering, and I assure you that on future tours that winter I did not bear down too hard on the point.

In those early days I met a lot of people who made deep impressions on me. One was George L. Mitchell, who had been promoted from superintendent of the syrup plant to branch manager of the Atlanta plant.

Mitchell had only gone to the third grade in school, and then he went to work for a living. He had been a convict guard on a road crew, which was a rough and tumble job in Georgia in those days. When he came to the Coca-Cola Company he was put in charge of the Negro crew that dumped sugar into the vats where syrup was mixed.

Mitchell was not only rough and crude, but he was also smart; one of the smartest and sharpest men I've ever known. He had a moralizing effect on everyone he came in contact with. He could walk through the plant and production would increase. He didn't have to say a word. If a man was repairing a barrel and Mitchell came through, the man began to work a little harder; and he kept working harder until he had the barrel finished.

Mitchell was a "cusser." You've seen people like that: They just curse. Every other word is an oath, and those who know them pay little attention because that's just the way they are. That was the way Mitchell was. It didn't present much of a problem down in the syrup factory where most of the work crews were made up of rough characters. But when Mitchell was promoted to branch manager, which was a white collar job, it did indeed become a problem.

Business was expanding by leaps and bounds, thanks to some changes Woodruff had made, some of which were key appointments like that of Mitchell. To make the operation more efficient, those in managerial positions who didn't already have them were given secretaries. The problem with giving Mitchell a secretary was that he cursed so much.

Harrison Jones knew I had taken a typing and shorthand

course at night school; so I got the job as Mitchell's secretary at twenty-five dollars a week.

I was a happy young man that day as I sat down in Mitchell's office to take the first letter he had ever dictated in his life. It was also the first letter I had ever taken; so you could safely say the blind led the blind that morning. *ALL* morning. We worked on that letter the entire morning.

When I took out all the cuss words and typed the letter, he didn't like it.

"It don't sound right," he said. "Let's do it again."

We did it again; and when I cleaned up the language and typed the letter, he still didn't like it.

"Take this out," he said, "and that," designating certain words and phrases. When I brought the letter to him again, he said, "No, that ain't what I want either."

Finally, he got up from his desk and went to a file cabinet. He rummaged in it a minute and came up with a letter he had received a day or two before.

"Here," he said, "write one that looks like this."

So I typed the letter to look just like the one he gave me, and he liked it and signed it.

He was a wonderful man to work for. He had nine children and sent eight of them to college. He knew kids and knew how to handle them.

He would look over at me during the day and see me nodding, and would say, "How much sleep did you get last night?"

"Well, I had to study until two o'clock," I would say.

"I don't have anything to do," he would say. "Why don't you go up and take a nap on the sugar bags. I'll come up and get you when I need you."

After giving me a couple of hours of sleep, he would wake me and we would get the work done.

One of the men Woodruff hired was a fellow named Hamilton R. Horsey, a vice president of the Travelers Insurance Company from Hartford, Connecticut. He had been a colonel in the first World War. Horsey was a martinet in that he expected everyone to do his work on time and to do it right; but he was a fine guy, a likeable person. He was single; I don't know if he was looking for a wife, but he looked every minute as if he had just stepped out of a bandbox. Maybe it was a throwback to the military, but he was perfect in appearance.

Mitchell was still in charge of the syrup plant. Even though he had been promoted to Atlanta branch manager, he was still the immediate supervisor of the syrup plant superintendent, the title Mitchell held before his promotion. He simply took on extra duties while retaining control over his former duties.

And every time Woodruff brought in a new man he sent him to us to train. Mitchell worked them in the syrup plant making barrels, or mixing formula, or whatever he could find for them to do.

Mitchell always admonished me, "Be good to him. He may be your boss tomorrow."

That's how it was with Horsey. When he finished his training, he became a vice president in charge of New Orleans. He also had duties in Atlanta where I was his secretary. I took his dictation in his room at the Biltmore Hotel in the morning, typed his letters in the office, then took them to the hotel at four in the afternoon for him to sign. Mitchell sent me over in the company car, and Horsey sat there in his underwear and signed the letters.

After three years of this, I went to take his dictation one morning and he said, "I'm going to make a trip around the world. Mr. Woodruff is giving me a new job to see if we can sell Coca-Cola in other countries."

He looked at me sharply, as if re-sizing me. "I need a young man to go along," he said, "to handle reservations and keep notes of what goes on and all of that. I would like to offer you that job. We'll be gone about nine months."

His offer thrilled me to my bootstraps. To think that a young man not yet out of college would be offered such an opportunity!

"Gee, that's great, Colonel Horsey," I beamed. "Let me let you know."

I talked it over with my mother that night, and she gave it a little thought, and said, "Sanders, you've only got one more year and you'll be graduating from Georgia Tech. You cannot accept that job."

That was that. I could tell by the look in her eye that no argument, no matter how powerful, could prevail. So I told Col. Horsey the next morning that I could not take the job and told him why. He agreed that I should finish my education.

He took another boy out of the office, a fellow named Dock Anderson. Dock got a lot more out of the trip than the experience of going. He eventually became vice president of export for the Coca-Cola Company.

Without question, George Mitchell was the finest man I ever worked for. But he was a practical joker, and he loved to play jokes on me.

One of Col. Horsey's duties, when he returned from his trip around the world, was to institute a budgeting system which the Coca-Cola Company had never had.

Department heads had to recommend things like capital outlays, equipment needs, and salary increases to Horsey, who had the final say in how much to budget for each item.

My salary was $27.50 at the time, and Mitchell recommended a five dollar raise for me. He recommended a ten dollar raise for Leo Wilson, who kept the stock books and made less money than I, and a modest raise for Breezy Wynn, an assistant chemist in the laboratory. I didn't like Breezy Wynn. We just didn't get along, and Mitchell knew that.

"Sanders," he cautioned me as I typed his recommendations, "you're not to say anything about this to anybody. I don't want anybody to know what I recommended them for."

"Oh, I won't," I said, "and I do appreciate your recommending me for five more dollars a week."

"That's all right," he said. "Horsey will probably fool you."

Two weeks later when I went in to take dictation from Mitchell, he said confidentially, "I heard from Horsey." He began rummaging on his cluttered desk. "I've got the letter here somewhere." And in a moment he said, "Oh, yes, here it is," and he came up with a letter on Coca-Cola stationery.

He opened it and scanned the page. "Here's Horsey's recommendation in response to mine for pay raises: Breezy Wynn, ten dollars a week; Leo Wilson, one dollar a week; Sanders Rowland, fifty cents a week."

Leo and I sat side by side in our office when I told him of Horsey's recommendations, and he said, "That pie-faced son of a bitch. He never did like you." He thought a few minutes, then turned to me and said, "Sanders, let me talk to you a minute."

We went up to the rest room and he said, "Are you going to quit?"

"I don't know." I said, "Do you think I should?"

"It's a hell of an insult," he said. "A dollar a week for me, and fifty cents for you! And word's getting around the office."

Mitchell had spread the word rather well. When I walked through the plant, I could hear folks whispering, "That's the boy got the fifty-cent raise." And to me they would say, "Fifty cents. That's twenty-six dollars a year. You can buy a new suit for that."

I ran into Horace Garner one afternoon. He was in the purchasing department by then.

"Horace," I asked, "what am I going to do about this fifty-cent raise?"

He said, "Did you see the letter?"

"No," I said. "Mitch had it."

"Go back and ask him to let you see the letter," Horace said.

So I went to Mitchell. "Mr. Mitchell," I said, "could I please have that letter from Horsey so I can attach it to the file?"

"Hell," he said, "I don't know where the damned thing is." But he had it all the time and was just pulling our legs. Both my raise and Leo's had come through as recommended.

Mitchell ran the syrup plant a long time before Coca-Cola hired a chemist. Mitchell was chemist and quality control wrapped into one.

Coca-Cola didn't have a chemist before Woodruff became president. A fellow named Arthur Ayers mixed the syrup. There were seven ingredients in the formula few people knew, and the seventh was the X ingredient. So much sugar, so much this, so much that, and then two gallons of X to twenty-five hundred gallons of syrup.

When Dr. Heath came on as Coca-Cola's first chemist, I worked vacation weeks in the syrup plant—two weeks here, two weeks there, two weeks somewhere else. A fellow named Dovis Austin helped Dr. Heath mix the "seven" behind iron doors in the basement of the syrup plant. They could mix enough in one day to last a week.

When Austin went on vacation, I replaced him. For two weeks I helped Dr. Heath mix the secret ingredient, but I didn't know what I was doing—or what he was doing, for that matter. He would say, "Give me that box number twenty-five thirty," or "Let me have some of that stuff." All I knew was that it smelled good, and when Dr. Heath got it mixed he would tell me how much water to put in it; and I would put in the required amount. Then we would put it in two-gallon cans to ship to the syrup factories around the country.

All of the seven ingredients in Coca-Cola were numbered— number one, number two, number three, and so on.

Before Dr. Heath came to work, Arthur Ayers would mix the

ingredients other than sugar and water. When he finished a batch, he would bring a glass of the mix to Mitchell.

Mitchell would sip it—sip, sip, sip.

"Let it go, Arthur," he would say. "It's fine."

One day I was in his office when Arthur Ayers brought in the sampling glass. Mitchell sat back and sipped, quietly smacking his lips.

He sipped it a second time, then said, "Arthur, I think you left out the five. Go back and find out."

A few minutes later, Arthur returned. "You were right, Mr. Mitchell," he said. "I left out the five."

Mitchell had that necessary taste. He could tell by a sip whether the formula was right. If he gave his okay, that was all that was necessary: They would put the mix in the barrels, weigh them, and ship them.

And just as there were men of Mitchell's cut all through the Coca-Cola Company, there were those of the other ilk, too.

I worked mostly as a secretary to several men during my four years at Georgia Tech. I was assigned for a while as secretary to the Traffic Department. Mark Emmert was traffic manager and he traveled a lot. When he was on the road, everyone in the department answered to Emmert's assistant, A. B. Carver.

In this department, there were four of us boys, two grown men, plus Emmert and Carver.

Carver was an impossible man. But he taught me lessons in reverse that I employed later in life when dealing with people.

There was a big clock at the door of the office, facing him. His desk was in the middle of the room arranged so that the other desks faced him, like schoolkids facing teacher.

Every time any of us was a minute late coming in—either coming to work or coming from an errand—Carver would call us up to his desk and bawl the hell out of us in front of everybody.

He enjoyed humiliating people. If I wanted to go to the men's room, I had to hold up one finger or two, depending on what I had to do. If he thought I stayed in the bathroom a moment too long, he called me to his desk and asked all kinds of questions. He was not that way only with me but with everyone in the department, grown men included.

We worked five full days a week and half a day on Saturday, and we were paid at quitting time. On Monday morning, each

boy who worked in the Traffic Department had to sit in a chair
beside Carver's desk and account for every penny we had drawn
on Saturday.

The lesson I learned from A. B. Carver was a negative one—
but I turned it around and made it positive. I told myself in no
uncertain terms: "If I ever have anybody working for me, I'm
not going to treat them like A. B. Carver treated me."

That might have been the best lesson I ever learned, and I
learned it from an impossible man. A. B. Carver was impossible—absolutely impossible.

I was awarded the high honor of becoming Master Counselor
of the Demolay, a Masonic order, during that time. In that capacity I had to attend the installation of a chapter from Atlanta at a
meeting in Savannah, Georgia.

Two weeks before the meeting, I told A. B. Carver about it.
"Mr. Carver," I said, "I would like to be absent on Saturday
morning two weeks hence." I told him why, that we were going
to drive to Savannah on Friday evening so I could help conduct
the ritual on Saturday.

He said he would think about it and let me know what he decided. I asked him two days later, and he said, "No, I haven't
decided yet." Three or four days later I asked the same question
and got the same answer.

He loaded me with work, so much work that I couldn't do it
all. Paul Bacon, a buddy who worked in the same department,
helped me out. He and I worked several nights to get caught up
on my work so I could make the trip to Savannah. But still
Carver kept me hanging until five o'clock that Friday afternoon,
just an hour or so before I was scheduled to leave for Savannah.

Even then he tried to keep me from going.

I went to him and told him that tomorrow was the day I had
asked to be off.

"Well," he hedged, "you haven't finished that work I gave
you."

I looked him straight in the eye. "Every bit of it is finished," I
said.

He knew it was, and he reluctantly let me go.

A man of the opposite cut—in every way—was Bill Greene.

I spent a part of the four years I went to Georgia Tech filling in
on Coca-Cola's vacation schedule. When anyone went on vaca-

tion, if I qualified to do his job, or if his boss thought I could handle it, I worked two weeks in the vacationing man's place.

There were two night watchmen at the Coca-Cola plant. Greene was the outside man, and a man we called "Old Man" Freeman was the inside man. They made regular rounds and punched time clocks on the way. If Bill Greene was scheduled to punch a certain clock at two o'clock in the morning, he had from ten minutes before two until ten minutes past two to punch it. If he didn't punch it in that twenty-minute span, a man on a motorcycle would check on him; and he would be penalized three dollars of his salary. One missed punch in a thirty-dollar-a-week job would cost these men dearly.

To make his rounds, Old Man Freeman had to walk forty minutes out of every hour. Bill Green had to walk thirty minutes to make the outside round, walking the perimeter of the fence and all the buildings. He walked it rain or shine.

Bill Greene was not an educated man. He signed the payroll with an "X" every week, but he drew the same pay—thirty dollars—that I got when I relieved Old Man Freeman for his vacation.

Once when Freeman became ill, Mitchell asked me to work for him until he was able to return. He was out almost fourteen weeks. I went to school in the daytime and worked seven nights a week, twelve hours a night—every night with no relief—until Old Man Freeman came back. I went on at seven in the evening and got off at seven in the morning.

All that for thirty dollars a week. But in those days thirty dollars was good money, especially for a college man. Besides, I was working toward permanency with the Coca-Cola Company. If I had been told to break rocks twelve hours a night, I would have tried.

Although Bill Greene had never darkened a schoolhouse door, he had reason about him; and he appreciated, perhaps better than most, the effort that anyone made to get an education.

He talked to me about education. He said he never had the opportunity to go to school and that a person should do everything in his power to stay in school. After three or four weeks on that job, I told him I was, indeed, doing everything in my power to go to school, and then some. He laughed, and since he had taken a liking to me, he began to show me ways that I could ease my load. He showed me how to walk my rounds in such a way that instead of having twenty minutes off every hour, I could have thirty. Sometimes when I dozed off during my thirty-minute breaks, he punched a couple of boxes for me and let me sleep forty minutes.

He was an absolute prince as far as I was concerned. He had something in his heart that many men of great education do not possess.

It was a fine moment for me when I received my diploma from Georgia Tech. I really felt I had accomplished a great task, and I had a deep feeling of pride.

My mother was dead. She passed away the previous year. And when I looked around at ten o'clock that morning when the graduation ceremonies began, there was my father and a couple of my sisters—and Bill Greene. I believe at that moment he was more proud of me than my father was. He was beaming.

As the years passed then, and I moved first to Memphis that fall, and then to New England, I would go back to Atlanta either for Christmas or for a part of my vacation each year. Every time I went out to the Coca-Cola plant and spent a night with Bill Greene, making his rounds with him and thoroughly enjoying visiting with him.

Each person can name certain people who bore great influence on his life during his early years. I can name three: my mother, Harrison Jones, and Bill Greene.

CHAPTER 6

Taking On the World

IN 1928 WHEN I WAS just out of Georgia Tech working for
Mitchell, one of the big problems in the Coca-Cola Company was
developing the right cooler for dispensing Coca-Colas. John Staton, one of Mitchell's assistant managers, was in charge of exper-
imenting with coolers.

Sometimes Staton's job seemed impossible to those who did
not stop to think of all the inventions and developments of that
day. No one had ever made a satisfactory refrigerator for soft
drinks. We had one called the "Icy-O," but it was not well insulated and required too much ice. The Liquid Carbonic Company
had a cooler in which bottles were pushed into tubes and ice was
packed around the tubes to cool the drinks. But when the tubes
became cold and too much pushing pressure was applied to the
bottles, the result was breakage—and, of course, a mess.

Staton had a big room in the back of the plant on North Avenue. He had all the cooling boxes manufactured by other firms,
and he had carpenters who made two or three dozen boxes of our
own. All together, there were about forty cooling boxes in Staton's room. He packed them with every sort of insulation imag-
inable. He had stacks of bags of cottonseed hulls, cotton, sugar
cane pressed together, cork, sawdust, and everything else he
could think of that might insulate a box.

He stuffed every box with a different insulation, or with different combinations of insulation, filled each box with the same
amount of ice, and placed bottles of Coca-Cola in each of them.

I was detailed to assist him. I weighed the chipped ice and made
sure each box had the same amount. I kept and recorded tempera-
tures on each box every hour, and at intervals I checked the tem-

perature of the bottles. One by one he eliminated the boxes in
which the ice melted quickest.

Soon we had eliminated thirty-nine coolers and had only one
left. It was made by the Glasscock Corporation of Indiana, whom
Coca-Cola awarded a contract for a great number of the boxes.

They were simple rectangular boxes on four high legs. The
insulated boxes were deep enough to hold the six and one-half
ounce Coca-Cola bottles upright with chipped ice spread over the
bottles to cool them.

Coolers were furnished to Coca-Cola bottlers around the country who sold them to their customers for fifteen dollars.

Later that summer of 1928 the Coca-Cola Fountain Department decided to put its own servicemen in the field. Coca-Cola
fountains were becoming so popular that full-time servicemen
who knew something about refrigeration and carbonation were
needed.

Ten of us who were employed in the office in Atlanta went to
school two hours a day, from four to six p.m., five days a week
for three months. Classes were held in the Coca-Cola building
where experts from the field came in to teach us how to repair
carbonators and draft valves, and everything about refrigeration.

In September we finished the course, and the company offered
all of us jobs in the field. My assignment was Memphis. I went
with Mitchell's blessing. My salary increased from $120 a month
to $160. I was furnished a little red Coca-Cola car with racks in
the back to carry advertising.

After a week following a fountain man on his rounds in Atlanta
to familiarize myself with the job, I went out to meet the world.

I thought I had a pretty good education. Not only had I been
graduated from Georgia Tech, but I was also well grounded in
secretarial skills; I could work in almost any department of the
Coca-Cola Company because of all those days I had spent reliev-
ing people on vacation; I thought I had the rudiments of salesmanship in my corner; and now I had been schooled in
carbonation and refrigeration.

My biggest success in Memphis, of course, was selling those
carloads of glasses to Bill Winters at Fortune's Drive-In, but my
duties covered a lot more than that.

I carried the latest advertising signs in my car. When I went in
to call on a customer, it was my job to see that he had good displays. If he didn't, I put them up for him.

One day in Jackson, Tennessee, I was putting up a decorated festoon over the soda fountain; and as I had been taught, I had several tacks in my mouth. That was the handiest place to carry them when I needed both hands for putting up a display.

As I hammered the tacks home, I noticed a woman and a little boy eating ice cream at the fountain watching me. The woman seemed to be hurrying through her ice cream, and the boy was fascinated at the way I was spitting out tacks and hammering them into the display.

When the woman finished, she urged the boy to hurry. But he was enjoying the little show I was putting on for him, and finally the woman lost her patience. She jumped up and said to the boy, "William, if you don't hurry up and eat that ice cream, you're going to wind up just like that young man, tacking up signs!"

I drove on to the next town and decided to put in a new crepe paper display at the drug store. I had been taught in another class how to handle crepe paper, which can be tricky. I decided to drape a window and put a display in the center.

I was enjoying myself, making rosettes and streamers. Then I filled my mouth with tacks, climbed up in the window, and began putting up the display. I dispensed tacks from my mouth and hammered them home with what I thought was a great deal of skill.

Some people stopped outside to watch, and one of them was an elderly woman. She watched for half an hour until I had finished the display. As I was putting the remaining tacks back in the container, she approached me in the drug store.

"Young man," she said, "I have just watched you put in a beautiful window, and you are an artist with crepe paper."

My chest swelled a bit with pride. I said, "Thank you, ma'am."

"I noticed you put tacks in your mouth," she said.

"Yes, ma'am, I do. That is the way we were taught to handle them because it's the fastest way."

"Have you ever swallowed one?"

"Oh, no, never. I am very careful. But if I ever do swallow one they told us to eat the inside of a loaf of bread and that would take care of it."

Her face grew extremely stern. "Young man, I want you to promise me something."

"What is that?"

"You must promise me that you will never put another tack in your mouth."

I was a bit dumbfounded, but I wasn't going to promise her a lie. "I'm sorry," I said, "I can't promise you that because my job depends on speed and accuracy, and I have to use tacks."

I didn't want to disappoint her, but I was truthful with her. Still, it didn't keep her from stomping off as if her mission had been unfulfilled.

When I went to Memphis, I was three months shy of my twenty-second birthday. I weighed about a hundred-forty pounds, and stood five feet seven or eight. I had no attachments to keep me rooted. I was unmarried, my mother was dead, and my sisters were caring for my father in Decatur. I was determined to make a success of whatever they gave me to do in Memphis, and I worked hard and long hours. The hours didn't bother me. I enjoyed my work.

On occasion, Coca-Cola would send company officials around to check on personnel like me. My first visit was paid by Ross Creekmore, the fellow who later thought I was drunk when I wired for a price for a carload of glasses. He spent a full day with me and may have had a little trouble staying up, I moved so fast. When six o'clock rolled around that evening and I was still putting up signs, he said, "Buddy, you gotta learn one thing: You can't do it all in one day."

Back home in Decatur, my mother had been a friend of a Mrs. Brownlee, whose husband worked for Coca-Cola. They knew each other at PTA in Glenwood School where my sisters and I had gone.

I had written home bragging about selling the carload of glasses to Bill Winters, and someone in the family told Mrs. Brownlee about it in idle conversation.

Mrs. Brownlee's husband was named William, but everybody called him "Pig-Iron." He was big and he was tough as pig-iron. The name was appropriate.

About that time, Pig-Iron Bill had been made a vice president of the Coca-Cola Company and put in charge of all the company-owned plants in New England. There were only six such plants, and Brownlee's office was in Boston; the rest of the Coca-Cola plants up there were franchised plants.

The company had decided to push Glasscock coolers in New England especially. When Pig-Iron Bill got word of my glass-selling success in Memphis, he figured I could sell coolers in Boston.

He telephoned me in Nashville and asked, "How would you like to work with me in Boston?"

"That sounds pretty good," I said, trying not to make a snap decision. "What would I be doing?"

"We'll talk about it tomorrow," Pig-Iron Bill said. "Take the night train and meet me here in Atlanta in the morning."

Floyd Judd, manager of the Nashville office, was in the office when Brownlee called me. He overheard the conversation, as did the cashier, a man named Short.

"Well, well," I mused aloud. "That was a call from a new vice president of the Coca-Cola Company wanting me to go to Boston to work for him," and then I said half to myself, "I wonder how much farther it is to New York from Boston."

To a Georgia boy in those days, the farthest place from Georgia was New York. Nobody ever thought of any other place being farther.

Short said, "I've got a map. Let's see where it is."

We poured over his map and couldn't find Boston anywhere between Atlanta and New York. Just as I was beginning to think they might have moved it, Judd said, "Here it is, away over here," and he pointed to the right of New York, and a bit to the north.

I remember thinking, "Well, what's it doing away over there?"

I didn't call my boss in Memphis to tell him I was going to Atlanta. I don't know why. I just bought a ticket and caught the overnight train. The next morning when I got to the Coca-Cola plant in Atlanta, my boss, D. Sales Harrision, stood on the front steps.

"What are you doing here?" he asked. "Your territory is in Tennessee. Why aren't you up there working it?"

"Mr. Brownlee called me," I tried to explain, "and asked me to meet him here this morning."

"Well?"

"Well, he is a vice president," I said.

"I'm a vice president, too," he said, and I didn't have an answer for that.

"I don't want you to talk to Brownlee," he said. "I want you to take the next train back to Nashville."

"I'm sorry," I said, "I'm already here. I don't know what it will hurt for me to talk to him."

Brownlee had been manager of the Cable Piano Company in Atlanta when he caught Bob Woodruff's eye by selling one million dollars worth of pianos in one year in Atlanta. That's a lot of pianos in a city of only a quarter-million people. So Woodruff figured Pig-Iron Bill was a supersalesman, and he hired him and made him a vice president. He operated that way. He surrounded himself with capable people; made them vice presidents; paid them well; and it paid off.

So I told my boss that I had made a mistake and I was sorry. "I should have telephoned you and told you right away," I said, "but I didn't. Now that I'm here. I've still got to see Mr. Brownlee."

"Well, all right," he said. "Go ahead. But don't make any rash decisions."

Brownlee leveled with me halfway. "I've got a sales job for you," he said. He stopped short to telling me it would be on a truck. He simply said he had a sales job for me and left it at that. He said he would pay me more money, but didn't say how much. (He later raised me from $160 to $195.)

He said he was new in the job and didn't know too much about New England or the people. He also knew nothing about the plants up there. But he said he was putting together a "team", and he wanted me to be a part of it. He said he had hired Cliff Hodson as production manager. Hodson was a relative of Mrs. Woodruff, who had been a Hodson from Athens, Georgia, and I had known Cliff when I worked in Mitchell's office in Atlanta. Cliff was a stock clerk when I had been a secretary, but now he was a very capable engineer.

I didn't know what to do; so I went to see D. Sales Harrison.

"What are you going to do?" he asked.

"Mr. Brownlee offered me a good job," I said.

"You've been doing pretty well in the fountain department," he said. "We have plans for you, too. I think you'd better stay where you are."

I still didn't know; so I went back to Brownlee.

"Mr. Harrison told me I ought to stay where I am," I told him, and he blew up. He cussed me over the coals right there.

"Can you make up your own mind?" he shouted, "Or do you have to have somebody else make it up for you? What are you going to do? Are you going with me or staying with Sales Harrison?"

Suddenly I made up my mind. "I'm going with you," I said.

"Then it's settled," he said, and shook my hand. "I'll call Harrison and tell him you're going to go with me."

"I would appreciate that," I said.

"By the way," he said. "I just bought my son, Bob (who was sixteen), a new Oakland All-American car with a rumble seat and a top that comes down. It's brand new, and I want you to help Bob drive it to Boston."

"Sure," I said. "Be glad to."

"Take a couple of weeks," he said. "No rush. I won't be getting up there for a couple of weeks; so you fellows have some fun. Have you ever seen Washington, Baltimore, and Philadelphia?"

"No," I said, "I've never been to any of them."

"Well, then, see them," he said. "There's a lot of things to see going up there."

"Thanks," I said, and I know I left there grinning ear to ear. I felt that a whole new chapter of my life was beginning.

CHAPTER 7

Breaking the Ice
in Boston

THE FIRST AIRPLANE RIDE I ever had was over the city of Washington. It cost five dollars. We saw the Lincoln Monument, the Washington Monument, and all the sights of Washington. Trains crawling into and out of the city looked like long black snakes.

On the ground we took it all in, taking our time. We wandered through the Smithsonian Institution and the Federal Bureau of Investigation.

In Baltimore we did the same, and there we prowled the waterfront. That was a treat; there aren't any waterfronts near Atlanta.

Philadelphia offered many sights including the Liberty bell. We were cruising down a boulevard there with the top down, enjoying the sights and the freedom of roaming leisurely, when a police cruiser pulled in behind us and turned on its siren.

No one had driver's licenses in those days. And states did not issue registration certificates for automobiles. Bob didn't have the bill of sale for the car; his father had it. So we were suspected of having stolen the car—such a nice, shiny, new car, and two kids tooling around in it.

We were hustled into the police station and from there Bob had to telephone his father collect in Atlanta. Brownlee told the police that the car did, indeed, belong to his young son, and told them to let us go, which they did, shaking their heads in wonder that a boy so young should have a car so hot.

We drove through New York and spent some time sightseeing and enjoying the biggest city in the land. By the time we drove to Boston, Brownlee was already there. We couldn't find the Coca-

Cola plant, and no one we asked—no one who could understand us—knew where it was. The plant was actually in Cambridge, but we didn't know that. We telephoned Brownlee and he said, "All right, hold on, I'll come out and get you."

He had a black chauffeur named Sponge Watkins, who drove him everywhere he went. Sponge's wife, a nurse, worked for the Brownlees, too. They were typical Southern blacks, good servants, and Brownlee had had them for quite a while. They had worked for him in Atlanta when he was manager of the Cable Piano Company.

They found us in short time. Brownlee told Bob to ride with him and said for me to drive Bob's car and follow. I thought we were going to the plant; instead, we drove out into the countryside and wound up in New Hampshire forty miles from Boston. We rolled into a place called Corbett's Pond where Brownlee had a cottage. In the cottage next door were Cliff Hodson and his family.

On the lake behind the cottage was a new speedboat Brownlee had bought for Bob. We spent an exciting afternoon aquaplaning around the lake. We had a great time, and when we came in, Brownlee had been watching us. He said, "I'm not ready for you down at the plant. Why don't you stay up here for a week or so and when I'm ready, I'll send for you."

That was music to my ears. That would stretch my leisurely time between jobs to a month—with pay. I didn't mind at all.

We spent several days lying around, getting a tan, aquaplaning on the lake, and eating ourselves silly. Each morning, Cliff would drive Brownlee to the plant in Cambridge and each afternoon would drive him back to Corbett's Pond.

At Sunday dinner a couple of weeks after we got there, Brownlee asked, "You about ready to go to work?"

"Anytime," I said. "Anytime you want me to."

"Okay, we'll take you down tomorrow."

The next morning, I dressed for work. I put on my white linen suit with blue stripes, a straw hat, sports shoes, and tie, got in the car, and was ready to go to work.

On the way, Brownlee briefed me—very briefly.

"You're going to work for the manager of the Boston plant," he said.

"What's his name?" I asked.

Cliff cut in. "His name is Mr. Hare."

"All right," I said. "Mr. Hare." I stamped it into my brain.

Brownlee didn't say anything more about the manager. He talked about the operation all the way down.

When we got to the Boston plant and went inside, we walked up to a man I took to be the manager.

"Clarence," Brownlee said to him, "this is Sanders Rowland, that young man I was telling you about. He's from Atlanta and he's going to work for us."

I stepped forward and offered my hand. "I'm glad to meet you, Mr. Hare," I said.

He gave me a stony look and said, "My name is Herr."

Cliff was about to split, and Brownlee was grinning. They were practical jokers.

Herr shook hands and turned away from the joke.

"Do you have any working clothes?" he asked, looking over my linen suit.

"I'm standing right in the middle of them," I said.

He couldn't believe his ears. "I mean *working* clothes," he said.

"Yes sir," I said. "This is what I intend to work in."

He shrugged. "Okay, Donovan," he called a big Irishman over and nodded toward me. "This is Sanders Rowland. Take him out and show him his route."

In the garage we walked up to a big Autocar 8 x 8 truck. I started to climb into the passenger side, and Donovan said, "Get around here. You're driving this thing."

"I've never driven a truck in my life," I said.

"Well, you're gonna drive this one; so you better get started."

"What do you mean, I'm going to drive this one?"

"This is your truck, Rowland," he said. "I'm going along to show you your route."

"You mean I'm just going to be a route man?"

"That's it."

"He brought me all the way from Atlanta just to be a route man!" I couldn't believe what I was hearing. I hadn't even been a route man in Tennessee.

Disappointed though I was, I was still game. I climbed under the wheel and before we had gone five blocks, I had mastered that truck.

We worked from early that morning until nine-thirty that

night. When I finally drove back into the plant, I had lost my hat, thrown my tie away, and ruined my suit.

The next day when I reported for work, I asked for a bit of time that morning and went out and bought some proper working clothes.

Donovan—his first name was George—spent a week with me, showing me the entire route. Donovan was one of three men who were titled "special salesmen." The other nine of us were "route salesmen," and I had the ninth route. I was at the bottom of the barrel.

My only chores were to work the six areas in my route once a week, selling Coca-Cola and coolers. The only Coca-Colas we had were the six and a half ounce bottles.

I quickly discovered that I had trouble with the language. I couldn't understand the people—they spoke so fast—and they couldn't understand me. There were motor parkways around Boston that permitted no truck traffic. After Donovan left me on my own, about once a day I got lost and invariably wound up on one of those infernal parkways. And always, somewhere along the way, there was a big Irish cop standing beside the parkway, or sitting on his horse there; and he blew his whistle and came over and bawled me out.

"You know better than to have this truck on this parkway, me boy," he said.

"I'm awful sorry, officer," I returned. "But I'm lost. I don't know how to get off this damned parkway."

When he heard my voice, he came back with, "Faith, but you're a damned rebel, aren't you?"

"Yes, sir, I am," I said, "but I'm still lost. Can you tell me how to get back to the Coca-Cola plant?"

Mostly, officers directed me back to the right road, and when I drove away I looked in the rear-view mirror and saw them standing there chuckling.

Once I learned the route, I was in pretty good shape. My route covered the same route that Paul Revere rode—Concord, Acton, Maynard. I sat up on that big truck and pretended I was Paul Revere, riding through the countryside. Once or twice, I shouted at passersby, "The British are coming! The British are coming!" And they looked at me as if I were a Southern fool!

Brownlee had brought me to Boston to sell coolers. I knew

that. He wanted someone who could sell the things and show the other salesmen how.

I had a cooler on the truck, and when I sold one I stocked it with Coca-Colas and ice. I got a block of ice and chipped it, and showed the storekeeper exactly how to do it to get best results.

All transactions were in cash, and I collected on the spot. The coolers cost fifteen dollars, and a case of Coca-Cola cost a dealer eighty cents, plus fifty cents bottle deposit. Coca-Colas sold for a nickel.

Unfortunately, when John Staton chose the Glasscock cooler for the Coca-Cola Company, he overlooked one important thing. In Boston, there were a lot of different cold drinks—soda waters—and the only two that would fit standing up in the Glass-cock cooler were the six and a half ounce Coca-Cola and a drink called "Moxie," which also came in short bottles. Everything else was sold in bottles nine inches tall, and the only way they would fit in the Glasscock cooler was lying down.

We experienced a lot of returns. I would sell a store a cooler, fill it and ice it, standing up the Coca-Colas and Moxies, and putting all the rest on their sides, and when I returned to collect the empties and replace them, the owner would say, "Take it back! Take it back! It won't hold my bottles."

There weren't any other good coolers around, and we really had to sell the storekeepers on the advantages of using our coolers. They were brightly painted; they attracted attention; and we firmly believed they increased business. The other boxes were made of wood, had practically no insulation, and to keep them from dripping water on the floor, the proprietor had to wrap the ice in beef paper and put it in the cooler. It kept the drinks only lukewarm. It wouldn't chill them at all. But you could take a Coca-Cola out of one of those Glasscocks, right out of the chipped ice, and it would be ice cold, just like we advertised it.

I had moved to Cambridge. I had a room in a rooming house in which John Hurt lived. John was from Atlanta, too, and Brownlee had brought him to Boston to be his purchasing agent.

I worked diligently. Every day, Clarence Herr, who became a close friend of mine, saw me pull that Autocar out of the shop at the crack of dawn—and he was always standing there when I returned anytime from eight to nine or nine-thirty at night.

Because I had trouble communicating with those Bostonians, I also had trouble selling them. After two weeks on the job, I overheard Brownlee ask Herr one morning, "How many coolers has Sanders sold since he's been here?"

Without waiting for Herr to answer, I spoke up, "I haven't sold any."

If looks could kill, I would have died right there. Old Pig-Iron looked a hole clear through me, and he said, "Why haven't you sold any? That's what I brought you to Boston to do."

I explained to him right then the problems I was encountering.

"People don't understand my language," I said, "and I can't understand theirs. Also, because I am a Southerner and this is the Depression, many of them resent my working when a lot of local boys are out of jobs. I've had customers fuss directly at me because I came up here and took a job that rightly should have been given to a New Englander. That's what they tell me to my face."

"Well. . . ." Pig-Iron started to say something, but I interrupted.

"That's not all," I said. "I can't even get inside the speakeasies—and they sell a hell of a lot of Coca-Colas."

"Why can't you get inside?" Pig-Iron asked.

"Because of this fellow Chandler."

"What fellow Chandler?"

"Asa Candler's brother. They call him Chandler. They know Asa Candler started Coca-Cola, and his brother, Warren Candler, is a Methodist Bishop in Atlanta—and a prohibitionist. I've been kicked out of several speak-easies because of a man I've never met."

Many of those people in Boston thought Asa Candler had caused prohibition. They had him mixed up with his brother, who hadn't caused it but certainly had furthered its cause. Asa Candler was on the other side. He drank whiskey.

"And that's not all," I thought I might as well lay it all out for him. "I'm in a new territory, and I'm having a hard time trying to compete with one product against all the competition preceding me."

I explained to Pig-Iron Bill that the fellow who had the franchise before Pig-Iron took it—his name was Robinson—had dealt in several different brands of soda water. He had sold Grape, and White Birch, and Lemon, and Strawberry and Cream Soda; and here I was, trying to sell nothing but Coca-Cola. They kept asking where my other flavors were.

Robinson had made deals with customers that I couldn't match. He sold them hundred-dollar stock certificates in his company. Anyone who invested a hundred dollars in stock got a ten-cent discount on every case of drinks he bought.

To every person who bought a share of stock, Robinson gave a Coca-Cola clock—a big clock that the customer hung on the wall.

The upshot of the thing was that Robinson went broke. And when he did, the Coca-Cola Company had to take over the franchise. That's when they sent Pig-Iron Bill in to straighten it out. So Robinson hadn't been gone more than a couple of months or so, and memories lingered.

When he went broke, the stock all those customers had purchased was no good. They didn't blame any one person—Robinson—for this folly. They blamed the Coca-Cola Company and anyone who worked for it.

The foreign element I dealt with—the Greeks and Italians and others—gave me the most trouble. They threatened me with physical violence. No one can imagine the abuse I took.

I reached the point that when I walked into a new place and saw a Coca-Cola clock hanging on the wall, I didn't say a word. I just backed out, with everyone glaring at me, got in the truck, and drove away.

Another problem we had was the way people thought about Coca-Cola. It had originated in the South, and I don't suppose that registered well with those who knew it. But the big drawback was that many people thought Coca-Cola really contained a narcotic—cocaine. "Dopes," they called them.

Moxie was the strong favorite. It was bitter as hell, made from an herb. It was like medicine, but people drank it. They thought it gave them "moxie," made them smart.

Moxie sold for a dime, twice the price of a Coca-Cola, and Moxie had a great advertising campaign. They would take a Rolls-Royce, or a Cadillac, or Pierce-Arrow, the finest cars you could buy, strip the body off and mount a horse's body on the frame. The driver would ride in the horse's saddle and push the stirrups to make the car go. He had a little steering wheel coming out of the horse's neck, and I had to admit, they had a whale of a gimmick.

Five or six of those Moxie horses went all around New England and became well known. They were the prettiest, shiniest things you ever saw.

A year later, when I had been named manager of the New Haven plant, one of our salesmen from Boston, a guy named Callahan who had switched over to Moxie, came to me in New Haven and asked if he could "park his horse" in my yard.

I said of course he could, and we went out to dinner. When we returned, every kid in the neighborhood was clamoring around that horse, just thrilled to death.

Faced with problems like that, Coca-Cola's battle in Boston was all uphill. And I was in on the fight from the beginning.

That first day, when George Donovan took me out to show me the first leg of my route, we made one hundred-eighty calls and sold six cases of Coca-Cola.

And that's the way it was for months.

Finally, through persistence and generally just trying to be nice and courteous to our customers, convincing them that we had a superior drink and certainly a superior cooler, we began to break the ice.

Boston had never experienced a day in which one hundred cases of Coca-Cola were sold. But we finally accomplished that several months after I came to work there. Nine of us who were working the sales routes sold one hundred and four cases one day. Pig-Iron Bill and Clarence Herr were so happy they took us all to the Lexington Hotel at ten-thirty that night and bought each of us a Littlejohn steak. Littlejohn steaks were the pride of Boston beef. They cost a dollar-fifty when steaks anywhere else sold for seventy or seventy-five cents.

In 1983, I was in Boston and had dinner with Bill Casey, president of the New England Coca-Cola Bottling Company, and told him about that day in 1929 when we nine sold one hundred and four cases, and he laughed and said, "Last Friday, we sold eighty-four thousand cases in Boston." Times have changed. We had something of a pioneering spirit in Boston in 1929, even though Coca-Cola was certainly a nationwide product. We felt as though we were plowing new ground, opening virgin territory, and indeed we were in many ways.

About seven o'clock on a Friday evening that October in Cambridge, I drove past Harvard Stadium and saw the lights were on. I knew that Harvard was playing Army the next afternoon, and on impulse I stopped the truck and went into the stadium and found the student manager in charge of concessions. I asked if I could put some Coca-Cola in his stands to sell at the game the next day.

The manager was agreeable. He said he had ten stands. "Okay," I told him. "I'll put ten cases in each stand, and I will ice down five in each stand. That will give you a start, and you can ice down the others as you need them."

At seven the next morning I loaded my truck with ten half-barrels—that's what we used to chill drinks in those days—and on the way to the stadium I stopped at the ice house and bought enough ice for the job. I paid for the ice, which was customary, but I would charge it to Harvard when we settled up. About eight o'clock I drove into Harvard Stadium with one hundred cases of Coca-Cola, the ten half-barrels, and all that ice. I began making the rounds of the ten concession stands, carrying a half-barrel up to each stand, returning to the truck for the ice, and returning a couple more times for the ten cases of Coke. I unloaded five cases and put the bottles in the ice and stacked the other five cases behind the barrels.

Having no help, I was tired when I finished the chore at noon, but I felt good because this was a break-through. No one had ever sold Coca-Cola at Harvard Stadium before.

The crowd came in. A lot of the men wore raccoon coats and hats with the brims turned up, and everybody was in a holiday mood. It was a fine afternoon, a bit on the chilly side, but sunny and bright. I bought a hot dog and a Coca-Cola and went up into the stands and watched the game, which started at two o'clock. Army won the game, and there were sixty thousand people shouting and screaming and laughing and crying and having a good time. I could see in my mind's eye all those people grabbing Coca-Colas down at the concession stands, but it did not occur to me that I saw nobody around me drinking Coke.

When the game ended and the crowd left, I got my truck and began making the rounds to pick up the empties. At the first stand, there was not one empty bottle. They hadn't sold a Coke! The second stand had sold two bottles. By the time I collected the leftovers from the ten stands, I discovered that sixty thousand people had drunk fourteen bottles of Coca-Cola!

The temperature had cooled considerably during the game and the crowd drank only coffee.

As I was loading the last cases on the truck, an inebriated fellow came along and apparently deciding to give me a hand, picked up a case of full bottles and threw it over the truck and onto the ground on the other side. I had to pay for the fourteen bottles he broke. My total sales that day were twenty-eight bottles of Coke, one of which I bought and drank with my pre-game hot dog, fourteen of which the drunk broke, and the thirteen that the sixty thousand other people had consumed.

I didn't even charge Harvard for the ice.

My working day ended about seven o'clock that evening—a twelve-hour day—and the next day when I had dinner with the Herrs, I told Herr about the experience at Harvard.

He chuckled and said, "Well, that's the first Coca-Cola ever been sold in Harvard Stadium. You made the first sale."

The main thing Brownlee hired me for, I felt, was to sell those Glasscock coolers, but after two weeks I hadn't sold a one. I knew if, rather, when I sold the first one, that would break loose the dam and a flood of sales would follow. But recording that first sale wasn't going to be easy, not the way things had gone for me.

I carried a cooler on my truck and demonstrated it at every opportunity. About ten o'clock in the morning a couple of weeks after I went to work, I unloaded the cooler at a Texaco station owned by John King in Waltham, Mass.

I showed him how the cooler worked and where he could put it outside his station to catch the eye of motorists and bring business into his station. I was convinced it would do that; it had been proved in many places.

He turned me down. He didn't even say, "I'm sorry." He just said, "No,"and turned his back and walked away. I loaded the cooler back on the truck and drove away. I did not see Clarence Herr in his little red Coca-cola car parked up the street observing me.

About an hour later he caught up with me still working my route.

This was about eleven o'clock. He said, "Sanders, have you sold a cooler yet?"

"No, sir," I said, honestly. "I haven't sold a one, and I've been trying, too. I just demonstrated up there at the Texaco station in Waltham."

"Tell you what," he said. "Let's go back to that Texaco station."

"I don't know anything else I could say to Mr. King." I said. "I used every sales pitch I know."

"Let's go back, anyway."

"Okay," I said. "You're the boss."

I turned the truck around and followed Clarence Herr back to the Texaco station.

"Bring the cooler," he said as he walked from his car toward the station.

"I've already demonstrated it the best I know how."

"Bring the cooler."

I took the cooler back into the station and waited for Herr to say something, but he looked at me and said, "Tell him what the cooler will do for him."

So I gave him the same pitch I had given him an hour before, and when I finished, he said, "Okay, I'll take it."

"I beg your pardon," I said. I couldn't believe my ears.

"I said I'll take it," he said. "Put me five cases in the cooler."

I hustled off to get the ice, loaded the cooler with five cases of Coca-Colas, chipped the ice into the cooler, showing John King exactly how to do it.

I drove away from there asking myself, "How in hell did he do it? How did he sell John King when I couldn't?" In my mind, I went over every angle of the sales pitch I had used and concluded that I could not improve on it.

Many years later, when Clarence Herr had retired to Florida and was well into his seventies, I visited him; and I asked him, "Clarence, please tell me how you got John King to take that cooler when I had given him the same sales talk an hour before and he wouldn't buy from me."

He laughed. "Sanders, I'm going to play straight with you. I figured all you needed was one sale to get you started; so I gave John King the price of the cooler and five cases of Coke and told him he didn't have to pay me back. I figured it would be a small enough investment in you."

"Well, I'll be damned," I said.

Herr's strategy had worked. It bolstered my confidence so that about two in the afternoon I sold a cooler to a fellow named Billy O'Brian at a Standard station.

And for the next seventy working days, I sold at least one cooler a day.

In all the time before I came to Boston, the eight route sales-men and three special salesmen had sold only fifteen coolers. They had been on the market a year by the time I got there.

Sometimes one sale—like the one to John King—will burst the dam. After that, all of us began to sell coolers, and business picked up considerably.

It's the same way with cases of Coca-Cola. You need to sell a few—make a big sale or two—to get your confidence built up, then your approach customers with a more positive attitude, and subconsciously they recognize that here is a man who knows what he's doing and really believes in his product. They are more apt to buy.

On those six routes of mine around Boston, I called on maybe a hundred-fifty to a hundred-seventy-five customers a day, and I was always on the lookout for new customers along my route. I was selling a cooler a day and thought business was good.

One morning I sold a cooler early, and our rules were that every time we sold a cooler we had to return to the plant and pick up another to demonstrate at the next place.

I pulled my truck back into the plant about ten that morning, and while someone loaded a cooler on it I stood talking to Clarence Herr. I saw Sponge drive Brownlee in a few minutes after I got there. Brownlee came over and looked at me and asked, "What the hell are you doing in here at ten in the morning? You're supposed to be working your route and selling coolers."

"I am selling coolers," I said. "I just sold one and came in for another."

"Bill Young in Waterbury sold three coolers yesterday," he said, and abruptly walked away.

I looked at Herr. "Who is Bill Young?"

He said, "He's a salesman in Waterbury. The old man was over there yesterday."

I hit the road again and about two o'clock I sold another cooler. When I returned to the plant, Pig-Iron Bill was coming in from lunch.

"I got two today," I told him.

He laughed. "Bill Young in Waterbury sold three yesterday," he said.

"Put me another damned cooler on the truck," I told the load-ers.

I went back out and about five-fifteen I sold the third cooler. I rushed back to the plant, not for another cooler, but to end my day. I figured I had done a good day's work.

When I pulled in, the old man was stepping into his car.

I rolled down my window and yelled at him. "How many coolers did Bill Young sell in Waterbury yesterday?"

"Three," he shouted back.

"I sold three today," I said.

He got in his car, rolled down the window, stuck his head out, and hollered, "I knew you would," and Sponge drove him away.

I was promoted from route salesman to special salesman, one of the three, and worked that job for a couple of months. I was glad to get off the truck. Now I had a car with advertising racks just like the one I had in Memphis, and I had three route salesmen working under me. All I had to do was supervise them and look for new business.

About the time I finished my first year in Boston, Herr was promoted to the managership of the Providence plant in Rhode Island, and he asked me to go along with him.

I mentioned this to Brownlee.

"What did you tell him?" Brownlee asked.

"I didn't tell him anything. I thought I ought to speak to you first. You brought me. . . ."

Still as gruff as ever, he cut me off. "It's your decision," he said.

"In that case," I said, "I'll go with him." It didn't really matter to Pig-Iron Bill. He was in charge of both the Boston and the Providence plants, plus New Haven and Hartford and a couple of others.

I really liked to work for Herr, and that's the reason I decided to go with him. But I didn't know what position I would get in Providence. I thought it might be sales manager. I had a good record of selling coolers, and he had asked me to go; so it was only natural that I should speculate about a promotion.

Meanwhile, I wound down my duties in Boston and began breaking in my successor. One morning when I came to work, Herr said, "Don't go out today. Mr. Brownlee wants to see you."

I waited in the sales room from seven till ten o'clock when Brownlee finally arrived. "I understand you wanted to see me," I said to him.

"Oh, hello, Sanders," he said. "Yeah, I want to see you, but I'll see you a little later."

I waited for him until noon, and when he came out of the office, he said, "Let's go to lunch."

Sponge drove us to Harvard Square, to a classy little cafeteria where a lot of Harvard students and professors ate. Brownlee was a great eater and he favored this place. He could eat more than any man I ever knew. That day he ate a five-pound lobster and had scallops and clam chowder. He polished it off in style, as I had seen him do many times before.

After lunch he wanted to go for a walk around the square. We came to a small tailor shop called Baron's. It had one window, and in the window was a bolt of blue cloth with a blue light shining on it.

"That's pretty," he said. "Let's go in and ask this fellow to bring it out and see if it looks as good in sunlight as it looks in that blue light."

When the tailor showed us the cloth outside, Pig-Iron Bill said, "It does look good."

"Yes," I agreed, "it's beautiful."

"Do you really like it?" he asked.

"Yes," I said, "I really like it."

He turned to the tailor. "Make him a suit," he snapped.

That was his way of giving me a bonus. He never said, "You're doing a good job," or "You're selling a lot of coolers." He just turned to the tailor and said, "Make him a suit."

I had to go for four fittings to get the suit, and it fit me like a glove. It was the first tailored suit I had ever owned, and I wore it fifteen years.

Soon after I got the suit, I moved to Providence, expecting to be made sales manager.

When I arrived, Clarence Herr greeted me, took me into his office, and said, "Sanders, we've had four routes here, and I've decided to open up a fifth one. I want you to take it."

No sales managership. Not even a special salesman's position. I felt demoted back to route salesman.

I put on a uniform again and climbed back onto a truck and began making rounds. If ever I felt like going home, that was the day. But I wouldn't go home and say, "I quit. I'm a failure."

Herr and I had a talk a couple of days later. "I know you must feel badly about being put on a truck again," he said, "but we need somebody who knows what he's doing to develop this territory. We've just opened South Providence, and you're the man to make it click. I also think you can set an example in salesmanship that will rub off on the others. I need you out there on the road worse than I need you here managing sales, and I hope you understand."

I felt better after that, and I worked hard to make that new territory profitable.

I spent six months in Providence, working day and night, and I got that South Providence territory going.

There I learned that position wasn't the important thing. The important part was to be able to do the work that had to be done. And that's what I did. When I left Providence after half a year, my route was successful and in good shape for my successor. I learned a good lesson from Herr: to put the proper people into positions of need, and when the job was done, then promote them.

My roommate in Providence was George Donovan, the big Irishman who broke me in on my first route in Boston. He was Catholic, and he prayed every night on his knees beside his bed. I had never known many Catholics. In Protestant Decatur we had one Catholic. His name was Morry Mabel, and every St. Patrick's day he hired a band and paraded around town. I remembered that Al Smith was a Catholic, and he ran for president, but stories circulated about him that made a lot of us in Georgia think he had horns growing on his head. George was a great guy, and he taught me that Catholics were just people.

When we found a difficult place to sell, several of us who were salesmen would get together and try to put some subtle pressure on. If George had a difficult place, I would go in and ask for Coca-Cola; and when they told me they didn't have it, I would say, "Well, I wanted six bottles. Are you going to get it?" And later another salesman or two would drop by and pull the same stunt, and pretty soon that place would give George an order.

Up the street from our boarding house was a diner that George had been trying to sell. He asked me to go there and order Coca-Cola.

I stopped in the diner the next morning and asked for a Coca-Cola.

"Sorry," said the proprietor, "we don't carry it."

"Well, I'd appreciate it," I said. "I live up the street in that boarding house, and I'd like to eat breakfast here. But I've got to have my Coca-Cola."

"I'll get a case," the man said, and later that day George made the sale.

So I began to eat breakfast there. The food was good. New England was filled with small, one-man diners like that in those days.

One morning when I came in the proprietor was at the end of the counter talking to the milkman and did not see me enter. I overheard him say, "Stick around a few minutes, and I'll show you the damnedest thing you ever saw. This Southerner comes in about six-thirty every. . ." he looked up and saw me and said to the milkman, "Oh, here he is now."

He came up the counter and asked of me, "The usual?"

I nodded. "The usual."

He brought me a bowl of cornflakes and a Coca-Cola. I poured the drink over the cornflakes and ate them with the milkman and the proprietor staring at me.

I have always eaten cornflakes and Coca-Cola. They're very good together. I have always drunk four Coca-Colas a day, sometimes more, and I've never had stomach problems. It lines my stomach and helps with digestion.

After six months in Providence I came to work one morning, and Herr told me not to run my route. "Mr. Brownlee wants to see you in Boston," he said.

I drove to Boston that morning. When I walked into Brownlee's headquarters office, he shook my hand and said bluntly, "My New Haven manager is leaving. I'd like you to go down there and be my manager."

Just like that! I made the jump from route salesman to manager of a territory in one morning. But Brownlee and Herr must have figured I was ready to make the leap. There were exciting days ahead.

CHAPTER 8

A Raise and a Little
Red Truck

PIG-IRON BILL EXPLAINED TO ME that day in Boston that as
manager of the New Haven plant I would be given a raise in
salary and a red panel truck with "Coca-Cola" all over it. He said
there were four salesmen and one man in the plant in the New
Haven operation. So it was a small plant, but still I was the manager.

"I'll meet you in New Haven next Monday," Pig-Iron Bill
said and dismissed me. That was in 1931. I was twenty-four
years old.

I left Providence on Sunday, rode the train to New Haven, and
took a room in the Taft Hotel across the street from Yale University. The next morning, Brownlee came to the Taft for breakfast
with me. We went to the plant after that and I met the German,
Wilhelm Hoffman, who had been manager of the plant. For reasons I never learned, Brownlee didn't like Hoffman and had
turned him loose. Hoffman went on to New London, got a job in
the Coca-Cola plant there, which was a privately-owned franchise, and worked there till he died.

The plant was small, so small that it was in the back yard of the
home of a man named Cary. The building was about five thousand square feet and was reached by a drive that came around the
side of Cary's house. In the plant was a Dixie bottling machine,
which could be operated by one man and bottled a case of twenty-
four bottles a minute.

The operator brought a case of dirty empties from the stack
and placed the bottles, two at a time, in the two cups on the

washing machine. The machine squirted caustic soda into the bottles, rinsed them, turned them over automatically, and sent them into the filling machine. There the machine squirted a little more than an ounce of syrup in each bottle and filled it with carbonated water.

That was all done automatically. The operator had to take the bottles off the machine, inspect each bottle individually, and put them in the case.

At that time, many Coca-Cola plants around the country depended on those little Dixie machines. There were then 1,350 Coca-Cola plants in the country; today there are less than six hundred.

They've been consolidated, modernized, and made so efficient that one plant can cover a wide territory.

Cliff Hodson, the production manager for Brownlee's New England operation, had driven Brownlee to New Haven that morning to introduce me to my new staff. I met the plant superintendent, Jerry Johnson, and the four salesmen, who immediately left to work their routes. Brownlee took me to the bank and introduced me to the people I needed to know there, and then he and Cliff left. They had business elsewhere, and they left me standing there. Nobody ever gave me any instructions about how to manage a plant. I had to learn for myself.

I had held most of the jobs in a bottling company and was no stranger to the work. I knew what each of my men was supposed to do, and I knew how much to expect of them.

Beyond that, I remembered A. B. Carver, the little emperor in the Atlanta office, and I was determined not to treat people like Carver had treated me. If I could always remember that, no matter what hardships came along, I would be able to get along with those who worked for me.

Only one of the four salesmen was married, and I was sure that I could be compassionate and understanding of the problems that the men would bring to me.

When my four salesmen checked in that afternoon, I knew I had problems of another nature. Together, they had sold sixteen cases of Coca-Cola in a working day that began at eight in the morning and ended at five-thirty in the afternoon.

I thought an average of four cases a day for each salesman was ridiculous in a territory that contained more than two million people.

One of our routes was seventy-two miles long, from New Haven to Kent. A salesman needed ten or twelve hours to work that route, and he should sell more than four cases. But my salesman didn't, and that was the problem I faced.

I settled into my usual workaholic routine, working from daylight until well after dark every day. Saturday night it would be eleven or midnight when I finished totaling up the revenue, making the deposit, and making sure the books were in order.

I took a late dinner at a place called "The Del," a delicatessen that served excellent food near the plant. After dinner, I fell into bed and slept till two o'clock Sunday afternoon. I dressed and went out for something to eat, then went straight back to bed and slept till Monday morning.

The Depression was at its height when I managed the New Haven plant, and nickels were scarce. Work was almost impossible to find, and those men who worked for me were happy to have jobs—even jobs that paid twenty dollars a week plus three cents for each case of Coca-Cola they sold.

It was not hard to find men to work, but it was extremely hard to find good salesmen, men who could go out and sell Coca-Cola by the case. Most of my salesmen were Southerners, either men I had worked with previously or men recommended to me by higher officials of the Coca-Cola Company.

The first man I ever had to fire was a big New Englander named George. He was a huge man, six feet three or four inches, and about two hundred fifty pounds. He was a likeable fellow, but as a salesman he fell flat. He simply could not sell, try as he might. I suspected that he was not trying too hard when he got out of sight of the plant, and it became apparent to me that I had to replace him.

Having no experience in such matters, I figured out what I thought was the best way to proceed. I told myself I had better hire his replacement first, a man who could go to work the day I fired George. Paul Bacon was available. He and I had worked together in the Traffic Department in Atlanta, both as secretaries, and it was he who had helped me do the mountain of work that enabled me to go to Savannah for the Demolay meeting.

On the day before Bacon was due to begin work, I called George in after he finished his route and told him how sorry I was but that I had to dismiss him and replace him with someone who could sell.

Suddenly, he burst into tears—this huge man—and fell on his knees with his hands clasped before him. He told me he had just announced his engagement and if he had no job he couldn't get married.

"You can't do this to me, Mr. Rowland," he cried. "You just can't! You just can't! God help me, what will I do?"

Well, I just stood there with my mouth open. I couldn't say a word, watching this big man groveling on his knees, crying real tears.

When I found my tongue I told him to get up. I told him he could keep his job, but that he would have to do better, work harder, and sell more Coca-Cola. He hadn't been selling enough to pay his twenty-dollar salary.

Then I telephoned Brownlee in Hartford and told him, "I've made a big mistake. I've got a man I have to fire, and I can't do it—and his replacement will be to work tomorrow morning."

"Why can't you fire him?" Pig-Iron asked, and when I told him the circumstances, he said, "I'll handle it."

He had a man in his office named Gardner Tillinghast, who had been with the Export Division and had worked for Colonel Horsey. Tillinghast was tough, about as tough as they came. Early the next morning Tillinghast drove up to the New Haven plant and in no uncertain terms dismissed George from his job, so that when Paul Bacon reported for work his truck was loaded and waiting for him.

When Paul started selling, business picked up. He so inspired the other salesmen that their sales increased too. We added a fifth route and hired a man named Walter Murray to run it. Pig-Iron Brownlee bought a new White truck for the route. Of course, Mr. Woodruff in Atlanta, who had been president of White Motor Company, was responsible for our purchasing White trucks; but they were big, serviceable, beautiful trucks - and expensive.

We soon outgrew the space we occupied, and I located additional space in the Smedley Warehouse on Brewery Street; so named because a large brewery had occupied most of the street, including the warehouse.

I rented enough space to move the entire operation into the warehouse. When I went to see our banker and told him that we would like to change our address and all our records because we were occupying new quarters, I didn't know that he was also executive director of the New Haven Chamber of Commerce.

He must have thought a positive announcement of business success might spur New Haven's depressed economy; so he contacted the newspaper and on the following day the paper came out with a big headline: "Coca-Cola Expanding—Moving to New Location."

We were already in our new quarters. When I came to work at seven o'clock the next morning, there were two hundred men looking for work standing in the alley leading to the entrance to our plant.

I suppose I had never known until then what real embarrassment was. We had no jobs; we were not hiring anyone. Yet the tone of the newspaper article had left the impression that there were jobs to be had at the Coca-Cola plant.

A terrible feeling overcame me. I spent the morning talking to men of every nationality and age, telling each that I was sorry but that we had already hired everybody we needed. I didn't say we hadn't hired anyone. I just said, "I'm sorry. Thank you for coming, but all the jobs have been filled, and here's a Coca-Cola for you."

When we did have an opening, we had our pick of men from every walk of life and with all degrees of education. There were so many people out of work that even good lawyers were looking for any grubbing job they could find.

So it was one day that Mr. Brownlee called me and said, "You remember Gene Stetson?" Of course, I remembered that Eugene Stetson was one of the three men who had purchased the Coca-Cola Company from Asa Candler for twenty-five million dollars in 1919.

"Yes, sir, I remember him very well," I said.

"Well, there's a young graduate of Yale," Mr. Brownlee said, "who graduated this year, and he's marrying Gene Stetson's daughter, Josephine. He wants a job, and you told me that you'd like to add another route."

"Yes, sir," I said. "We need six routes."

"Will you give this young man a job?"

"If you want me to," I said. "I'll be happy to have him."

The young man's name was Bob Hatcher, and he came to see me to apply for the job. He had been captain of the Yale baseball team and appeared in every way to be a fine young man. He was from Macon, Georgia, and was engaged to a girl who lived in

Coscob, Connecticut. There wasn't a place in Coscob at that time under twenty or thirty acres, all with tremendous houses. Coscob represented country living at its best—at its most expensive best. Swimming pools, big cars, and plenty of money. Stetson was a vice president of a bank in New York and Coscob was about thirty minutes out of the city.

The interview did not seem to be awkward for Bob Hatcher, but it was for me. Here I was, manager of a small Coca-Cola plant, offering a twenty-dollar-a-week job to a young man who was marrying a girl from Coscob, Connecticut. That's one for Ripley, I thought.

But Bob Hatcher was glad to get the job; so I told him to come to work the next Monday.

We had a great team spirit in the New Haven plant. We had five routes. Paul Bacon had one. Don Cowan, another Southern man whose father had asked me to give his son a job in the presence of Mr. Woodruff in Atlanta, had another. We had an Italian named Lou Inzero on a third route, and Walter Murray and Eddie Dwyer, a graduate of Fordham, worked the others. When Hatcher came, we added a sixth route.

We didn't sell as many cases of Coca-Cola as we thought we should have, but we had a good time. In retrospect, I suppose we sold about as much as could have been sold because of the depressed times, but young, single men who had jobs then usually thought they should accomplish more than they did. Murray, Inzero, and Dwyer lived at home, and Don and I had rooms.

We were such a close-knit group that not any of us would leave the plant at night until all trucks were in and loaded for the next day's runs. We loaded the trucks ourselves. Then I would make up the deposit to take to the bank the next day and put it in the safe.

On the Monday morning that Hatcher reported for work, no one left the plant to work routes until he came. He was there early; so no one was delayed. He rolled up in a big limousine with a chauffeur, and he unloaded golf clubs and tennis racquets and a lot of other paraphernalia.

"He'll never use those," Don said, looking at the golf clubs and tennis racquets. And he never did—not while he worked for us at New Haven.

Hatcher settled into the routine with us; and for weeks we all
arrived at work together in the mornings, and no one left in the
evenings until all could leave.

One night, Don said to me, "Mr. Rowland, I haven't been to a
movie since I've been up here. Would it be all right if I go to a
picture show tonight?"

It was about eight o'clock. I laughed and said, "Well, we've
got about everybody loaded. Sure, go ahead." I was busy making
up the deposit and working on the books, and about nine-thirty I
saw Don still hanging around.

"I thought you were going to the picture show, Don," I said.

"I thought about it," he said, grinning, "but I'd feel like a heel
leaving so early."

Don became our leading salesman in the summer. He had a
beach route, about twenty-five miles out to Saybrook, and he
put off more Coca-Cola than anybody else. We did a good business
in the summer.

Don was a heavy sleeper. He overslept often until I made him
take a room just across the street from the plant. Then I would go
and wake him and make sure he got to work on time. When it
snowed he had a penchant for turning over in bed and going
back to sleep. The first thing I did on a snowy day was go across
the street and wake Don and make sure he dressed and came to
work.

One summer day, Don's mother and Mrs. Woodruff came to
New Haven and checked into the Taft Hotel. They came in a
chauffeured limousine. On their first day in town, they came to
the plant. I seated them in my office and gave them Coca-Cola. It
was about one o'clock in the afternoon.

"Where is Don?" Mrs. Cowan asked.

"He's out on his route," I said. "Today he went to Saybrook."

"Could I go out there?" she asked.

"Of course," I said. "I'll be glad to take you out there. I know
where Don is, and we can pick him up easily."

She told Mrs. Woodruff to go back to the hotel and she would
see her at dinner time; so I drove Mrs. Cowan to Saybrook and
found Don. She got on the truck and finished the route with him,
making all his calls; and when he rolled in to the plant that evening, she was worn out. But that was a mother's love for her son.
She simply wanted to be with him and to see what he was doing.

Eddie Dwyer was a smart fellow. He was a graduate of law

school and had passed the Connecticut bar, but he couldn't get a job with a law firm. There were no jobs like that available. So he did the best he could, and the best at that time was with the Coca-Cola Company. We were expanding rapidly in our new plant on Brewery Street, and when business reached a certain point, I pulled Eddie off his route and made him a special salesman like I had been in Boston. He was a detail man, which made him a good lawyer, I'm sure, in later years. He paid attention to the smallest detail and was proud when he accomplished small things.

One thing we tried to do was plaster New Haven with big, beautiful Coca-Cola signs. We tried to put up a new sign somewhere every day. Occasionally I rode with Eddie just as I rode the routes with my route salesmen, keeping myself familiar with everything going on in the territory.

Riding with Eddie one day, we approached O'Brian's Grocery. One of the outside walls of the building was big and bare.

"Eddie, that wall needs a Coca-Cola sign," I said.

"I've tried," Eddie said, "but he won't let me put it up."

We had a big sign, 32 by 56 inches, that would be perfect for the wall.

"Well, keep after him," I said.

"I am," Eddie replied.

About two weeks later, Eddie came into my office late one afternoon, grinning. "Can you come with me a few minutes?" he asked. "I've got something I want to show you."

We got in my panel truck and drove over to O'Brian's, and there on the wall was the big Coca-Cola sign.

"I kept after him" Eddie said. "Doesn't it look pretty?"

That was how much pride Eddie took in his job, enough to take me on a twenty-minute drive to see a new sign he had put up.

Eddie was second in command under me in the New Haven plant, and when I went home to Atlanta the Christmas before I got married, he drove me to the train.

Before I boarded, Eddie asked, "Now, what can I do for you while you're gone?"

"You can sell a hundred cases," I said. "We've never sold a hundred cases in a day in the winter. See if you can do that. It would be great if you could."

"How will I let you know?"

"Send me a telegram."

"Collect?"

"Yeah, send it collect. I'll be glad to pay for it."

I had to pay for three telegrams while I was home for Christmas.

When I promoted Eddie Dwyer to special salesman, Don Cowan talked me into hiring his cousin from Birmingham, a car salesman name Ike Feagin.

"I've got this cousin in Birmingham," Don said. "He's not doing anything because he can't sell any cars, and I'd appreciate it if you'd give him the route job."

That was fine with me. I called Ike on the phone, and he was willing to come up for twenty dollars a week and three cents bonus a case.

That gave us an almost all-Southern sales staff. I had hired another Atlanta boy named Joe Eckman, a tall, skinny basketball player from Georgia Tech. Everybody called him Papa Joe. We had Bob Hatcher, who was originally from Macon, Georgia, Don Cowan from Atlanta, and Paul Bacon from Atlanta. The other three salesmen, Dwyer, Murray, and Lou Inzero, were from New Haven. Jerry Johnson ran the plant; his assistant was another Italian named Phil Salso, and both were from New Haven.

At one time, our six Southerners, Hatcher, Papa Joe, Cowan, Feagin, Bacon, and I, all lived at the YMCA. The Y building was new, built about the time I came to New Haven.

We all rode together to and from work in my panel truck, four in the rear, one in the front seat, with me driving. We ate together, usually at the Del; and we played together, especially on weekends.

Every Saturday night we hustled to the Y, quickly showered and dressed, and went in the panel truck to Cheshire, Connecticut, about twenty-five miles from New Haven to a large inn that was a speakeasy. There we spent the night, drinking beer and whiskey, playing cards, and having a big time. I didn't drink the hard stuff at the time, but the speakeasy kept a good supply of Coca-Cola, which satisfied me. On Sunday morning we drove back to the YMCA, singing and happy as a half-dozen larks, and everybody sacked out for the rest of the day.

In the 1920s and early-thirties, the University of Georgia and Yale played each other in football, and every other year Georgia came to Yale.

Before the Georgia-Yale game when I was in New Haven, I decided to sell some Coca-Colas at the Yale Bowl. I knew that with a Georgia crowd on hand, sales would be much more brisk than they had been the day I sold the first Cokes in Harvard Stadium.

Concessions at the Yale Bowl were leased by an Italian fellow named Andy Spinnelli. He stocked the stands, supplied the manpower, paid Yale for the lease, and kept the profits.

I drove over to the Yale Bowl and met Spinnelli and told him that when Georgia played at Yale there would be a lot of Georgia people on hand. I was sure they would want to drink a lot of Coca-Colas.

He laughed. "Mr. Rowland," he said, "I've got all the drinks I need here. I've got Simpson Springs, and I've got Canada Dry Ginger Ale. That goes well. They use it to mix their drinks. And, you know how cold it gets up here. Cold drinks don't go as well as coffee, except for chasers."

His big problem was room. "I just don't have room for any more drinks," he said. "If you could find some way to store and dispense the Coca-Colas, I would be glad to handle a few."

I mulled that over for a few days and finally settled on an old Ford truck chassis that had been sitting in the yard of the warehouse when we leased it and moved in. The chassis had wheels and rims but no tires. I bought four old used tires for three dollars each from the people who sold us tires for our trucks, and I hired a carpenter to build a container to fit on the chassis. He built a tongue on the front of the chassis that hooked to the rear of one of our pickup trucks. All I had in the rig was twelve dollars for the tires and the money for the carpenter's labor.

On Saturday morning of the Georgia game, we filled the container with Coca-Cola, iced them down, put a big Coca-Cola sign on the container, and drove to the stadium. We parked where Spinnelli told us to, near the stands in which the Georgia people would sit; and a couple of my men spent the afternoon manning the Coca-Cola stand.

Our success was nothing to write Atlanta about, but it was better than I'd had at Harvard Stadium. At that first Georgia game, we sold twelve cases of Coca-Cola, for which Mr. Spinnelli, of course, got the profit. He was so pleased that he told us if we wanted to, we could sell Cokes at all of the Yale home games, which we did. We brought a double staff of men, and while half sold Coca-Cola, the other half watched the game. Every now and then we switched.

Soon, Spinnelli began putting Coca-Cola in some of his regular concession stands, and by the time I left New Haven he was a regular customer.

So the first sales of Coca-Cola at Yale Bowl, like those at Harvard Stadium, didn't amount to much—but in time they led to a lot of business.

CHAPTER 9

Doubling Up

THOSE WERE GOOD DAYS in New Haven. For me, that was a learning period. I learned more about management and about people than at any other time in my life.

All of us at New Haven worked too much. We were happy to have jobs that brought in steady paychecks, small though they were. Thousands of men were out of work, and there was little or no work to be found.

I had been a workaholic since I went to work full time for the Coca-Cola Company, and I didn't mind because I was in a learning process and had no one to look out for but myself. I had no ties, no strings attached. I loved my work. I believed in Coca-Cola. So that's where I spent my time.

During the week, when all the salesmen had their trucks on the routes, I had some spare time. As long as the Dixie machine was going full blast everything was fine. We were bottling with that one small machine as much Coca-Cola as we could sell.

Sometimes I went downtown for lunch breaks and occasional shopping. On one of those breaks I met a wonderful girl named Betty Lee. She was half Chinese. Her father was manager of the Yale School of Music, and her mother was a beautiful Chinese lady who had been an opera singer when Betty's father had met her during a performance at Yale. They were later married and had the one daughter.

Betty was conscious of her lineage. Her eyes were beautifully shaped, but she told me she would never have children because she would not subject them to the problems she had had "growing up with slanted eyes."

We dated for a while, and I suddenly realized I was becoming quite serious about her. I was twenty-five and had saved some money, and my thoughts kept turning toward the fact that it was time I got married.

I had never had true romantic inclinations before. I had never really thought about getting married, and if I had had such thoughts I probably would have thought of getting married to a Coca-Cola bottle.

The Brownlees had moved to Hartford, and they occasionally invited me up for Sunday dinner. I telephoned Pig-Iron and asked if I could bring Betty up on the following Sunday. I told him I was thinking of marrying her and wanted them to meet her.

The Brownlees welcomed her and made her feel at home all Sunday afternoon, and when we left I thought we had had a good time and that the Brownlees liked her very much. I was quite pleased with the day.

But the next day—Monday—Brownlee came to New Haven to see me. He was still Pig-Iron Bill; no beating around the bush. Just bring it into the open and lay it on the line.

"Sanders," he said when he walked into my office, "you'd better not marry that girl."

"I what?" I was amazed.

"You can't marry her," he said. "She's Chinese, and you can't marry a Chinese girl. Oh, she's a fine girl; we really liked her. But you can't marry a Chinese girl. You've got your career as well as your life to think about."

I had no comeback. I was dumbfounded. I didn't want to argue with him because I had solicited his opinion.

"I know a girl you ought to marry," Brownlee continued unabashed. "Her sister goes with my son, Bob. We'll have her over soon when you come up, and we'll introduce you to her."

He talked only a few more minutes, then abruptly left and returned to Hartford.

I didn't know what to do. I had cultivated Betty's family until I knew they expected me to marry her. Her grandmother—her father's mother, who lived with them—knew I was thinking of matrimony and had told me she wanted to give me her own mother's diamond ring to give Betty for an engagement ring. It was a beautiful ring. "I want you to give this to Betty," she said, "And you don't have to tell her that I gave it to you."

Believe me, I gave marriage a lot of thought for the next few weeks. The upshot was that I decided not to marry Betty, for several reasons. I am sure what Pig-Iron Bill said made an impression on me, but the big factor was that Betty refused to have children. When I made up my mind, I told her. I broke the news to her gently, and she seemed to understand.

"I don't blame you," she said. "You are the kind of person who should have children because you will make a wonderful father. But I will never have children. I do not want them."

After I was married, Betty wrote my wife a sweet letter, and Mimi really appreciated it. I didn't see Betty again after I told her we could not be married.

A couple of weeks after Brownlee told me he wanted to introduce me to the sister of his son's girlfriend, he called and invited me to come to Hartford for Thanksgiving. It was 1932, and that was the day I met my future wife.

She was a beautiful girl. Her name was Helen Kenyon, and she was of an old, established West Hartford family.

There was a crowd at the Brownlee home that day. Paul Bacon was there, and so were two other Southerners whom I do not remember. They worked for Brownlee in Hartford. The Brownlees' son, Bob, and his girlfriend were there.

And Helen Kenyon was there with her date, a young fellow named David Bowes of the Pitney-Bowes Bowes.

After spending the afternoon with that crowd—a non-drinking group by the way—I discovered that I liked Helen Kenyon very much. We all talked and drank Coca-Cola, and no one even thought of hard liquor.

But as much as I liked Helen that afternoon, I felt that she disliked me. Rather, I thought she liked Paul Bacon better. I couldn't tell how much she liked David Bowes. I thought she didn't like me because I wore spats and a derby. I also had on a Navy blue coat, but the thing she liked least about me was that I smoked cigars. I had smoked cigars since I was sixteen.

She refused to date me, much as I asked. I talked to her several times in the weeks before Christmas, and she still wouldn't date me. I became even more intrigued.

For Christmas, I went to visit my family in Atlanta and spent most of the time thinking about Helen Kenyon. On Christmas day I telephoned her to wish her Merry Christmas. I had never called her on the phone before, and she liked my voice. She liked my Southern accent. Too, she was impressed because she had never had a long-distance call of that long a distance before.

"Look," I said, "I'm going to be back about January second. How about let's go bowling with Marian and Bob, or something?"

She hesitated only a moment, then said, "All right," and I walked about two feet off the ground until I returned to New Haven.

So we went bowling on our first date, and her father made her be home by ten o'clock, and he made me leave as soon as I got her home.

She was working as a secretary, making ten dollars a week, and David Bowes was her steady beau. He was on Pitney-Bowes payroll as a salesman, making fifteen dollars a week.

She and I dated each other a few more times, and one evening she told me she was engaged to David Bowes and intended to marry him.

"Well, when are you going to marry him?" I asked. I was a bit taken aback, but also angered at such a direct statement.

"Just as soon as we're making forty dollars a week between us."

"How long will that be?" I asked.

She said she didn't know, and I did a bit of calculating in my head and said, "Tell you what. You make ten dollars a week and he makes fifteen. He needs to make thirty. Send him over to my place, and I'll put him to work at thirty dollars a week; and you'll have your forty dollars. You can get married right away."

"Would you do that?" she asked.

"Yes. I would do that because I want you to be happy."

"Can you really give him a job making thirty dollars a week?"

"Absolutely, and I'll do it too. You tell him to come and see me tomorrow and I'll put him to work."

I left, feeling quite dejected. I had made up my mind that I would put David Bowes on the payroll.

But he didn't show up the next day. Nor the next, nor the next. He didn't come at all.

I took that as an encouraging sign.

We continued to date, and I began to forget about David Bowes. I thought she was forgetting about him, too.

In March, I asked her to marry me; and, to my surprise, she accepted my proposal.

Suddenly I was on the verge of having another family. Helen's parents, Frederic Hatheway and Caroline Maslen Kenyon, had lived in West Hartford for many years. He was general manager of the Hartford Steam Boiler Inspection and Insurance Company for more than thirty-five years and was also a well-known singer and soloist in several churches.

Helen's mother was the daughter of Stephen and Harriet Brown Maslen of Hartford. Stephen was a skilled craftsman from Trowbridge, England, owner of a monument works that is still in business in Hartford. Some of his works decorate the Capitol building there. Harriet was of the Rhode Island Browns.

One of their claims to fame was that they were friends of Mark Twain. I remember Helen telling me before we were married how she remembered a ride in Reverend Twitchell's electric car when she was a mere child. Reverend Twitchell was a close and dear friend of Twain's.

Helen and I became engaged in March and scheduled our wedding for April 15. That was 1933, the year Roosevelt took office as president. The depression was at its height, but strange things happen to some people during terrible times. The strange thing that happened to me was that I got promoted again.

Pig-Iron Bill told me he wanted me to become manager of the Hartford plant, which was much larger than New Haven. At the same time, he said, I would still be responsible for New Haven, even though New Haven would have a new manager.

I asked who the new manager would be, and Pig-Iron said he wanted his brother-in-law, Bud Connor, to be the new New Haven manager. Connor didn't have a job and Brownlee, maybe at the insistence of his wife, was creating one for him. That's often the way things worked in the Depression.

Bud Connor was not my kind of man, but Brownlee had been so nice and good to me that I agreed to take Connor under my wing and spend enough time with him to show him how to manage the New Haven plant.

Later, Brownlee was transferred back to Atlanta and was succeeded by A. M. Day, Roosevelt Day's brother, as vice president in charge of company-owned plants, and the first thing A. M. Day did was to fire Bud Connor. Connor was one of those unfortunate guys who depended on everybody else to look after him. I did all I could for him; but he just wouldn't work, and I was glad Mr. Day had to fire him and not I. I owed Brownlee more than that.

For some time, however, I divided my time between Hartford,

where I ran the entire plant, and New Haven, where I still had to do most of the work. It was no picnic.

Helen and I were married in the Congregational Church in West Hartford as scheduled on April 15, 1933. Our wedding reception was held in her parent's home—without us.

One of their neighbors was a fellow named George Jones, whom I did not like. When we parked on the street by Jones' house and went into the Kenyon home for the reception, I noticed a few minutes later that Jones had other cars parked in such a manner that my car was blocked in.

The guy was a nuisance, and I knew he was up to something. As soon as Helen had changed into her traveling clothes, I told her to come on.

"We're leaving," I said. "George Jones is up to something. He's going to do something to my car. He has me blocked in now, and the only way we can get out is to drive over his lawn—and I'm going to do it."

She didn't want to, but she came along. We got in my car, and my anger was so great then that I gunned the car over Jones' lawn and left deep ruts in the soft April ground.

I was already ticked off because when we came out of the church after the wedding, Helen saw an old boyfriend, Paul Blakesly. She cried out to him, and he came over and put his arms around her: I didn't like it worth a damn.

So I was ready to leave the reception when we got there—and the thing about Jones blocking my car in was the last straw. So we left.

That was the day that Pig-Iron Bill showed his colors as a sadist. He had told me to spend the first night of our honeymoon at the Bear Mountain Inn in Bear Mountain Park, New York. We were going to drive to Atlanta.

Bear Mountain was about two hours from Hartford, and I had taken Pig-Iron at his word and made a reservation.

We arrived there about seven-thirty in the evening and—I'm sure Brownlee knew this—the only thing open was the inn's upper floor—just cots under a window; no bathrooms in the rooms; only a place for campers to sleep with one toilet down the hall.

That's where we spent our first night—the facilities were truly terrible. Helen sprained her ankle making the step down to the hallway from the toilet, and about eleven-thirty a bunch of drunks came in and awakened us and caroused all night.

I thought, what a helluva way to start a marriage. I'm sure Helen's thoughts were stronger than that.

We drove to Washington the next day and stayed that night in a fine hotel, and the third day we drove to Greenville, South Carolina, and checked into the Poinsettia Hotel. It had all-Negro help, all in white gloves, and the most genteel atmosphere you could ever imagine. That was Helen's introduction to the South, and she loved it. She especially loved the huge chandelier in the dining room of the hotel.

We went on to Decatur the next day and stayed two weeks with my family, then drove to Birmingham and spent a week with one of my classmates, Ernie Smith, who had married Brownlee's daughter, Jane.

When we returned to Hartford after a month, we settled into an apartment on Collins Street. We paid forty-two fifty a month for a living room, den, kitchen, one bedroom, and a bath. It was a fairly new apartment and very nice.

We lived quite well. Steak was twenty-five cents a pound, eggs ten cents a dozen, bread five cents a loaf, and all the fresh vegetables you could eat for practically nothing. Helen would take ten dollars to the store and buy our week's groceries and have change left.

She also believed in Coca-Cola. When she went to a store to get groceries she always asked for six bottles of Coca-Cola. If the proprietor said he didn't carry Coke, she would huff out without buying the groceries. If this happened often enough the store usually called us and asked if we would stock it with Coke.

When I came to Hartford, I brought Joe Eckman and Don Cowan with me as salesmen. In Hartford, as everywhere else, I rode the routes to familiarize myself both with the territory and with my salesmen.

I knew what Eckman and Cowan could do; so I rode with them for pleasure.

Sometimes a salesman would trade a case of Coca-Cola to a store for four packages of cigarettes. It was a fair trade since cigarettes sold for twenty cents a pack and Coke went for eighty cents a case. Trades like that were a good way to sell Cokes because a salesman like Joe Eckman who smoked would make the trade and then pay for the case of Cokes himself and draw three cents in return for selling the case.

One day when I rode with Joe, he stopped at a store where the

owner wanted a case of Coca-Cola but had no money to pay. He
dealt in live chickens, and we wound up trading a case of Coke for
two live chickens. We punched holes in a cardboard box, put the
chickens inside the box, and I took them home with me.

We had been married about two months, and when Helen saw
the box with holes in the side, she was sure that I had brought her
a puppy.

"Oh, Sanders," she cried happily, "a puppy!"

"A puppy?" I asked. "Oh, no, this is no puppy." I opened the
box, and she saw the two chickens and almost fainted.

"What," she said, "do you intend doing with those things?"

"Oh, I'm going to wring their necks in the bathroom, and you
can cook them for supper," I said.

"You," she said sternly, with fire in her eyes, "are not going to
wring any neck in my bathroom."

"Nothing to it," I said. "I've seen our cooks do it many's the
time. All you do is just wring their necks."

"Not in my bathroom," she said again, speaking very slowly,
and this time I got the message.

I wound up giving the chickens to a fellow who sold fresh eggs,
and he was happy to get them.

While in Hartford, I learned the truth of that old saw, "it isn't
what you know, it's *who* you know."

One of our neighbors was a classmate of Helen's. She was married to a lawyer named Joe Cooney, and I didn't know at the time
that he was also a member of the State Senate. He was a young
man in the law office of Hartford's mayor, and that was impressive enough for me.

I had begun to drink a little socially at that time—a taste of gin
now and then. I could call a fellow I knew in East Hartford,
and he would deliver a bottle of gin to me for one dollar. I had
also begun to make a little bathtub gin in our apartment which
was pretty good; but not as good as the East Hartford stuff. On
occasion we got together with Joe and Mallie Cooney and had a
drink or two and some good conversation.

One day Pig-Iron Bill came to see me and said the State Legislature had proposed a one-cent a bottle tax on soft drinks, which
was an extremely stiff tax, amounting to twenty percent of the
purchase price. Brownlee told me the legislature was holding a
hearing on the tax that afternoon and for me to get all of our

employees over to the State House at two o'clock to attend.

I herded everyone to the State House and went into the hearing room. The chairman of the committee holding the hearing was Joe Cooney. Several of our people spoke at the hearing, but I did not. At the conclusion of the hearing, Joe said, "Sanders, what are you doing here?"

I told him we had a tremendous interest in the soft-drink tax, and he said, "One cent won't make that much difference."

"What are you doing tonight?" I asked him.

"Nothing," he said, and I told him not to plan anything. I called my bootlegger in East Hartford, got my dollar bottle of gin, and Joe and I had a few drinks and a long conversation that evening—and the tax bill later died in committee. It didn't even get to the State House floor.

That's when I learned how important it was to know the right people in the right places.

Old Demon Rum got me in hot water with the company in Hartford once. It almost got me fired.

The Shriners had a circus every year in Hartford. A fellow named Bob Mellard, who was manager of the Hartford Club, was the Shriner in charge of refreshments at the circus. I visited him and asked him to sell Coca-Cola in his concession stands.

"I'll do it on one condition," he said, "that you fix me five cases of a very special kind of Coca-Cola."

I asked him what kind, and he explained. "We have about ten men who work in the refreshment stand, and just for them I want you to bottle five cases of Coca-Cola with an ounce of rum in each bottle. I have the rum here at the club."

I laughed and thought quickly and could see nothing wrong with such a request, especially since it would be a private matter just between us. "I think I can do that," I told him. It was a chance, I thought, to sell a lot of Coca-Cola.

Mellard came over to the plant one evening before the circus, and I asked the superintendent to stay, and the three of us opened five cases of Coca-Cola, put an ounce of rum in each bottle, then recapped all the bottles, and set those special cases aside.

Mellard, who had promised to buy all of the circus's soft drinks from us, then ordered five hundred cases of Coca-Cola for the circus.

He iced the special Cokes down in a small container the day the circus started, and his concessionnaires had a lot of fun selling hot dogs and Coca-Cola.

Unfortunately, in a big rush between acts of the circus, one of the concessionnaires got hold of two special bottles of Coke and sold them to a woman and her young son.

Pretty soon the woman was dizzy and the son was walking around like a rooster, crowing, and carrying on.

When the mother found out what had happened, she raised Cain and threatened to sue the Shriners, the Coca-Cola Company, and everybody else she could think of.

Fortunately for us, the woman's husband was a Shriner, and when Mellard explained to him what had happened, he talked his wife out of suing.

Brownlee heard about the fracas a few days later and was ready to fire me until Bob Mellard drove to see him and explained that it was he, Mellard, who was responsible both for putting the rum in the Coke and for selling two bottles to the woman. Actually, he was overstating it a bit because I carried responsibility for the whole thing, too. Even at that Brownlee might have fired me had not Mellard reminded him that the Shriners had sold five hundred cases of Coca-Cola, and if Brownlee wanted them to sell any more at future events he would find a way to keep me on the payroll.

It was touch and go for a while, but the business of selling Coca-Cola in Depression days overcame all obstacles.

I had never seen a New England blizzard. Being from the South where a three- or four-inch snow is a whopper, I didn't know what a real blizzard was—and never really gave it any thought.

One morning in Hartford I got up with the wind howling around the house and snow piled knee-deep in the streets. We lived six or seven miles from the plant; and as I got ready to go to work, Helen said, "You can't go to work today."

"Why can't I?"

"Nobody will be out today," she said. "The snow is over your knees now."

"I am going to work," I said.

She said nothing more, knowing by then how hard my head

was. She let me find out for myself what a real New England blizzard is like.

I left the house with a bag of laundry that I was taking to the laundry across the street from the Coca-Cola plant. We lived in West Hartford, about three blocks from downtown. On across the Connecticut River and about five miles out in East Hartford was the Coca-Cola plant.

First, I couldn't get my car out, the snow was so deep. But that didn't faze me: I walked down to Farmington Avenue, the main street, thinking I would catch a streetcar; but no streetcars were running. So I walked on a few blocks to the railroad station to take a taxi, and there were no taxis out that morning.

Few people were on the streets, only the most hearty, or foolhearty, however you look at it. I walked on through town and across the bridge. There over the river the wind really whistled— straight from the North Pole it came with ice in its whiskers. Fortunately, I had that bag of laundry, and I held it before my face to break the wind.

I left home about seven that morning, and at ten I arrived at the plant. It was a helluva walk on a good day. When I arrived, I was the only one there. All the Yankees knew better than to get out in weather like that. But I was a stubborn, hard-headed Southerner, and no storm was going to stop me.

About noon a couple of other Southern boys who lived across the street showed up at the plant. Since we couldn't find anything else to do, we broke out the shovels and began clearing snow.

It was a good thing we didn't get the trucks rolling that day. Our trucks in Hartford were covered only with canvas, and on a cold day, those bottles of Coke froze and burst by the hundreds in the back of those trucks. Some of the trucks arrived in late afternoon with nothing but broken glass. We just scooped everything out and threw it in the trash barrels.

I learned that day to cease production during blizzards and just let nature have its way. Two or three days later we would be back to normal.

We had two Dixie machines in the Hartford plant, and we didn't have quite enough business to keep the machines busy.

Colonel Horsey had been opening up foreign markets, and the

Coca-Cola Company was shipping bottled Coke out of New York
to some of those places. Since we were not operating at capacity,
we were assigned to produce some of the shipments for the overseas market.

We bottled the specified amount in special green bottles—
Export Coca-Cola, we called it—and shipped it to New York
where the bottles were put in cardboard sleeves and packed
in sawdust in sealed wooden cases. We bottled Export Coca-Cola
one day a week to be shipped all over the world. Coca-Cola was
sold in eighty foreign countries in 1933.

Two other momentous things occurred when we lived in Hartford: Roosevelt closed the banks, and our only son was born.

In March of 1933, Roosevelt closed all the banks in the country, trying to help bring the country's economy back onto an
even keel.

I don't remember why, but the night before the morning that
all banks closed, I failed to make our deposit. All the business we
did in those days was in cash, and I had two days receipts—about
four hundred dollars—on hand.

I telephoned Mr. Brownlee and told him what I had done, and
that I had some cash on hand, and he said, "I don't have any. Let
me have a hundred dollars."

By the time I got the money to Brownlee, he told me of two or
three other companies that needed some cash quickly; so we
spread that money around. When the banks reopened, Brownlee
and all those companies paid the money back to me.

Henry, our son, was born in Hartford Hospital May 16, 1934.
He weighed around six pounds and was a lively little rascal.

But shortly after his birth, something happened. Something
ran through that hospital, and ten of the fourteen babies died.
Henry and three others survived, I think, because we had one of
the finest doctors in New England, a Dr. Brayton, working with
Henry. His weight dropped to three and a half pounds, and we
almost lost him.

I have always credited Dr. Brayton with saving Henry's life.

Henry stayed in the hospital six weeks and for a long time his
skin was like a cloth draped over bones. At Dr. Brayton's request, I gave Henry several blood transfusions; and miraculously
he pulled through. We had no more problems with him.

We were then a family—more than just a married couple—and
life took on new meaning for both Helen and me.

*   *   *

One of my route salesmen in New Haven, Otis Wells, was a fraternity brother of mine at Georgia Tech. He was from Georgia, but he had been in Texas selling Bibles with a buddy named Robert Carlton Downs. They were good salesmen, and when I got the opportunity to hire Otis Wells, I jumped at the chance. He was happy to come to New Haven and work for a steady paycheck, even if it was just twenty dollars a week.

Otis did such a good job for me in New Haven that I promoted him to route manager, and when Brownlee needed a manager for the Springfield, Massachusetts, plant, he put Otis in that job.

Otis called me from Springfield one day after I had been promoted to Hartford and asked if I would come over and meet Robert Downs, his buddy. Downs needed a job and Otis was thinking of putting him to work. But he wanted my opinion.

I drove to Springfield and met Downs, and he was a thoroughly likeable fellow. His nickname was "Doc." His father had owned a large Georgia farm and had a lot of black tenants. When some of his tenants were sick, the elder Downs would send Robert to give them a dose of castor oil, or whatever; and the tenants began calling him Doc. The name stuck.

If Doc Downs had a problem, it was his strong will. He didn't believe in second place. He didn't believe in non-accomplishment. If he set out to do something, he did it—one way or the other.

I approved of Downs, and Otis hired him.

Periodically, Otis would telephone me and talk over his problems. I brought him to New England, and when something went wrong he felt better if he talked to me.

He called one day and said, "Sanders, I've got a problem."

"All right," I said, laying aside what I was doing. "What is it?"

He spoke slowly and very carefully. "What do you do," he said, "when one of your salesmen hits a dealer in the head with a hammer?"

I said, "Get the hammer and put it in the safe."

"I'm serious," he said. "Doc was putting up a sign on a dealer's store, and the dealer didn't want the sign. Doc said he was going to put it up anyway. The dealer grabbed the ladder and shook Doc off of it. When Doc picked himself up off the ground, he hit the dealer in the head with his hammer."

"You do have a problem," I said. "And if you haven't already
been out to see the dealer, I suggest you go see him and apologize. Tell him Doc has a violent temper—and tell him you'll
bring Doc to apologize to him if that will help."

"And then?"

"And then you take Doc over there and tell him if he doesn't
apologize you're going to run his butt all the way back to Georgia."

So Otis took Doc and made him apologize, and the dealer accepted the apology. But he never did let them put up the sign.

Otis was transferred to manage the Oakland, California, plant
a few years later, and Doc succeeded him as manager of
Springfield. After that Doc straightened out the plant in Flint,
Michigan, which had been in bad shape, and stayed with Coca-
Cola until he retired to Hendersonville, North Carolina. After I
went to Asheville, just twenty miles from Hendersonville, a few
years ago, I visited with Doc and tried to talk him into helping
me solve some of the problems in Asheville; but he wouldn't do
it.

"No, sir," he said, "I'm not going to do it. I worked all my
life, and I'm just not going to work anymore."

And he didn't. He didn't have to. He had been very lucky
buying Coca-Cola stock and owned more than a million dollars
worth of it when he died.

For sixty-five years I have drunk at least four bottles of Coca-
Cola every day, sometimes more. I can remember only one time
when I was saturated to the point that I couldn't drink any more.

I was riding a route in Hartford with a salesman named Ralph
Thompson. We had company funds set up for sampling, which
was a way to get people to taste Coca-Cola. We believed if we
could get them to drink one bottle, they would be hooked.

If I saw a storeful of people and nobody drinking Coke, I'd just
buy a round. Sometimes the dealer would sell me the Coca-Colas
outright, and sometimes he would let me have them cold out of
his box. I would replace what we used with Coca-Colas off the
truck.

Thompson and I walked into his father's store one day, a general store out in the Connecticut countryside. Eight men sat
around a stove, enjoying the warmth, for it was a rather cool day.

No one was drinking anything; so I said, "Gentlemen, belly up to the bar and let me buy you a round of Coca-Cola."

I bought eleven Cokes, one for each of the eight men, one for Ralph's father, one for Ralph, and, of course, one for me.

When we finished, I looked at the eight to see if any were smacking their lips, eager to get another Coke. Apparently one was, for this man spoke up and said, "That was fine, my friend. You bought that round. I'll buy the next one." So he bought eleven Cokes and we all had a second drink.

Then a third man, and a fourth, and a fifth bought rounds—and all of us wound up drinking five Coca-Colas. That's more than two pounds of Coca-Cola per man.

Let me tell you, I sloshed when I walked out of there.

Coca-Cola today tastes the same to me as Coca-Cola did in 1920 when I went to work. Some people say the six and one-half ounce bottles of Coke—the small ones—taste different than larger bottles. And they do, but not because the mixture is different. It's the carbonation. The same three and one-half volumes of carbonation are put in a twelve-ounce bottle that are put in a six and a half ounce bottle.

Six and a half ounces make the perfect sized drink. The carbonation is just right for that size bottle, and all other bottles, regardless of size, seem to taste differently; but it's the same mixture.

The minute Coca-Cola hits your stomach it is absorbed by the lining of the stomach; it's broken down quickly and you get the immediate effect of the sugar.

If you drink a grape or an orange at nine in the morning and I come along at ten and say, "Let's go get a Coke," you're ready. You know it will be soothing to the stomach. But if I said, "Let's go get another orange," you'd balk. You wouldn't be ready for an orange or a grape.

Part of the huge success of Coca-Cola is that the stomach breaks it down quickly. That's why I can drink so many and enjoy all of them.

I have been asked many times if Coca-Cola ages; and the answer is yes, any soft drink will age. After about six months, any of them will change taste. There are no preservatives in soft drinks—at least not in Coke—and since all the ingredients are natural, they will age.

Those were good years for me in New Haven and Hartford, because I was learning how to manage a Coca-Cola company.

I had success in both places. In New Haven, our four salesmen sold sixteen cases the first day, and when I left we were selling about three to four hundred cases a day steadily. We had increased from four routes to eight, and all eight routes were going well. That was a healthy increase for two and a half years. Our main competition in New Haven was "Iron Brew," and we outdistanced it easily.

Hartford was a going concern when I got there. The salesmen had already cracked the one-hundred-cases-a-day barrier. But I managed to expand the nine routes, put a warehouse in Waterbury to relieve the crush on the Hartford warehouse, and to shorten some of the routes.

I thought my learning—and my accomplishments—were pretty sound, especially for a Southern boy on Northern soil.

CHAPTER 10

Providence

WE HAD BEEN IN HARTFORD more than three years, and we were happy. We had started our family and things were going well at home. At the office, I felt comfortable running a Coca-Cola plant. I knew the work from the ground up. I knew all the personnel, knew their strengths and weaknesses, and felt that I had placed each person where he could do the most good for the company.

Things were running smoothly and business was growing rapidly.

In September of 1935, Helen awakened in the middle of a night. She had a nightmare.

"I just had a dream that you had been transferred to Providence," she said. Providence was larger than Hartford, and the company there was a good-sized plant.

I laughed. "I don't think that will ever happen. Gardner Tillinghast's home is in Providence; and since he came home after his stint with Export, I don't think he'll ever want to leave again."

We forgot the dream in the succeeding days; at least I did—until Christmas day.

On Christmas Eve, I received a call from my boss, A. M. Day, whom we called "Bum" Day. He had been an All-American football player at Georgia Tech.

"Sanders," Day said over the phone, "I'm arriving in the morning at nine at Hartford Station. I'd appreciate it if you'd meet me."

"Yes, sir, I'll meet you," I said. "I'll be standing right there."

This was not an unusual request from Bum Day. He was Eastern Regional Manager for the company-owned plants, and he traveled around all the time. He was an old bachelor and Christmas day didn't mean a whole lot to him. It wasn't the first time he had asked me to meet him at the station and drive him home. He lived in Hartford.

Next morning at nine, I stood on the platform of the railroad station. When the train came in, Bum Day and Gardner Tillinghast stepped off. Bum shook hands with me and I shook with Gardner.

Bum didn't beat around the bush. "You can shake hands with Gardner again," he said, "and congratulate him. He's the new manager in Baltimore."

I congratulated him. Baltimore was a big plant in comparison to Providence—and Providence was that much bigger than my plant in Hartford.

As we walked to my car, Day said, "You meet me in Providence tomorrow morning at ten, and I'll make you the manager of Providence."

Just like that. No bargaining, no fencing. Just a flat statement. "That's great," I said. "I'll be there."

On the way home, he said nothing more about it.

I drove the seventy-four miles to Providence the next morning and Bum Day installed me as the new manager. In the new operation, I had nineteen employees, a plant on Smith Street, and a bottling machine that turned out three hundred cases of Coca-Cola every hour. This machine was five times more productive than one Dixie machine, which would bottle sixty cases an hour. I had employees filling positions in Providence that I had never had in my two previous plants. I had a cashier, a big Irish girl name Catherine Cooley. She checked the trucks in and handled the money; and believe it or not, she loaded and unloaded trucks, throwing Coca-Cola around with ease. A girl named Marie Delay from Pawtucket, was my secretary.

One of the things that enticed me to Providence, other than it being a bigger operation than Hartford, was that Providence had a sales manager. I had never had a sales manager in my operations; that job I had handled myself.

Day transferred the present sales manager out of Providence and recommended that I hire a Pennsylvania Dutchman named Herb Myers, who had grown up in Lancaster, Pennsylvania. He sent Myers up to see me and I hired him.

A phenomenon occurred that first year in our business in Providence. I had heard other managers talk about it but had never seen it happen.

We had ten sets of routes, each worked by a different salesman when I came to Providence. Few of them had to come back to the plant on any day for a second load. If they did, it was late in the afternoon; and they would take on fifty cases or so—never a truck load.

When summer came, however, our business increased. I was in the plant one morning about ten o'clock, and the trucks had been gone for three hours. Suddenly, the doors opened and in came a truck for a second load. No sooner had the doors closed than they opened again, and two more trucks came in empty. I couldn't believe what was happening. By eleven o'clock all ten of our trucks had loaded up again, and in the afternoon some came back for third loads.

The phenomenon was that when this increase in business hit, it stayed. It was not a fluke. The routes stayed strong and our sales grew so quickly that by July we were running that bottling machine at night. To keep up with the route salesmen, we had to bottle day and night.

The increase in business drew Bum Day's interest, and he came to Providence and spent some time watching the operation. He decided that the business was there to stay, and the only way we could handle it was to build a new and larger plant.

He immediately began to make plans for the expansion. He handled the whole thing: I had nothing to do with it. My business was to sell Coca-Cola and I was doing it. It kept me busy almost day and night.

Day brought in an architect named Jesse Shelton from the Atlanta firm of Roberts & Company. Chip Roberts, who ran the firm, was a good friend of Bob Woodruff's and an alumnus of Georgia Tech. He was quite a guy in the Democratic Party. He had been treasurer of the Democratic Party in the South, and Jesse Shelton had been vice president at the same time.

Shelton brought another friend of Woodruff's with him, Frank Adair, who was in the real estate business. Adair bought all real estate for the Coca-Cola Company.

I had already picked out a choice piece of real estate, just about the size we needed and in the approximate location we wanted.

Adair brought a young man with him named St. Elmo Massingale, whose job it was to visit locations where Coca-Cola was planning new plants and figure the center of distribution. This was important. If a plant was located, say, twenty-five miles from the center of distribution and it operated fifty trucks, those trucks were rolling fifty unnecessary miles every day—and that amounts up in operating expenses.

When Massingale figured the center of distribution in Providence, it was 1.2 miles from the property I had chosen, so Adair bought it. The price was right, but it was in a part of Providence that had once been under water. At one time the bay covered that area. In order to put up a strong building, we had to sink two hundred eighty piles from thirty to seventy feet in the earth.

Coca-Cola built a building of eighty thousand square feet for $350,000, and the land, including the price of the piles, was only $80,000 more. Bum Day figured it was a bargain.

A Yankee construction engineer named Riley got the contract to build the new building. He was a good, honest man. As a consequence of the work he did in Providence he later built several other plants for the Coca-Cola Company. However, he could not understand why Coca-Cola let Jesse Shelton design New England plants from Atlanta.

"Look here," Riley told me one day, "the roof of this building is not designed strong enough to hold the snows it'll have to hold. And he has outlets for fans in every room. We never use fans in Providence. We don't need 'em."

Riley complained to Shelton about the roof and the fans; and Shelton changed the roof, designing it stronger to the specifications Riley outlined for him. But he wouldn't budge on the fans. When the building was finished, we had fan outlets all over the place—and we never used them.

Providence had a city ordinance that a building had to have a fire wall around every ten thousand feet of floor space, and Shelton had designed fourteen thousand feet of garage space for us without a wall. When faced with the ordinance, Jesse didn't want to change his plans.

"Go politic a little," he said to me.

I did a little snooping around City Hall and found that the man I needed to see was Kelly Mangianti, Secretary to the Building Board.

Jesse Shelton and I took the plans and went to see Mangianti.

Sanders Rowland's father, Henry Sanders Rowland (right rear) at work in the Atlanta Coca-Cola Company's accounting office at turn of century.

Just before the turn of the century the Coca-Cola administrative force in Atlanta was photographed on the company steps. Asa Candler, who started the company in 1886, stands at front right. Beside him is Frank Robinson, his accountant who named Coca-Cola and wrote the name in Spencerian script. In second row from top, third from left, with head cocked to his left, is Henry Sanders Rowland, the author's father.

This was Coca-Cola's mail room force in 1921 (right) Sanders Rowland at left, Louise Neal, Gatewood Workman, and "Miss Margaret" Landers. Below, a Coca-Cola baseball team of the mid-1920s in Atlanta. Judging by the man's expression at center right it was a fearsome nine. Sanders Rowland, the manager, stands at left rear.

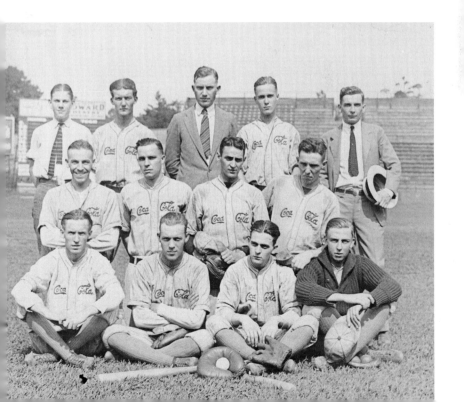

Above, Main Street in Memphis in 1928. Note Coca-Cola's neon sign in center. Left, Uncle Jim Pidgeon, Memphis bottler, in Rome with Italian bottler. Below, the Memphis sales force in Uncle Jim's favorite uniforms, riding pants, shoes, leggings, white shirts, bow ties, and Coca-Cola caps.

Sanders Rowland and his red Coca-Cola truck in New Haven, Conn., 1930.

This is the portrait Robert W. Woodruff autographed for Sanders in 1931.

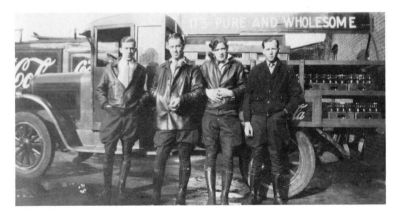

Above, New Haven salesmen in 1930, L-R, Bud Yarnell, George Driscoll, Bill Tierney, and Sonny Robinson. Below, shoveling snow at the Hartford plant in 1933, L-R, Charles Adams, Angelo Della Rocco, Don Cowan, Bob Hatcher, Joe Eckford, Jake Mitchell, and John Cannon.

Above, a 1937 Ford Coca-Cola truck being used in a World War II scrap metal drive in Providence. Below, note the clean lines of the new Coca-Cola Bottling Company plant in Providence, opened in the summer of 1937.

With gasoline hard to get in World War II, the Providence plant employed hayburners to pull Coca-Cola wagons for the duration. Below, a Providence sampling crew made rounds in 1943, giving sample Coca-Colas to residents. Such crews improved sales by introducing the product to new customers.

One of the kings of swing, Tommy Dorsey, entertained the military at Quonset Point in a Coca-Cola production in May of 1945.

Sanders Rowland reaches into box to get Bandleader Les Brown a Coke, above. That's Doris Day sitting on the box. Below, Bandleader Sammy Kaye goes through serving line at Quonset Point before show in 1945.

Above, Sanders Rowland, left, with singer Morton Downey, center, and Mason Dunn, in March 1944. Coca-Cola sponsored Downey in a daily radio show.

Sun-drying bottle caps, called "crowns," made from old tin cans during World War II. Right, Bandleader Xavier Cugat penciled this caricature of Sanders Rowland when Cugat played for troops at Providence during the war.

Ludford Eagan, center, receives keys to new car from Sanders Rowland for selling 102 coolers in a month in Birmingham in 1955. At right is Birmingham Coca-Cola sales manager Cecil Parks.

Crawford Johnson, Jr., who brought Sanders to Birmingham.

Crawford Johnson, III, one of the two best men Sanders trained.

Sanders poses proudly with triplet grandchildren, then 8 years old, in 1971. L-R: Andrew, Sara, and Bruce.

Tom Nash, the Asheville president trained by Sanders.

Sanders Rowland at age 79, whose life with Coca-Cola has been an adventure.

We told him what we wanted and asked if he could get an ease-
ment that would prevent our having to section off four thousand
feet of garage space with a wall.

"Leave the plans with me," he said. "The committee will
meet Monday night, and I'll let you know if I can get this
through for you."

Shelton stayed over the weekend, and on Tuesday morning we
went back to see Mangianti. He was smiling when we walked in.

"You're exempted," he said. "You don't have to put in the
extra wall."

That was a relief. It was also a financial saving for the Coca-
Cola Company, and it speeded completion of the building.

When the plant was completed in summer of 1937, we had a
public opening. We invited all the dignitaries—the mayor, police
chief, fire chief, city and county officials, and a lot of other people. The public turned out in good numbers and organized tours
took people through the plant.

At the end of the tour on which Mangianti saw the plant, he
came to me and said, "Nice place you got here, Mr. Rowland."

I said, "Thank you, Mr. Mangianti, you helped us a lot."

And he said, "I'd like to speak to you privately."

We went into my new office, closed the door, and sat down.

Mangianti didn't hesitate with what was on his mind. "I have
a son named Vincent who graduated from Brown this year," he
said, "and he hasn't got a job. He's been looking for a job since
June. This is August and he still doesn't have any prospects."

"Well, well," I said.

"Jobs are hard to find," Mangianti continued. "I would appreciate it if you would interview my son and give him a job."

That was the one thing I could do. We had opened the new
plant in June, got the kinks out, shaken down the crews, and now
we could use two or three new people in certain positions.

"Mr. Mangianti," I said, "I would be happy to do that. Yes,
I'll give your son a job. Just send him to see me."

I have never seen such relief wash over a person's face.

"You are expanding here," Mangianti said. "You're adding
here."

"Yes, we're doing that," I said. "Tell you son to come and see
me tomorrow."

There was a lot of back-scratching done during the

depression—you scratch my back and I'll scratch yours. But some of it paid off. That one certainly did. Mangianti was the man I had to see in City Hall when I needed anything done.

His son, Vincent, was a big, fine-looking man who was eager to work. I put him on the payroll, and he pitched in with a vigor that a lot of young workers did not have in those depression days. He was such a good worker that I also hired Mangianti's other son, Bob.

When the war came on in 1941, I had to let Bob Mangianti go, but Vincent stayed on. He became a fine route salesman, a route supervisor, later a plant manager, and finally president of a Coca-Cola company.

Politics continued to work for us. Our new plant was on Pleasant Valley Parkway, a beautiful divided street with trees planted in the median. The street was paved, but the side street leading to our new plant was not.

I paid a visit to Mangianti and said, "Mr. Mangianti, how will I get that street paved?"

"That's not my baliwick," Mangianti said, "but do you know Ray Shawcross? He's your councilman over there."

"I don't know him."

"I'll introduce you."

A few days later Mangianti called and asked me to come to City Hall. There he introduced me to our councilman, Ray Shawcross. I told him that I would like to get our street paved and explained the volume of Coca-Cola truck traffic on it. He saw that in bad weather the street could be a major problem for us.

Within a week the street was paved.

Within the next week, Shawcross came to see me. "I have a son named Raymond Junior," he said. "I would appreciate it if you would give him a job."

I began to wonder how many city officials had sons out of work.

But all I said was, "I'll be happy to interview him and see if we have an opening."

Young Raymond came over the next day. He was not the sales type; he seemed to be more suited for work in the plant. So I gave him a job in the plant, and he worked out very well. He did not progress any further in the Coca-Cola structure; eventually he quit and went to work in his father's business, but he got valuable experience from us.

We had tremendous production in the new plant. Our two bottling machines turned out two hundred forty bottles a minute—ten cases every minute. At our grand opening, the mayor's chauffeur was a man who had worked briefly for me when I came to Providence. When he quit, he told me, "Coca-Cola will never sell up here. Maybe in Atlanta, but this isn't Atlanta. And I can't make it trying to sell Coca-Cola."

When he walked around the new plant with the mayor, he inspected it closely; and he later said to me, "I don't believe you built this plant. There is no way you can ever sell enough Coca-Cola to justify a plant like this."

The depression lingered, though there were strong signs of its end. But for the next year or two after we opened the new plant, I had access to all the quality help I wanted. The first person to call on me was the head of the job placement bureau at the University of New Hampshire. He had a list of graduates of his university who were available for employment. I hired two of them, and both turned out to be excellent employees. One became manager of our plant in Worchester, and the other later managed our plant in New Bedford.

The personnel placement manager from Boston College came to me and showed me a picture of the Boston College football team of 1937. "You could just about take your pick," he said. "All the seniors are looking for work." I hired Warren McNamara and Dick Van Iderstein for twenty dollars a week and three cents a case, same as I paid everybody. They were happy to get jobs and were good salesmen.

Business grew so fast between 1936 and 1941 that I opened warehouse operations in Woonsocket and Peacedale, Rhode Island, and in Attleboro and Fall River, Massachusetts. We built a new plant in New Bedford which we opened just as World War II broke out.

We expanded so quickly in those immediate pre-war years that the Providence company operated eight sales distribution points in Rhode Island and southern Massachusetts. Some of those grew so large that I had to appoint sales managers to oversee the route men. There was no production at those sites. We delivered the product on transports, stored it in the warehouse, and the trucks worked out of those distribution points. They were busy places.

We didn't just sit back and wait for this business to come to us. We went out looking for it, and we had to work hard to get it.

When I was in Boston I spent a day in Cambridge, Massachusetts, at a grocery store giving away samples of Coca-Cola. I took a cooler with seventy-two bottles of ice cold Coke and started to work at eight in the morning. I offered a free Coca-Cola to every customer who came in the store, and by five in the afternoon, I had only given away half of my bottles.

We did door-to-door sampling in Providence. We had special sampling crews, dressed in uniforms. There were eight men, a driver, and a supervisor in each crew. They loaded a truck with coolers; and when they reached the area they wanted to work, each man carried four to six bottles with straws. They fanned out, four on each side of the street, knocking on doors and offering Coca-Colas to everyone. They chalked the sidewalks in front of the houses they'd already worked so no one would duplicate.

We paid these sampling crews five dollars a day, six days a week—thirty dollars a week. And they got all the Coca-Cola they wanted to drink free.

Some of those samplers became very clever. A lot of people wouldn't come to the door, or would ask "Who's there?" through the door. When the man said, "I'm from the Coca-Cola Company," it was easy for the person in the house to say, "Go away. I don't want any."

So some of the fellows would answer "Who's there?" with "C.O.D.," and when the lady would come to the door she would invariably say, "I haven't ordered anything C.O.D."

"I know," the sampler would say, giving her his biggest smile. "C.O.D. means 'Come on Down'."

Some people simply would not drink Coca-Cola. They still thought, even in 1938, that Coca-Cola contained dope.

New England weather continued to intrigue me. After that bout with the Hartford blizzard, I learned how to cope with New England snow.

I had never been in a hurricane. In Atlanta we sometimes got the tailend of hurricanes, a hard wind and rain, but never the real thing.

I had never been in a hurricane until one struck Providence in 1938. Our family had been enlarged that year with the birth of our daughter, Polly, and I now called Helen "Mimi." That's what little Polly called her; she couldn't say Mama—she said "Mimi."

One afternoon in September, after rain had fallen almost all day, Mimi called me and said the window had blown out of Henry's upstairs room. I told her I would send someone right away to fix it, but when I went outside the wind was really howling, bending trees, whistling around the corners. I telephoned Mimi back and told her I couldn't find anyone to fix the window, to put something over it until I got home; and I would fix it.

By then it was raining hard, and the wind was increasing in volume. I watched out the window, thinking this was some storm, and suddenly several trees within my sight were uprooted and overturned. My immediate concern was for the big plate glass windows in the plant, and before I could detail someone to cover them with something, one of them blew out. It just seemed to explode.

I called Mimi back to tell her to stay inside and keep the children in, and I said, "This is bad. This wind is really bad. It's uprooting trees over here."

"There's a hurricane on," Mimi said. "I heard it on the radio."

It was a hurricane, all right, and a strong one at that. A wall of water came roaring up the Providence River and inundated the town. Streetcars were covered with water. The high water mark of the 1938 hurricane went above the high water mark of the Hurricane of 1815, which was a doozy. The 1815 mark had been placed on the side of the Baltimore Hotel when it was constructed—a long time after 1815, by the way.

More than five hundred lives were lost in that hurricane of 1938. One of our route salesmen, Ed Regan, was working a downtown route when the wall of water hit the city. It was so deep in the street that cases of Coca-Cola floated off his truck. He was caught in an alley and had to swim out. On the way he dove into the basements of several buildings and dragged people to safety. The newspaper later ran a story about how he saved many lives that day. He said the water came up without warning.

Our home was only eight or ten miles from the plant. I left the office about six o'clock. I was not too worried about Mimi and the kids. We had visitors from Worchester that day, and they spent the night.

Every way I turned, streets were blocked either by water or by fallen trees. Several times I waited until crews axed through trees blocking the road. No one had any power, but we were lucky in that respect. We had a gas refrigerator, and Mimi cooked with gas. She had a huge store of candles and had the house lighted with them when I finally reached home about ten-thirty. Driving home that night was an ordeal.

We survived in relative comfort, considering the plight of many others.

Next morning I had as much trouble getting back to the plant as I had the previous evening coming home. I arrived about ten in the morning, and there was concern that some of the places we served had contaminated water because of the hurricane.

We had about a three-day supply of Coca-Cola already bottled and stacked in the warehouse; so we loaded all trucks and fanned them out in all directions. Before long, the trucks began coming back for second loads. "They're taking Coca-Cola by the case right off the trucks," one salesmen told me. The people had seized upon the idea of drinking Coca-Cola when there was no water.

We had no electricity at the plant, no way to bottle Coca-Colas. Our supply would be exhausted the next day at the rate the salesmen were hauling Cokes out of the warehouse.

The National Guard was patrolling downtown Providence keeping all unnecessary people out. One of our production foremen was a captain in the National Guard and was on duty. I knew if I could find him, he could give me permission to get into City Hall; so I walked downtown—conditions were so bad I couldn't drive, and it was only about a mile away. I found the captain and he let me into the city. The president of the electric company was a good friend of mine, a fellow Rotarian, whose office was on the seventh floor. I walked up the seven flights of stairs and went into his office. Luckily, he was there.

"Hello, Sanders," he said, "what in the world are you doing here? I had trouble getting to the office."

"Well, I had trouble getting here, too," I said, "but we need electricity."

"Everybody needs electricity," he said.

"We may need it worse than others," I said. "What our problem is, is we are sending Coca-Cola to Warren and Wickford and all these places that don't have drinking water. I need electricity to bottle more Coca-Cola, or we're going to be out."

He saw my point and thought a minute. "We're running a line up to the hospital," he said, "and that's right above you. We're coming right by you on Pleasant Valley Parkway. Hmmmm. I'll have them cut you in on that line."

We were bottling Coca-Cola the next day, and we kept our two machines running twenty-four hours a day, turning out ten cases a minute. That went on for a week, and we moved every case we bottled.

In the days that followed the hurricane, we saw what a storm like that can do. Another Rotarian named Arthur Angel owned a home at Green Hill on the ocean in South County. His was one of three hundred beautiful little homes down there, and when the hurricane of '38 struck, it destroyed every home there. Fortunately, no one was there. It was September and everyone had locked up these houses and gone back to their regular homes for the winter. The hurricane also destroyed a yacht club at the foot of our street, washing all the boats away, and there were two or three tankers stranded on dry land. I remember that one of them rested across a busy highway.

The only things we lost at our home were the window that broke out in the early stages of the hurricane and a sandbox in the back yard. The sandbox had an umbrella on it. Mimi was looking out the window when it took off, and she said it flew away like it had a motor on it.

Another devastating hurricane hit Providence in 1944, but without the loss of a single life. By then communications were so improved, partly because of World War II, that everyone got word in time and battened down.

Vending machines were properly perfected before World War II. Machines came on the market that would accept a nickel and deliver a Coca-Cola—the kind of machines we had been searching for for years.

The Mills Novelty Company, which manufactured slot machines, built a vending machine that would hold two hundred-forty bottles of Coca-Cola—ten cases. It was a big, beautiful machine, and I bought ten of them and looked around for a young man who could sell them. He then presented himself. I hired a young fellow named Ford McGowan, a graduate of Providence College and Harvard Business School. He was smart as a whip; but like all the others, he came to work for twenty dollars a week and three cents a case for what he sold.

He wore a uniform like all my route salesmen, and he was a handsome young man, in or out of the uniform.

After he finished his route one day, Ford came to my office. "Mr. Rowland," he said, "I notice that you're working awful long hours and you're busy all the time. I think you need somebody to assist you, and I would like to be your assistant manager."

"Ford, that's very fine," I said. "That was a good speech, and I'm glad you're looking out for me, but I don't need an assistant manager. What else have you got on your mind?"

"Well, have you got something," he said, "that I can do without wearing this uniform?" He told me how his girl's parents wouldn't let him marry her as long as he wore a uniform and drove a truck for a living.

His timing was perfect. I had that day bought those ten vending machines. I took Ford to see them.

"What I want to do," I said, "is place these machines in plants, filling stations, anywhere like that where they will be used. Now, you're a likeable guy; you're an Irishman, and you have all the charm of the Irish. You get along well with people. Do you think you've got enough blarney about you to call on industrial plants and other places and get them to let you put coolers in for their employees?"

The idea intrigued him, as it did me. "Yes, sir," he said. "I can do that."

"All right," I said, figuring in my head. "We've got ten coolers. I'm going to take you off your route for six weeks to let you try to place these machines. If you place them in six weeks, I'll keep you off the truck."

He placed all ten machines in the first week. He was so determined to marry his girl that he made the extra effort. Later, I recommended him for sales manager in Boston, and he did a good job there. Then he went to Miami and wound up managing Coca-Cola plants in Florida.

We worked out deals with local plants in which we would put a machine in and keep it stocked. We charged eighty cents a case for the Coca-Cola and fifteen cents a case for rent of the machine. So we received ninety-five cents and the plant twenty-five cents for every case sold in their vending machines.

This was all new business, and some of the vending machines sold ten cases a week.

In a few years we would amortize each of the machines.

When we moved into the new plant in 1937, we really went after the full service business. We would install machines in a plant, stock them, collect the money, and each month we would send a check to the account for twenty-five cents a case for all the Coca-Colas sold in its machines. That way the plant had little responsibility, no work, and it realized a good profit. We also made good money on the machines.

We had several routes, each serviced by a route salesman, on which there was no business but vending machines.

Down the street from the Coca-Cola plant was the Nicholson File Company, which employed three thousand people. The vice president of Nicholson File was Foster Hunt, who was active in the community. In 1939 he was named chairman of the Providence Community Chest. He called me and asked if I would head the food and beverage division of the Chest, which included all the soft drink and beer distributors, cafeterias, restaurants, hotels, and food companies.

I was assigned a quota, and was given some good men to work for me on the committee. We met quite often to make reports and keep up to date. Foster Hunt was a good fellow who smoked a pipe. He did not like cigars; so when I was around him, I kept my cigars in my pocket and I, too, smoked a pipe.

I met a little Frenchman one day who made nice-looking pipes out of applewood. They smoked sweet and tasty. I bought a dozen of them unfinished for ten cents each and I polished them. One day I took three of different shapes and styles and showed them to Foster Hunt and said, "Select one. You smoke a pipe. Select one of these. I want to give it to you."

He chose one he liked and over the next few weeks he called and told me how pleasant it was to smoke that pipe.

When the Community Chest campaign was over, I checked our books and found that we had no vending machines in Nicholson File; and there were three thousand employees going thirsty. I found that several of our salesmen had called on the superintendent of Nicholson File and had been turned down on the subject of vending machines. So I called on him myself, and in no uncertain terms he told me: "We don't want our people spending their money for frivolous items; wasting their money on something they don't need; plus the fact that we're paying them one dollar an hour in wages, and I shudder to think how much time they would take away from their jobs to go to these machines and drink Coca-Colas. We're not going to have that going on in this plant."

I waited until the weather warmed up to ninety-five in June and telephoned Foster Hunt. "Foster," I said, "could I come down and see you if you're not too busy?"

"Oh," he said, "come on down, Sanders; I'll be glad to see you."

I had chilled twelve bottles of Coca-Cola in a picnic cooler, and I took them with me to see Hunt. No one in Providence had air conditioning in those days, and the Nicholson File offices were broiling hot.

As soon as I sat down, I opened a bottle of Coca-Cola and gave it to Foster. He drank it with relish and called in his secretary and I gave her one.

When the Coca-Colas were gone and only Foster and I were in the office, I said, "Foster, we've been trying to let your employees enjoy what you've just had as a break from work. When they get refreshed, they'll do better work—and Coca-Cola definitely refreshes. It has sugar in it, and sugar picks you up. They'll do a better job with Coca-Cola available."

"Nothing wrong with that," Foster said.

"There's one thing wrong," I said. "Your superintendent downstairs won't let us put any machines in here."

"Oh, George is a hard-nosed Yankee," Foster laughed.

"You're a Yankee, too," I said, "but you understand what I'm talking about."

"Yeah," he said. "Wait a minute."

He called up Gus Sanders, the office manager. "Gus, it's hot in these offices. Rowland wants to put a machine in here that will let our employees buy Coca-Cola for a nickel a bottle."

"I think that would be fine," Gus said. He had obviously enjoyed his Coke.

"Thanks," I said to Foster. "I'll bring a machine right down."

I hurried back to the plant and had the men load a machine on a truck. I took three men with me, but when Foster said he wanted the machine on the third floor where the executive offices were, and we had to carry it up the stairs, I called two more men; and all six of us were required to get that heavy machine to the third floor.

I told Gus Sanders we would service the machine every day if necessary—and it was. That was one of our busiest machines.

Gus called me a couple of days later. "Sanders, the people downstairs are fussing that they'll have to walk up three flights to get a Coca-Cola. Can you put another machine on the first floor?"

"Yes, sir," I said. "We'll have it over there today."

We put it beside the door that led from the offices to the plant, and what I hoped would happen did. The workers in the plant kept coming, through the door and buying Cokes. The machine was emptied once or twice a day. Gus kept calling me to come and restock the machine.

"Gus," I said, "you'd better get Mr. Nicholson to let us put some machines in the plant."

"We'll have to talk to the superintendent," Gus said.

"He won't listen to us. We've talked to him several times already."

"Let's go see him together," Gus said.

Gus was a vice president and chief accountant or treasurer of Nicholson File, and I went with him to see the superintendent.

Gus delivered the knockout blow as we walked in the door. "George," he said, "your people are drinking my Coca-Colas. I want it stopped."

George's mouth dropped open.

"Either you put a machine on your side," Gus said, "or we'll lock the door."

I made the pitch again. I told him how Coca-Cola refreshed the workers and how much better they worked. . . .

"It's true," he said. "It's true."

"Well?" Gus asked.

"All right," George said. "How many machines do you want to put in?"

I said, "Ten."

"Okay," he said. "Go ahead and do it."

We put ten vending machines into Nicholson File and the three thousand employees consumed a hundred cases a day—twenty four hundred Coca-Colas a day. We had to assign a man to work nothing but Nicholson File.

A heavy machinery plant named Brown & Sharp was down the street from Nicholson File. Brown & Sharp made rifles for England during the war. Henry Sharp was the owner, and he was a tough old Yankee. I tried for the entire twelve years I was in Providence to sell him on the idea of putting vending machines in his plant—and I never managed to sell him. The year I left, somebody got to him and sold him. I never found out who, but he must have been some salesman!

Ford McGowan did a terrific job on the plants in Providence. Providence is a jewelry center with a lot of jewelry plants. There were some rubber plants and textile plants, and Ford cornered most of that market. We wound up with twelve or fifteen route men doing nothing but servicing machines.

That increased our business tremendously, and it was all new business.

It was a competitive business within our company. We had no competition from other companies in the vending business. I organized contests for our salesmen and made the prizes for selling the most Coca-Colas or the most vending machines worth winning.

We had one salesman who was so good he almost furnished his house with prize furniture.

Westinghouse began making red Coca-Cola machines, and we were selling them around Providence faster than Westinghouse could make them. Other Coca-Cola companies were selling them, too, but we were far out front in that race.

We had several unfilled orders waiting and no coolers in sight; so I telephoned Chink Watts at Westinghouse and asked, "Chink, who could I talk to about getting some more vending machines tout de suite?"

"I'm the boss," he said. "You're talking to the top right now, and I just can't get them for you, Sanders. We'll fill your orders as they come up."

I even said, "Please, let me have them"—we were that desperate—but he was stubborn.

"Can't do it," he said. "Sorry, but I just can't."

I had an idea. I got out an old bill of lading and noticed that a shipping clerk named Steve Ziwicki had signed it. I called person to person to Steve Ziwicki in Chicopee Falls where the plant was located.

"Mr. Ziwicki," I said, "this is Sanders Rowland, the Coca-Cola bottler in Providence."

"Oh, yes," he said. "I've shipped you some coolers."

"That's why I'm calling," I said. "We're out, and we're desperate. We need a carload of machines right away. Could you please get me a carload?''

He paused and hedged. "Well. . . ." he said.

"Just let somebody else wait," I said. "I've already got these sold. I know all your other orders can't be like that."

"Okay." he said. "I'll bend the rules a bit and ship them to you."

He sent them out that afternoon, and we placed them all the day they reached Providence—but my little escapade almost got Ziwicki fired. Chink Watts found out about it and lowered the boom. He couldn't take the machines back since we had already distributed them. But I had to call Watts and talk very sweetly to save Ziwicki's job.

CHAPTER 11

Big Bands and
Tin Cans

SUDDENLY, IT WAS 1940. May 30 to be exact. Twenty years had
slipped away since I went to work for Coca-Cola at eight dollars a
week, carrying mail and running errands for Miss Margaret
Landers in the Atlanta office.

Gardner Tillinghast showed up in Providence that morning of
May 30, 1940. His father still lived in Providence and he came
home occasionally. He came to the plant and reminded me that
this was my twentieth anniversary, and he said he wanted Mimi
and me to have dinner with him and his wife that evening at a
certain hotel.

He said nothing about a party, but when we walked into a private dining room at the hotel that evening, all of our Providence
employees were there, and Gardner and the managers of our
plants and distribution points in other towns were at a management table.

They had genuinely surprised me. I really expected to have
dinner only with Gardner and his wife, but it was very pleasant to
have all of our employees come to my party.

I was still in Providence in 1945 when my twenty-fifth anniversary came around. That time all of my employees surprised
me with a beautiful silver service which I keep in a bank vault
today. It is valued at several thousand dollars.

Two things I value as much as the silver were the telegrams I
received that day.

The first was from Harrison Jones, vice president in charge of

sales when I was hired in 1920 and now chairman of the board of
the Coca-Cola Company.

He wired: "Twenty-five years ago a kid twelve years old called
on a man and asked for a job. His face was good and his smile was
fine, and behind it the man thought that there was a mind—and
he got the job. Through the years he has moved apace from job to
job and place to place. He has grown in strength as he went his
way, and he has kept the smile he had that day. The man takes
pride in the race he has run, in the progress made, in the growth
attained, first because the old man was right, and second because
the old man loves kids."

That shook me. Yes, sir. Just to think about Harrison Jones,
six feet seven or eight, two hundred seventy pounds, and a
bruiser of a man who used the strongest cuss words—and here he
was showing his soft side.

The second telegram was from Mr. Woodruff. He sent it to
Mason Dunn, our sales manager in Providence:

"Only the fact of inescapable engagements elsewhere prevents
me from joining with you there in saluting Sanders Rowland on
Thursday. For many reasons, I look back with genuine satisfac-
tion on his quarter of a century of service with the company. One
gratifying result is that he has learned how to gather about himself the able group of associates he has. Another is that the attachments formed in these twenty-five years make it fair to assume
that we may anticipate a continuation of this relationship through
a good many more years. I'm almost willing to disregard the haz-
ards and list him right now as a permanent member of our corporate establishment. In getting along with him, I figure that the
first twenty-five years are the hardest, but I could be mistaken.
We shall see. Give my warmest regards to Sanders, to
Mrs.Rowland, and to everyone at the Club."

These telegrams were most gratifying because I knew that both
men were sincere in what they wired. They genuinely cared
about people; they cared deeply about the people who worked for
them; and they always had their employees' welfare at heart.

Mr. Woodruff visited me in Providence in 1938 just after we
opened the new plant. He came with his wife, a charming lady,
and with Holland Judkins, president of company-owned plants.

They made a special trip to see our new plant because it was
the first one built in a long line of planned expansion plants.

Later, new plants were erected in Boston, Worcester, Springfield, and many other places, but ours was first.

They spent the night at the Biltmore Hotel, and Mimi and I asked them to let us take them to dinner. First, however, Mr. Woodruff wanted to inspect the plant. We walked through it that afternoon and he liked the layout.

"How much land do you own that isn't covered by the building?" he asked.

"Very little," I said. "Just the parking spaces out here."

"Let's go outside," he said and we walked out.

"Who owns this land back of the plant?" he asked.

"I don't know," I said.

"Find out and buy it," he said. "Don't care what it costs. Buy it."

Judkins was beside him. "Holland," he said, "Sanders will get you the information, and I want you to buy that land."

The land in question measured two hundred by five hundred feet, about two and a half acres, and it was an exceptionally good piece of property.

We found out who owned it and bought it. Before many years passed, we had expanded the plant all over those acres. Mr. Woodruff was a man of intense foresight. He could see Coca-Cola bottles in the future.

Mimi and I drove the Woodruffs and Holland Judkins to the Lobster Pot in Bristol, Rhode Island, for dinner that evening. It was a lovely night. We had a fine dinner, and Mr. Woodruff gave Mimi a beautiful pin. She was pregnant with Polly at the time, and he noted her condition.

"All I have is money," he said to Mimi. "I don't have any children. I would give all the money I have to have what you and Sanders have."

And I think he meant it. He was crazy about children.

The next morning I met them in the lobby of the Biltomore Hotel before they left to return to New York.

He maneuvered me off to one side and asked, "How many days are you working?"

"Six."

"Cut that back to five."

And I did. That was the start of the five-day work week in the Coca-Cola bottling companies.

*   *   *

During 1941 we kept making record sales in Providence, but everyone knew the war clouds were piling up and it was just a matter of time until we went to war.

My thirty-fifth birthday passed four days before the Japanese bombed Pearl Harbor, launching the United States into war. The nation immediately banded together in a great war effort; and almost overnight, it seemed, we were producing the material to fight the world.

In the Providence plant, we produced a lot of Coca-Cola for the war effort. Coca-Cola was shipped overseas to our fighting troops. We found other ways to aid in the war effort. We participated in all of the scrap iron drives and paper drives and in every way we could contribute.

Several military bases sprang up in the Providence area. There were the Walsh Kaiser Shipyards going day and night building warships. Out on Quonset Point stood the naval base of that name and a naval air station. Also in the area were Camp Miles Standish, a staging area for Europe-bound troops; Camp Endicott, a Seabee base; and Camp Thomas, the base from which supplies were shipped all over the world.

Early in the war, the Coca-Cola Company established a program of entertainment for military installations and civilian war producers. With so many bases in our area, the Providence plant became one of the leading sponsors of big-time entertainment for the troops.

Our first such effort was bringing Les Brown and his Band of Renown to the Providence City Auditorium for a concert for the military. Brown's singer that evening was Doris Day, and she was absolutely charming. Brown was a little distant, as many of the bandleaders were. Forty years later I saw him and asked if he remembered playing for the troops in Providence, Rhode Island, and he said he did not. The big bands played so many engagements during the war that half the time they probably didn't know where they were.

Over a period of months, we had many of the big bands come in. Some of them played in Providence and some played on base. Both Tommy and Jimmy Dorsey brought their bands in and played at two of the bases. They were grand gentlemen, a delight to know. Ina Ray Hutton, the girl bandleader, had a terrific band. She really entertained the troops.

We brought Abe Lyman and his band and Vaughn Monroe and

his band. I don't remember much about Lyman except that he had a good band. He didn't fraternize with the officers, didn't even come to the party that we threw for the dignitaries after the show. Usually we had these parties after the show in the Bachelor Officers' Quarters and invited the commanding officer, the ship's service officer, the PX officer, and any other bigwig on base. Sometimes we would have the mayor of Providence attend and other civilians of that stature.

I remember one of those parties that twenty-two people attended. We had a full hour of social drinking and then a full lobster dinner, and the bill presented to me was for eighty-eight dollars.

Vaughn Monroe was a pain in the neck. Nothing suited him. He fussed about all the arrangements. If everything was just right, he still looked until he found something he could crawl on someone for. He was the least likeable of all the bandleaders I met—and he was not popular with his own band, either. They cursed him roundly behind his back, and I couldn't blame them. I don't know how they put up with him.

Buddy Rich was popular. He was a drummer, and could he ever beat his drums! When he picked up the sticks and began to play, whoever was in the vicinity quit what they were doing and watched and listened.

Henry Fonda was a ninety-day wonder going through Quonset Point. At one of the parties we threw following a show, Fonda was a member of the commanding officer's party, and the captain asked Mimi and me to come over and meet him. When we were introduced, Fonda looked right past us. He shook hands, didn't say a word, then turned his back and walked away. The captain told us that Fonda had trouble keeping his uniforms together. WAVES working in the base laundry stole his underwear for souvenirs, and Fonda was forever having to buy new underwear.

Usually during the big band shows, they would cut a thirty-minute radio transcription that was broadcast to our troops all over the world. Many of these were done at Quonset Point. In fact, most of the shows were at Quonset because there was a great turnover in personnel and there were always fresh sailors to entertain.

The band usually played for about an hour and they did the radio show. Before the band began to play on the radio portion, the director of the show introduced me. He usually said, "Ladies and gentlemen, may I introduce Mr. Sanders Rowland, manager of the Providence Coca-Cola Bottling Company, which is responsible for bringing this band here tonight."

Then he beckoned me to the microphone, and I said a few words in my Southern drawl, which was very distinct in those days. At one of those shows, just after I said a few words, a sailor, obviously from the South, sitting in the tenth or twelfth row, shouted, "From Providence? He's no Yankee. He's a Southerner!" That broke up the audience, the captain, and the band, and they left it in the show when it was broadcast.

I still owe a debt of gratitude to one of the big band leaders, Sammy Kaye, who came to Quonset Point for a show.

Sammy and his band, as all of them did, came to Providence on the train. I arranged for a bus to take the band on to Quonset Point and brought my personal car to drive Sammy Kaye and the director of the show and perhaps the girl singer to the base. Quonset Point was down on Narraganset Bay, twenty-two miles from Providence.

This time, the singer turned out to be married to one of the trumpet players; so she rode on the bus with him. I shook hands with the director of the show, whom I knew from previous shows he had directed at Quonset; and he introduced me to Sammy Kaye. Both the director and Kaye had cards in their hands. They had been involved in a card game on the train and were reluctant to give it up until they finished it.

"I'm going to lead the way," I told the director. "We'll have a couple of motorcycle cops leading us, and the bus will come just behind us."

"Fine," he said, still studying his cards.

We walked to my car, and I opened the right side front door for either Kaye or the director to get in; but they said, "Thanks," and both got in the back seat and continued to play cards. Things were pretty quiet in my car on that ride. I could hear the cards slapping on the back seat, and occasionally one or the other would say something or laugh.

We reached Quonset Point, and they went inside and continued to play. The orchestra set up its equipment on stage and moved in for rehearsal. Sammy's assistant director began putting the band through its paces, and Sammy and the director were still slapping cards down on a couch.

When they finished a hand, I asked them, "What in the world are you playing that's so interesting?"

Sammy said, "We're playing gin rummy. You ever play it?"

"No," I said, "but I want to learn a game as interesting as that. I play poker and bridge, but I've never played gin rummy."

"When we finish this game," Sammy said, "I'll teach you to play."

When the director got busy, Sammy said, "Here sit down," and he shuffled and dealt the cards. In a few minutes I had the hang of the game, and it was exciting. It is not a difficult game, but it requires a certain amount of brain power if you play it well.

That was in 1942, and in the years since, I suppose I have whiled away more spare time playing gin rummy than anything else. I play in tournaments and have won several. And Sammy Kaye was responsible.

The Walsh Kaiser Shipyards were within a mile of our house in Providence. It was a shipyard in which Liberty Ships were made, and three shifts kept the shipyard going day and night around the clock. The lights in the shipyard were never dimmed.

Not only was that a nuisance when we were trying to sleep, but I knew that if the German Luftwaffe ever came over to bomb America—and in 1942 we did not *know* that this wouldn't happen—then that shipyard would be a prime target.

I knew that Earl Stringer, one of my associates at the plant, had been talking about buying a weekend place in the country. So I went to him and suggested that we look for a place together.

He liked the idea, and in no time at all we found a two-hundred-year-old Cape Cod cottage on seven acres of land nineteen miles from Providence and bought it for fifteen hundred dollars. The house had no furniture, no electricity, and no running water. But it did have a good well with a pump that pumped water into a big barrel on top of the outhouse. Pumping the pump one hundred times would fill the barrel. Henry was big enough to pump; and since he liked the chore, he did most of the pumping when we used the cabin. From the barrel, a line ran into the kitchen where a spigot drained the water from the barrel.

We stocked the place with sugar and kerosene and cans of vegetables.

We dubbed the place "On The Line" because it stood near the Massachusetts state line. The land was not cleared and was rather primitive; so we had a lot of privacy. Only one road came into the place.

Earl's family and ours shared the cabin on alternate weekends. I don't recommend that type of ownership and sharing. It's hard to make work. Despite our being good friends, things often got mixed up over who used this and who used that. Finally I said to Earl, "You're either going to buy me out, or I'm going to buy you out. I don't care which."

"You buy me out," he said, so I paid him seven hundred fifty dollars for his share and became sole owner of this beautiful place. We spent some nice summers out there, every summer during the war. We were near some little country towns in which the Fourth of July celebrations were always fun, and it was nice being away from the city.

When I ran out of gasoline for my car, which I often did during the war when gas was strictly rationed, I rode the bus to work and back. The bus ran on the road that passed near our property, and it was about an hour's ride to work and an hour back. Usually, when I got home in the evening, Mimi, Henry, and Polly would be waiting for me on the side of the road. They enjoyed the walk of about a mile from the cabin to the road to meet me.

At first, I had bought a two-wheeled vehicle similar to a Moped to ride back and forth to work, but when rain caught me on the road, I arrived either at work or at home in a mess; so I quickly got rid of that thing and rode the bus.

My personal car wasn't the only one that lacked for gasoline in wartime. The Coca-Cola Company was not considered an essential industry and was not allowed enough gasoline, tires, or manpower to do its job properly.

Four good customers of our Providence plant were race tracks, two horse tracks and two dog tracks. One of the horse tracks had sold one thousand cases one day. I wanted to be able to deliver Coca-Cola to them, but when I drew ration cards for our company, I was advised by the ration board that the gasoline could not be used to deliver Coca-Cola to the race tracks. Neither horse nor dog racing was considered essential to the war effort.

I thought a lot about how we could deliver to those tracks, and an idea came to me one day when I was thinking back about Coca-Cola's history. What had Coca-Cola done before automobiles and trucks were invented?

Deliveries had been made with horse and wagon. We could use hayburners instead of gasburners!

I found a company that could build wagons and had four sturdy wagons built, each capable of holding a hundred cases of Coca-Cola. Two of the wagons were built to be pulled by a team of two horses, and two others were one-horse jobs.

I rented a stable within a block of our plant and stabled seven fine work horses in it. A man who knew horses slept in the stable watching over our animals.

Since none of our route men knew anything about horses, I hired four hostlers, one for each wagon. Each morning the hostlers hitched the horses to the wagons, drove them to the plant, and loaded them with Coca-Cola. Then the hostlers drove the wagons on their daily rounds, and salesmen accompanied them to make the sales.

Our wagons ranged as much as five miles out of town, hauling Coca-Cola to the race tracks and to a lot of other customers who might not have been served by our trucks because of gas shortages.

Our horse-drawn Coca-Cola wagons became popular sights around Providence. We used them from the beginning of the war until the end, even though gas rationing eased toward the end of the war.

Wagons were not as fast as trucks, and horses not as clean as gasoline engines; but all in all they were successful additions to our operation.

We had few real problems with them, but on occasion the problems they created were amusing.

One of the hostlers drove a salesman and a wagonload of Coca-Colas to the naval base one morning. While the salesman made the rounds inside the command headquarters, the hostler snoozed in the wagon seat out front.

The base commander left his office and walked down the whitewashed stone path toward the Coca-Cola wagon. Just before he reached the wagon, the horse raised his tail and vacated with a Plop! on the whitewashed stones.

The commander lit into the hostler with a passion, raking him over the coals this way and then the other; and finally the nonplussed hostler raised his hand and asked, "What did you want me to do, cap'n, hold my hat for him?"

Once for a war bond rally in Providence the rally chairman asked if he could borrow our single-horse wagon to ride in the bond-drive parade. We were happy to let him have it, and furnished a hostler to drive it. The chairman hooked up a battery-powered microphone and amplifier in the wagon and rode in the parade urging the citizens to buy war bonds.

The parade curled around the Providence Mall. On its second turn around the Mall, the horse, which had apparently foundered itself eating that morning, dropped dead in the middle of the street.

We had a tough time figuring out how to move the dead horse. It was so limber and so heavy that a hundred men would have had trouble lifting it, if they could have gotten hold.

We finally fashioned a canvas saddle, worked the horse into it, and picked it up with a wrecker.

We participated in all sorts of scrap drives—scrap iron, scrap paper, scrap whatever could be used in the war.

Denny Roberts, the mayor of Providence, asked me to be chairman of the first paper drive in the city. He appointed a committee to help me, and we organized that paper drive as well as it could have been organized.

We put out the word telling people how to bundle paper and what kind of paper we were looking for. Then we arranged for trucks, mostly from the furniture industry, and for crews to cover the city picking up the paper.

The drive was successful in every way but one. Pickup day was windy, and when we finished, the streets were littered with paper the crews had dropped. You should have seen the streets on Monday morning after that Sunday afternoon drive. Charlie McElroy, in charge of the Sanitation Department, spread his crews all over town on Monday morning and cleaned the city up before anyone could raise a cry.

I headed two paper drives and one scrap metal drive, and all were successful. Once, I was carrying something metallic out of our basement to give to the drive, and Polly watched me. She was about four years old, maybe five, and she still had trouble saying her "esses." She would say, "Papa, look at the 'nake," or "look at the 'moke." On that day, she startled me by asking, "Papa, where are you going with that 'crap?"

*   *   *

In 1944 with the war going strong, a young lawyer named Jake Russo was a member of the Rotary Club. He was with Liberty Mutual Insurance Company of Boston. One Monday morning he telephoned me: "Sanders, we have the first bottling claim for Canada Dry; and there is not a Canada Dry plant in Providence, and our lawyer has never been in a bottling plant. We're being contested, and he has to represent us in court."

I asked, "How can I be of assistance, Jake?"

"Could I bring him to your plant and let you show him how you bottle Coca-Cola?"

"Why, Jake, fine. How about ten o'clock in the morning?"

"We'll be there."

Next morning Jake introduced me to a distinguished-looking gentleman in his sixties. I met them in the lobby. "Shall we go to my office?" I asked.

"Let's start right on the tour," the lawyer said.

I began to show him the plant. We passed the superintendent's office, and there was the superintendent asleep on a cot.

"He stays here," I said. "He just goes home occasionally. He spends most nights here because we are bottling twenty-four hours a day."

We walked into the bottling room, and I pointed out some men I had gotten from the penitentiary when they were let loose. I described the trouble we had finding good help with all able-bodied men going into the armed services. I told him of our problems obtaining enough gasoline to run the trucks and about the problems we encountered running the machinery around the clock seven days a week.

"The only time we stop the bottling machines," I said, "is every seventy-two hours to clean the soakers. We bottle all the time."

We were packing what was then known as V-3 cases to be shipped overseas to the military. They had thirty-six bottles instead of the twenty-four we packed into our own cases. The bottles were put into sleeves in the cases. The cases were made of wood, and we sealed them by nailing wooden lids on. Then we banded them with wire strapping and stenciled their destination on them. This operation required five extra men; two to pack the bottles, two to stencil, and one to strap the cases.

But all of these went to the military, and when we bottled for Uncle Sam we got all the sugar and tinplate we needed—and those two items were hard to come by for civilian use.

We shipped the V-3s from Camp Thomas. When we got an order for five hundred V-3s from New York, we packed them and loaded them onto two transport trucks. Since our transports could only carry three hundred V-3s because of weight restrictions, we would split a five hundred order between two trucks.

I showed the Canada Dry lawyer our transports, and we were loading one at the time. I said to him, "Yesterday morning, I got here at seven a.m. At midnight last night I was still here working. We had to get the last two hundred cases on a ship at Camp Thomas. The driver of the transport, a fellow by the name of Raymond Quirk, had driven as far as he could. He had been on that transport since six in the morning—he had worked eighteen hours. He said to me, 'Mr. Rowland, there's one more load to be made to that ship, and I just can't do it.'"

"I told him I had never driven a transport, and he said, 'Well, you don't have to back it. You just pull alongside the ship, and they'll unload it. Then you can drive right around and come back here.'"

"Well, I was the only guy here who could take the load; so I got in the transport and hit the road. There was little traffic at midnight. I hadn't gone far when I began to get the feel of the truck, and from there it was easy. I went right to Camp Thomas and pulled up on the dock, and they unloaded me. I had somebody sign for the load, then I drove back here. I got back at two o'clock."

We went on through the plant. I showed him the whole operation: how we cleaned the bottles with caustic soda; how we inspected them; bottled them; and capped them.

By that time, I was tired. "Gentlemen," I said, "Let's go sit in my office and have a Coca-Cola, and I will try to answer any questions you have."

I had been with this lawyer for an hour, constantly describing our operation, trying to give him an idea of how a bottling plant worked.

Sitting in the office, Cokes in hand, he looked at me and asked, "Do you live in Cranston?"

"Yes, I do."

"And your name is Rowland?"

"That's right. Sanders Rowland. I live at Eighty Glen Street in Cranston."

"Well, Mr. Rowland," he said, "I am the chairman of your draft board, and we drafted you last night."

The statement startled me, and when I recovered my composure, I said, "Well, I was offered a commission when the war started. I was offered a majority by Bill Webster, the vice president of the power company. He was an Annapolis graduate who was looking for people. I didn't take that majority because I figured I could do better supplying the soldiers and sailors with Coca-Cola. We have so many men in service that I have had to hire these prison guys."

I was not rambling, simply explaining my position to him.

"I don't regret turning down the majority," I said, "because I sincerely feel that I have made major contributions to the war effort right here. I am almost thirty-eight years old; I have two children, but when I get my greeting I will go in as a private."

He was silent a minute, maybe two. Then he said, "May I use your phone?"

I handed him the telephone.

He called the draft board and asked, "Have you mailed out those notices to draftees from last night?"

Apparently she said no, for he said, "Hold the one for Sanders Rowland."

I never heard another word about the subject. I think the thing that convinced him was that I had been at the plant from seven in the morning till two in the morning the previous day; and that I had driven that load to Camp Thomas at midnight; and, of course, that we were bottling for the military twenty-four hours a day.

The only thing he said to me when he hung up the phone was, "I think we're better off with you where you are than being a private in the military."

Bottling for the military, it was not unusual for us to get orders for a half-million V-3 cases. That's eighteen million bottles, packed thirty-six to the case. We needed fifty-two days, bottling full blast, to fill an order that size.

We used all the tinplate we got on military bottles, and we had no trouble getting enough. For our civilian bottling, however, we often had to use iron crowns. The iron crowns left a lot to be desired, but they served the purpose because most of our bottling for local consumption was used quickly.

Somehow, by pure accident, a truckload of the iron plates got mixed in with our military tinplate supplies. We used them un-knowingly on a shipment of one hundred thousand V-3s to be shipped to China. When they arrived, after having been in the hold of a ship for all that time, all the crowns were rusted; so the military promptly refused delivery and shipped the hundred thousand cases back.

My people had to remove all the crowns, dump the Coca-Cola, and clean the bottles for reuse.

There was a question as to how the mistake was made, whether it was the fault of our bottling plant in Providence or of the Crown, Cork and Seal Company. So I went to New York and met with the president of Crown, Cork and Seal. The army asked us for $50,000 damages, and in that meeting, when no one could decide who was ultimately responsible, we decided to split the damages and pay $25,000 each.

We did not always get Coca-Cola bottles back. During the war they were used all over the world for insulators on power poles.

At one time, Coca-Cola had thirty-six bottling plants around the world bottling wholly for our servicemen. My old friend from Atlanta and New Haven, Paul Bacon, was in charge of that opera-tion in Europe.

Having so many problems getting crowns during the war, Coca-Cola plants all over the United States experimented with anything they could lay hold of. The Number Ten tin can was the same thickness as the bottle crown; so we collected these cans and stamped them into crowns. We took the cans wherever we found them, mostly out of garbage cans. They came in to us by the truckload, greasy with tomatoes and corn and goodness knows what else; cockroaches crawling all over them.

We had to cut the cans, spread the metal flat, then put them in caustic soda to clean them. We punched the crowns and pressed them into bottle caps. We worked four and sometimes five people on that.

The scrounging operation kept us from losing a good part of our civilian business during the war, but it was a dirty business.

Mason Dunn, my sales manager in Providence, would go to local restaurants and search through their garbage to get the cans. Dunn was a graduate of Brown University and an extremely intelligent man. After a week of searching through garbage with another man, he came to me and said, "I didn't hire out here as a garbage man, and if you want me to keep this up, you'll have to accept my resignation."

He smelled so bad I couldn't stay around him. He was dirty, and he was mad.

"Mason," I said, stifling a laugh, "show the other guy the route and forget it."

In the bottling business, we really had to scrounge to keep bottling for the civilian population during the war. We had no problems with the military, but the civilian side of the business really suffered.

We had trouble with customers, too, when we had to ration. We would ration customers to, say, half of what they had been buying, and several would scream and holler and threaten to sue us because they said we were cheating them on how many cases they had been buying. But we had extensive and accurate sales records, and when a customer yelled loudly enough, we showed him the records and that was the end of that.

The war sent men from our company to the far corners of the globe. We kept up with all of them, keeping their addresses as current as we could, and each month one of our department heads would write a newsletter to our service men. We called it "Tobits," which stood for "To Our Boys in The Service." We mimeographed it and mailed it to all of the military personnel from our company—the Providence Coca-Cola Bottling Company.

In the letter we would include addresses of all the guys so they could write to each other.

Sometime in August or September of 1944, after the invasion of France, I received a telephone call from the father of one of our men in service. He said he had not heard from his son in quite a while, and that the last thing he had heard was that his son was missing in action. He wondered if I could find out anything for him.

It was only by luck that I did. I had no channels to go through to get special information, but the same week I got the call from the father I also got a letter from the son. He was in a hospital in England. He had gone into France on D-Day and had been shot in the leg and captured by the Germans. The American forces had overrun the German unit that held him, and he was freed and sent to a hospital in England where he was recuperating nicely. His name was Possum McClain.

I called the elder McClain and told him the news, and the father and mother were very happy. Possum returned after the war, but he didn't stay with us. He went back south to his home state.

CHAPTER 12

Practice What
You Preach!

AN ORGANIZATION KNOWN as the Coca-Cola Bottlers Association has done a lot for the independent Coca-Cola bottlers. I was
elected to the board of governors of the bottlers association in
1946 to represent the New England bottlers, the only man on the
Board of Governors who did not own a Coca-Cola plant. At that
time, I had worked twenty-six years for the parent Coca-Cola
Company.

The first meeting I attended was in Savannah, Georgia. When
the treasurer read his report, I was surprised to learn that the
association had several hundred thousand dollars invested in various stocks but not any in Coca-Cola stock.

I asked the question, "Mr. President, I would like to know
why the association does not buy some Coca-Cola stock? It's as
good as any stock on the market, and it's certain to give a good
return on our money."

The president did not know why the association owned no
Coca-Cola stock. No one in the room knew, but several thought it
would be a good idea to purchase some.

"Mr. President," I spoke up, "while we're on the subject I'd
like to ask another question, perhaps for my own edification, being the new member of the board of governors."

"Go right ahead, Mr. Rowland."

"Why does the association need all that money, anyway?
We've got several hundred thousand dollars, and you keep col-
lecting dues from everybody."

It turned out that Crawford Johnson, Sr., the Birmingham,

Alabama, bottler, had organized the association in 1920 or 1921. He had organized it to insure bottlers against claims that people got bugs and mice and such things in bottles of Coca-Cola. Too, bottlers needed insurance against broken bottles doing damage to people.

Until that time, no insurance company would write insurance to protect manufacturers of soft drinks, but this association had been successful in getting adequate insurance.

Before the president or anyone else could answer my question as to why we needed all that money, Walter Sams of Richmond, Virginia, who owned eighteen Coca-Cola plants in Virginia and Pennsylvania, said, "Don't answer him!"

"Why not?" the president asked. "Why not tell Sanders why we've got this much money?"

"He's nothing but a spy," Sams said emphatically. "He works for the Coca-Cola Company, and he's the first man we've ever had on this board who is with the parent company. He'll go back and tell everything we say here. Don't talk about anything in front of him that you don't want to get back to Atlanta."

Sams was a good bottler and a respected man. And quite a man he was! He was in his sixties, but he could bend over and put his hands flat on the floor and then swing his legs into the air and stand on his hands. He often demonstrated his ability in bar-rooms. In fact, we had a few drinks together the night before, and I saw him perform.

"Well, now," the president said, "I don't think Sanders is a spy, and I think he's entitled to an answer to his question. I'm going to tell him."

What he told me was this: In 1923 when Bob Woodruff was elected president of Coca-Cola, he wanted to change the perpetuality of Coca-Cola franchises. Since franchises had been sold, they had been sold as perpetual franchises that could not be canceled. That protected each bottler's territory, and that spelled out how much they would pay for syrup by the gallon.

Mr. Woodruff wanted the price of syrup to be flexible, and he wanted franchises issued for five- or ten-year periods.

The Coca-Cola Bottlers Association, which was made up of elected representatives from each state, entered into litigation with Woodruff and the Coca-Cola Company, and the bottlers raised a lot of money to fight the case.

The bottlers won the court fight, and apparently won it with-

out having to spend nearly as much money as they thought they
might have to; so all that extra money remained in the association
treasury.

Woodruff did not get his way with stateside bottlers; but when
he expanded Coca-Cola worldwide, he issued term franchises, re-
newable every so many years, and made the price of syrup flexible.

Only five or six years later, the Coca-Cola Bottlers Association
owned several hundred thousand dollars worth of Coca-Cola
stock.

During those post-World War II years, I was also a member of
the Marketing Committee of the Coca-Cola Bottlers Association.
I chaired this committee for fifteen years. I was elected chairman
after having been a member for eight or ten years, and I knew
everybody on the committee and on the parent association.

We met once in Atlanta, and the agenda was mostly taken up
by sales and advertising people from the Atlanta offices of the
Coca-Cola Company demonstrating new sales pitches to us. They
talked all morning and illustrated their talks with advertising
signs about how well Coca-Cola goes with food. They had some
attractive displays of Coca-Cola and roast beef, Coca-Cola and
potato chips, and Coca-Cola with assorted foods. We were all impressed at the end of the morning session. No one before that had
concentrated on selling Coca-Cola as a drink to be taken with
meals.

Several of us went to lunch together in the hotel dining room,
and I ordered Coca-Cola with my lunch. So did Paul Roberts,
who represented Hartford, Connecticut. The waiter told us it
would take a few minutes, that he would have to get the Coca-
Cola from the bar.

The Coke was good with lunch—I had been drinking Coca-
Cola with meals for a long time—but I was still mad about having
to order Coca-Cola from the bar when we got back to the meeting
rooms.

I found a big piece of cardboard, and on it I put the letters
"B-G-O-Y-A."

When I reconvened for the afternoon session, I held up the
sign in front of the committee and I said, "Now, gentlemen, you
all elected me chairman of this committee, and this is the first
meeting I have presided over. We spent the morning hearing
about how good Coca-Cola goes with food. I was the first one

who ordered Coca-Cola for lunch, and I had trouble getting it because they didn't have it in the dining room downstairs. They had to go to the bar to get it. My friend, Paul Roberts, was the only other member out of twenty on this committee who also ordered Coca-Cola for lunch."

I held the sign higher so that all could see it. "This is what we're going to have to do to make this campaign work. What does BGOYA mean? Gentlemen, it means, 'Bottlers, get off your asses!' If I'm going to be chairman of this committee, we're going to practice what we preach. We're going to ask the Coca-Cola Company why a major hotel in the middle of Atlanta serves Coca-Cola only in its bar—and I'm going to ask why you gentlemen don't start drinking Coca-Cola with your meals, especially when you're attending a Coca-Cola convention.

"Those are not unreasonable questions to ask, and if you're not willing to answer, then I resign as your chairman."

I really meant what I said. I believed in Coca-Cola.

July of 1947. We had a summer place on the seashore at Buttonwoods, a community of seventy-nine houses started sometime in the nineteenth century as a religious community. There are a lot of places in that area that began as religious colonies— Martha's Vineyard, Nantucket.

A friend named Bill Abel told me just before the war ended that this place was available, and I bought it. I sold the two hundred-year-old Cape Cod cottage, and we moved into this one for the summers. We were on a street, not the beachfront. I avoided buying on the beach because of the hurricanes.

Paul Bacon had returned from Europe and was Eastern Regional Manager of Company-owned plants for Coca-Cola. He telephoned and asked if he could spend a weekend with us. We had been swimming and were sitting in our bathing suits having a drink when he popped a question that totally surprised me.

"Sanders, the plant that I'm having the most trouble with is Pittsburgh, Pennsylvania," he said. "I know you and I know what you can do. I want you to go to Pittsburgh and manage that plant. Will you go?"

My first reaction was negative. "I appreciate that, Paul," I said, "but I'm perfectly happy here in Providence."

I thought another moment, then added, "Henry is in a good school." He was in a private school called Moses Brown School, an old New England prep school of the first order. "And Polly is happy in her school. Our beach home here is only nine miles from our city home, and I can commute from here all summer with no problem at all. No, I don't think I want to go to Pittsburgh. . . ."

"I'll give you five thousand dollars more a year."

That rang my bell. I was making sixteen thousand; he was offering twenty-one.

"Now, that sounds all right," I said. "That's more like it." I had not been fishing for more money. Money hadn't even entered my mind. I was thinking of how much we liked Providence, how happy we were, how accustomed we were to everything. It was home.

There is no question about it: The twelve years we lived in Providence were the happiest years we have ever lived.

Mimi and I had a lot to talk over after Paul left, and at the end of our discussion, she said, "Well, I've come with you this far. If you think Pittsburgh is the thing to do, I'll go to Pittsburgh."

I telephoned Paul the next day and told him I would take Pittsburgh.

He said he did not want me to go until the end of the year. That gave me more than five months to wind up my business in Providence.

I hated the thought of leaving Providence but liked the idea of making a more comfortable living for my family. Pittsburgh was a steel center and should be a good Coca-Cola town.

I had the Providence Coca-Cola Bottling Company on the move. Business was growing in every way; we were able to give promotions and increases in salary when such were due; I had been able to train people and see them succeed in the business. I had never lived in a community where the people were nicer to our family and especially to me, a Southerner with a Southern drawl that I could in no way hide if I wanted to. And on top of that, I thought so much about the great seafood restaurants and all the fresh lobster that I wouldn't be able to eat in Pittsburgh that my mouth began to water.

I did not delay announcing that I had taken another job. For fairness's sake I wanted all those who worked for me to know that I would be leaving.

All my managers in the Providence operation—and we had a bunch of them by that time—gave me a party and presented me with a beautiful set of golf clubs and an eight-sided poker table. It was such a large table that I couldn't get it in the house we bought in Pittsburgh and had to leave it stored in Providence until we moved on to Birmingham in 1949. The table was so big that Polly uses it for a dining room table.

I was president of the Providence Chamber of Commerce in 1947, and by staying until the last of the year, I was able to complete that term.

Leaving Providence was hard to do, and I went to Pittsburgh alone. Mimi and the kids stayed in Providence to finish out the school year. They moved to Pittsburgh in June.

CHAPTER 13

The Pits

BEFORE I LEFT FOR PITTSBURGH, I knew I would encounter
union problems there. Pittsburgh was a union town, and the unions ran the Coca-Cola Bottling Company. I had no idea to what
extent they ran it, but it didn't take long to find out.

Only once had I had an encounter with a union. In Providence
the Teamsters tried to organize our plant when I first got there,
when we worked out of the old plant on Smith Street. A representative of the Teamsters said we were putting vending machines
in some unionized plants, and the union thought it would be
better for all concerned if Coca-Cola was unionized. He said we
would do a lot more business that way.

Very quietly, but very strongly, I said, "I am not going to put
these men in a union. If a man wants to join a union, that's up to
him. But I will not instigate it. In fact, I will fight it."

He said, "I'll just talk to some of the fellows and see what they
want to do."

At quitting time I saw him standing outside the plant, handing
out cards and talking to employees as they left. He was not on
company property, and there was nothing I could do about it.
Not in that way. What I did was talk to the men myself. I told
them that we did not want the union, and I did not think the
union could do as much for them as we could. I told them I had
worked for Coca-Cola for fifteen years without benefit of union,
and things had gone very well for me. I told them that things
would also go well for them if they let Coca-Cola run the bottling
operation, and not the union.

The union finally called for an election, and nineteen of our
employees voted. Five voted for the union and fourteen voted

against it. Just after the vote, two of the five who voted for the union quit. They were union plants, put in their jobs to try to promote the union.

As long as I was in Providence, the subject of unionization never came up again.

At Pittsburgh, we had bottling plants in Pittsburgh and McKeesport to the southeast of the city and warehouses and distribution centers scattered around the territory. It was a large operation but should have been larger.

Six unions were involved with the six hundred Pittsburgh employees of the Coca-Cola Company. All the unions were Teamsters, American Federation of Labor, and all met in the same building. One of the unions only had three members. That was in the Sign Department in which all advertising signs were painted and erected. Another union for garage mechanics had only five members. The other unions were for office workers, production people, and sales personnel.

When I arrived, I discovered that the sales manager in Pittsburgh had been transferred and had not been replaced. So for the first few weeks while I was trying to get my feet on the ground as a manager, I also doubled in brass as sales manager. That was not easy, but it gave me a better grasp of the impossible situation I faced.

We had a sales meeting every Monday morning. I outlined what I wanted the sales personnel to do that week. The union steward sat in the same seat on the center aisle. Before anyone in the room agreed to do what I asked, he would look at the steward, who would shake his head yes or no. Frequently, he would veto what I wanted done simply by shaking his head, and there was nothing I could do to get the workers to do it.

My only accomplishments with the unions in Pittsburgh were compromise. I don't remember ever getting done what I asked in the way I wanted it done. Somewhere along the way I would hit a brick wall with the union and have to compromise.

I don't mind saying that I got sick—absolutely sick—of unions in Pittsburgh. I have no love for them to this day and never will.

That summer of 1948 was hot in Pittsburgh, and we could have sold all the Coca-Colas we could deliver. But the unions blocked the sales. They held them to a certain level.

Our trucks had a carrying capacity of two hundred cases of Coca-Cola, but the union would allow only one hundred ninety-six cases to be loaded. Four empty spaces were on every truck that went out every morning. They were for the first cases of empty bottles the salesman brought out. We had thirty-five trucks going out, and that was one hundred-forty cases less than we should have been carrying.

It was also in the union contract that the salesmen only carried one load per day. Not any of the trucks came back for a second load as my trucks always had in New Haven, Hartford, and Providence. If a salesman sold his cases before he finished his route, he would wait until next morning to finish the route, no matter how many customers needed the Coke. Because of that, our routes were never on schedule. A store might get Coca-Colas on Wednesday this week and Thursday next week. If the store ran out on Tuesday, it just had to wait till Thursday to get restocked.

During one particularly hot spell that June, I watched the trucks roll in empty in early afternoon and knew that customers were out and were begging for Coca-Cola. I told my assistant manager, Charlie White, "I'm going to load the trucks tonight. I'm going to put two hundred cases on every one. That'll give us a hundred-forty more cases, and it's a shame if we don't sell them. People are out there wanting Coca-Cola and can't get it because of a damned union."

"You're going to get in trouble," Charlie said.

"Well, I'm going to try it."

I waited until the night crew came on and went to the head shipper and told him to load the trucks and put two hundred cases on each. Of course, he went straight to the phone and called the Teamsters to tell them what I was doing.

Next morning I went to the plant before seven o'clock to watch the trucks roll out. Charlie came in about seven. He grinned at me and said. "You know you're not going to have any salesmen show up this morning, don't you?"

At nine o'clock, not one salesman had come to work. The telephone rang, and it was Mel Humphries, Teamsters 249, AFL.

"Sanders, you got any salesmen at your plant?" he asked.

"No Mel," I said. "You got them all down at the union hall." He chuckled.

"How about sending them on over and getting them started," I said.

"You take those four extra cases off the trucks, and I'll send 'em over," he said.

There was no way I could win.

"I'll take them off," I said, and hung up.

I had the men remove four cases from each truck, and that afternoon I called a meeting and told the union heads how ridiculous that rule was. I asked whether my men were working for the Coca-Cola Company or the Teamsters Union, and I never got a straight answer. But we reached a compromise and reduced the number of empty spaces on each truck from four to two. That gave us seventy more cases going out every day.

I was in Pittsburgh fifteen months, battling the union every day, and sad to say, I managed to beat it only once.

Even then, it was not a company victory. It occurred over a personal matter.

One day I was driving to McKeesport, northeast of Pittsburgh, to have lunch at noon with our manager. About fifteen minutes out of McKeesport, I saw one of our trucks parked on the side of the road at a rest area. I drove into the rest area and got out and went over to the truck. The driver, Charlie Taten, was asleep in the seat of the truck, snoring gently.

I didn't wake him. I thought perhaps he was sleeping his lunch hour away, which was his business. I drove on to McKeesport, had lunch with our manager, then drove back to Pittsburgh.

On the way back, our truck was still parked in the same rest area. I drove in again and Charlie Taten was still asleep in the seat. This time I awakened him. I was angry.

"Charlie," I said, "you can't sleep on the job when I'm the manager here. You got to work to earn the money I pay you."

"I don't like your attitude," he said, rubbing sleep from his eyes.

"I don't care," I said. "I'm calling a meeting of the Union Committee this afternoon, and I want you at the meeting. You're going to tell them I caught you sleeping on the job."

"I won't be at your meeting," he said. "I don't have to come."

When I got to the office, I telephoned Mel Humphries, the business manager of the union, and said, "Mel, I want a meeting of the committee right now."

"I can get 'em together at four o'clock," Mel said.

"All right," I said. "Why don't we meet here in my office?"

Mel got hold of the other five members of the committee, and they gathered in my office at four. Charlie Taten, as he promised, didn't show up.

I told the committee what I had found, that Charlie Taten had been asleep in his truck on the side of the road to McKeesport for at least two hours and fifteen minutes.

When I finished, Mel looked at the other committee members, then looked me straight in the eye, and said, "We haven't talked to Charlie. We'll have to talk to him and see what he has to say. See?"

"Yes," I said, "I think I see."

I dismissed the committee and went home, knowing I had lost another round.

The next morning Charlie Taten brought in a doctor's report saying he was ill and if he had driven a truck and not stopped to "rest himself," he probably would have wrecked the truck and damaged it, and surely would have lost the load of Coca-Cola.

"You can't fire a man for protecting your property," Mel Humphries said. "He was only looking out for you."

So there was nothing I could do about Taten. However, I kept the incident in the back of my mind.

Another of our drivers was Chuck Schmidt, a good German boy from Pittsburgh. When I got to Pittsburgh I had ridden with all our drivers to familiarize myself with both the routes and the personnel. Chuck Schmidt was a decent kid who tried to do a good job for the company. He had a wife and three small kids, and he worked hard to earn as good a living as possible.

Charlie White told me one day, "Chuck Schmidt is at home sick. He's been out a week."

I said, "I think you and I ought to go over there and see about him—see if he needs anything."

We drove to the two-level house in which Chuck and his family occupied the ground floor. Chuck was in bed, and the children had colds—a pitiful sight. Chuck had no groceries and no coal. He worked under a no-work-no-pay contract, which was the only thing, I was convinced, that kept some of the route salesmen on the job.

When we left, I took fifty dollars out of my pocket and gave it to Charlie. "Will you please go buy some coal and take some groceries to Chuck's house?"

The coal and groceries pulled them through until Chuck could come back to work, and word apparently spread around the plant what Charlie White and I had done.

About two months later, in the midst of a union meeting that

Mel Humphries had called to reem me out about something, Humphries suddenly said, "By the way, did you know Charlie Taten is sick?"

"No," I said. "Nobody saw fit to tell me."

"I guess you haven't been to see him, then?" Mel asked.

"No, and I don't intend to go.!"

"Well, we've talked it over, and here's what we want you to do," Mel said, indicating that he and the other committee members had spoken of this before the meeting. "We want you to go buy Charlie Taten a ton of coal and some groceries like you did for Charlie Schmidt."

I looked at him coldly; and he added, smiling, "If you don't, we'll walk out."

I blew my top. That was the last straw—and my only chance to beat those bastards.

"Walk out, you sons of bitches," I said. "That was Sanders Rowland's money that I spent—not the Coca-Cola Bottling Company's money. I bought that coal and those groceries for Chuck Schmidt. Now, go ahead and walk out, you bastards."

And I walked out.

That was the only time I beat them in fifteen months. These men were absolutely unreasonable, impossible to deal with. Mel Humphries had been educated through the third grade, and he was vice president and business agent of the largest union in our plant.

While I was in Pittsburgh, The Taft-Hartley Act was made law; and I thought we would finally get some relief. But the first incident after passage of the law showed me differently.

Westinghouse made the vending machines we used. They did not dispense bottles, but cups. To mix Coca-Cola in a dispensing machine, we had to have carbonic gas in about a ten-pound cylinder connected to the machine. The syrup was poured in the top from gallon jugs. The man who serviced the machines had to connect the CO_2 with a wrench.

Ironically, it was in the Westinghouse plant where this incident occurred. Our serviceman reported to the union that he had to turn a wrench to connect the CO_2; and the union, in turn, informed me that our salesmen were not allowed to use wrenches and I would have to send a member of another union with each route salesman who serviced these machines just to turn the connecting sleeve to connect the CO_2.

I called the Chicago headquarters of the company-owned bottling plants and asked to speak to our attorney. I explained the situation to a lawyer named Joe Collins, and he said, "I'll send you an opinion by mail. You will have it in the morning."

His opinion came the next morning, and it bluntly stated in a two-page letter that Taft-Hartley covers this in our favor. So I called the two unions concerned with this into my office and started reading the letter from Joe Collins. Before I was halfway through the letter, one of the union leaders stood and said, "To hell with Taft-Hartley. We'll tell you what you can do—not Taft Hartley."

"I beg your pardon. . . ." I said.

He stabbed a finger at me. "You put that man on to handle the wrench, or we'll put this whole plant out."

He did not equivocate. I understood very clearly every word he said.

I called a recess and phoned Joe Collins and told him what the union man said. And Collins said, "Well, we don't want them to shut us down for just one man here and there, and you do have twenty-some machines from Westinghouse."

I said, "Yes?"

"Tell them you'll put the extra man on."

I went back to the meeting and said, "Joe says to get a wrench-man."

They walked out of the room laughing.

The union wasn't my only problem in Pittsburgh. I succeeded a young man named Joe Hefner, who seemed to be quite interested in getting away as quickly as he could. He was going to Japan to work for Coca-Cola, and he had a house in the Swanpoint section of Pittsburgh. It was located on the old Heinz estate, the estate of the man who made the fifty-seven varieties. Joe was anxious to sell the house at a reasonable price; he wanted to cut all ties with Pittsburgh and get on to Japan.

He made me so good an offer on the house that I couldn't refuse it; so I bought it without consulting Mimi. It was either buy it then or maybe not get it; he really intended to sell it that day for almost any price.

I telephoned Mimi and told her I had bought a house, and explained why I had to buy it so quickly. She came to Pittsburgh on the train. When I met her at the station not far from the house, I said, "It's only seven o'clock. Let's go have some breakfast."

Now, my wife is strictly a night person. She doesn't get up till ten or ten-thirty, and if she's awakened earlier she is a pretty grumpy person. That morning, of course, she was awakened early.

"I don't want any breakfast," she said. "I want to see the house."

So we drove to the house. There was not a brightly-painted house on the street, no blues, no yellows, no whites; only browns and drab, dark colors. Mimi stopped in front of the house and said firmly, "I won't live in that house. I won't even go in!"

That was the beginning of Mimi's problems with Pittsburgh. She never liked the town; she didn't like anything about it.

Eventually she had a nervous breakdown there.

I didn't like Pittsburgh, either, but I kept it to myself because I was working. I had been transferred there supposedly as a promotion, but Paul Bacon, who had promised me a five thousand dollar raise, was fired soon after I got to Pittsburgh. His successor, Harry Kippe, who had been a football coach in Michigan, said he didn't know anything about a raise. He said he thought sixteen thousand, which I was making at Providence, was about right for the Pittsburgh job.

That really stuck in my craw.

Anyway, I had to beg Mimi to go in the house, and when she finally did, the inside was so dark and dull that she almost cried. I'll have to admit it was not a particularly desirable house. But it was the house I could afford—and it was fairly close to my work.

Until our furniture arrived, our family lived in a hotel for about two weeks. The hotel we chose was a sort of headquarters for three of the six unions I had to deal with. Scotty Marshall, Mel Humphries, and some other equally obnoxious union people hung out in the hotel bar. When they found that we were living in that hotel, if they wanted to talk to me about something, we would meet in the bar and have a few drinks. I thought perhaps in that atmosphere I could talk some sense to them.

I really thought we were making progress; so one night I asked Scotty if he had a wife. "Oh, yes," he said, "I have a wife, and I have children."

"So do I," I said.

"Let's get our wives together," he suggested.

That might pave the way to better relations, I thought. So we invited them to have dinner with us. I thought we had a nice time, but Mimi said later she couldn't stand Scotty. He was a rough character and both he and his wife used foul language. Mimi was miserable with them.

I tried everything I knew to make friends with some of the union people. Somehow, I had to break the ice. We could not live under such conditions that existed—not after being so happy in Providence.

Some of the union people who frequented the hotel bar at ten and eleven in the morning asked Mimi and me to join them.

"Let's do it," I suggested. "I've got to make this job work. I want to be successful here." I was ready to try anything.

So we joined them on two or three occasions, and Mimi and I had a terrible time. We were not cut out for such as that. That was not what the Coca-Cola business was all about. She finally reached the point that she would not go back—and that's when I began to think about getting out of Pittsburgh.

We had plenty of competition in Pittsburgh: 7-UP, Pepsi, and two or three other lines were unionized, too, but in a much better way. They had all joined together and dealt with the unions as a group. But Coca-Cola didn't join the association, and it cost us ten percent more in just about everything we did. Someone, somewhere along the line, got Coca-Cola out of step in Pittsburgh.

I must admit that I made very little if any progress in Pittsburgh, and apparently no one else did after I left. I went back twenty years later and business had increased only ten percent over what it was when I was there.

The wonder is that it increased at all, considering some of the shenanigans the route salesmen pulled. I rode with one, a fellow named Ernie, who had sixty customers. He was scheduled to call on them three times a week. That was a fairly easy route and should have been lucrative. But it wasn't producing like it should, and I rode with Ernie to find out why. At noon, he knocked off. He announced to me, "I'm through. Now I have lunch, and after lunch I catch the show at the burlesque."

"You're through for the day? You haven't covered half your route," I said. "What about these other thirty customers?"

"Oh, them," he said. "Well, I don't call on them but once a week."

"You're supposed to call on every customer twice a week."

"That's a lot of bull," he said. "No need to pester them to death."

It made no difference to Ernie that I was manager of the plant. He had the union behind him.

I'd be lying if I said Pittsburgh was an absolute twenty-four-hour disaster for us. The town had its good moments, though they were few.

One of the good moments came with the visit of James A. Farley, the man who had been in Roosevelt's government. I had met Farley in 1937 at a Coca-Cola meeting in Philadelphia. Mr. Woodruff hired Farley and made him chairman of the board of Coca-Cola Export. Farley got around quite a lot.

During the war when the mayor of Providence, Denny Roberts, enlisted in the navy, I wanted to do something for him. So we threw a dinner for him, and I got Farley, a good Catholic like Denny to come to Providence and make a speech.

Farley was a gentleman if ever I knew one. He called his wife every night wherever he was; he never used a curse word that I heard; he didn't smoke; he didn't drink—but he didn't condemn those who did. He was such a busy man and had so much correspondence to keep up with that he employed two secretaries in his office at 515 Madison Avenue in downtown Manhattan.

He telephoned me one morning.

"Sanders," he said, "I'm going to Portsmouth, Ohio, to make a speech, and I'm going to have a long layover in Pittsburgh tomorrow. I'll get in at seven in the morning and won't get out of there till late in the afternoon. Will you meet me at the train?"

At seven the next morning I was standing on the platform waiting for the train to come in. When Farley arrived, we shook hands, and he said, "Take me to the barbershop."

I don't think he ever shaved himself. The first thing he did in every town was go to the barbershop for a shave; the second thing was to call the number one Catholic in town, and the third thing was contact the Coca-Cola bottler. Since I was the Pittsburgh bottler, he only had two things to do that morning.

When he was shaved, he said, "Sanders, how about taking me over to see Monsignor Corrigon?"

"Mr. Farley," I apologized, "I can't take you, but I'll arrange for someone to."

"Why can't you?"

"My son, Henry, is in the hospital for some tests this morning. He got kicked in the head playing football, and he blacks out."

He asked, "Where is he?"

"He's at St. Joseph's."

"Well, let's go see him."

We drove to the hospital. I had been unable to get a private room from Henry; therefore, he was in a ward.

When Farley walked into the hospital, Mother Superior and all the nuns recognized him right off the bat, and they all came around beaming.

Mother Superior asked him why he was at the hospital.

"I'm over here to see Henry Rowland," he said, "and by the way, I understand his father was unable to get a private room for him."

"We'll take care of that right away, Mr. Farley," said Mother Superior, and before we left Henry was wheeled to a private room.

After the tests and treatment, Henry continued to black out; a year or so later when we were in Birmingham he ceased to faint.

That afternoon Farley took the train on to Portsmouth, and the following morning he called me on the phone. "Sanders, this is Jim Farley. How's Henry? How'd he make out yesterday? What did the doctors say?"

He was a caring man.

I made a trip with him once to a Coca-Cola convention, and we rode the train for two days together. I learned on that trip that he was a memory expert. He taught me the rudiments of memory work.

A man walked up to him on the train, shook hands, and said, "Mr. Farley, You don't know who I am, but we met once at . . ."

"Wait a minute," Farley said. "Didn't I meet you in Schenectady?"

"Why, yes," the man beamed.

"You were on the platform when I was up there talking for Roosevelt, weren't you?"

"That's right. My name is. . . ."

"Wait a minute," Farley said. He thought a moment. You could see his memory discs turning. "Your name is Brown."

He absolutely shocked the hell out of the man.

When he was coming to Providence for Denny Roberts' going-away party, he had me send him the names of everybody who would be at the head table and at the party for distinguished guests. I sent him a short paragraph about each one, and when he got there he could call each person by name and ask about the kids, or whatever.

On the train he taught me how to remember things by association, and his method was really quite simple. If he met a Mr. Jones, he managed to call the man's name at least three times in conversation, and anything Mr. Jones said to him he stored and could recall it when he needed to.

We worked most of those two days on his method. When I went to Birmingham later I practiced what he had taught me and found that I could remember the names of all six hundred of our employees, their wives' names, and their children's names.

And that shocked the hell out of me!

Crawford Johnson, Jr., became an acquaintance of mine at the National Soft Drink Convention in Atlantic City, New Jersey, in 1933.

I was newly married but didn't make enough money to take my wife to the convention. At night at the convention I usually sat in the suite rented by Herbert Thompson of the Bond Crown Company of Wilmington, Delaware. He always had a slab of beef and plenty of shrimp and Virginia ham, and all the whiskey anybody could drink. So his suite was usually pretty crowded.

A friend of mine named Jim Warren, of Tampa, Florida, introduced me to Crawford Johnson, Jr., of Birmingham, Alabama. Crawford's father owned eleven Coca-Cola Bottling companies in the South. We talked for a while, then someone suggested we go out for something to eat. We took a taxi to a restaurant called the Knife and Fork, had dinner about nine-thirty, and Crawford picked up the check. We were enjoying after-dinner drinks about eleven and enjoying the music of a three-piece band and a girl singer.

Suddenly the band ceased playing and began packing instruments. Crawford beckoned the waiter. "We'd like to hear that band and that singer another hour."

"Sorry," the waiter said. "They're union. They only play till eleven."

"Get the bandleader over here," Crawford ordered, and when
the bandleader came, Crawford waved a hundred dollar bill under his nose. These were Deep Depression days, remember.

"Will this keep that girl singing and you playing another
hour?" Crawford asked.

He didn't have to ask twice. We enjoyed the music for another
hour. And that was the first hundred dollar bill I had ever seen!

I spent time with Crawford Johnson, Jr., every year at the soft
drink convention, and we became good friends.

In 1946, Crawford and his younger brother, Allen, and I attended Coca-Cola's first Manager's School in Atlanta. Al Steele,
a vice president of Coca-Cola, taught us how to manage Coca-
Cola bottling companies.

During that school, the Johnson brothers asked me up to their
hotel room and offered me the job of general manager of the Birmingham operation at twenty-five thousand a year. That was nine
thousand more than I was making, but the Birmingham plant
was an independent operation, a Coca-Cola franchise, and I was
on the actual Coca-Cola Company payroll.

Birmingham was one of the oldest franchises in existence.
Crawford Johnson, Sr., a man of vision, had established the operation in February 1903, in a building twenty-five feet by fifty feet
at First Alley and Twenty-fourth Street North. He started in the
bottling business as a one-man, one-mule operation. The man
was named Sam Whitt and the mule, Bird. Whitt operated a foot-
powered bottling machine capable of turning out thirty cases of
Coca-Cola per hour.

Crawford Johnson, Sr., worked in the court system and the
food brokerage business in Chattanooga, where the earliest Coca-
Cola franchise was established when Asa Candler put up the first
bottling franchises for sale. Knowing a good thing when he saw
it, Johnson borrowed the money and bought the Birmingham
franchise.

By 1904, the company outgrew its original location and moved
into a two-story building fifty by one hundred fifty feet on Avenue B South. Three years later, with business growing by leaps
and bounds, Crawford Johnson, Sr., built a new plant with four
foot powered bottling machines at Avenue E and Twenty-second
Street South. Four one-mule wagons, carrying sixty cases each,
delivered Coca-Cola around Birmingham.

Johnson automated the Birmingham plant in 1913 with a low-pressure bottle filler, one of the first of its kind. It produced two hundred forty cases of Coca-Cola per hour.

I knew the Birmingham plant had been one of Coca-Cola's forerunners and one of its most progressive franchises. But I turned the Johnsons down with reasoning like this: "I'm sorry, fellows, but I'm awfully happy where I am. I appreciate your offer, though. My son and daughter are in good schools, we've got a summer place at the beach, and I'm not really hurting for money. Oh, I'd like to have more money, yes, but I don't think I want to leave the Coca-Cola Company."

After thinking about that statement a few seconds, I thought I should qualify it. "My father left the Coca-Cola Company, and my mother told me it was the greatest mistake he ever made in his life."

Unfortunately, a year later, I let Paul Bacon talk me into moving to Pittsburgh, but I thought the job, in such a large city as Pittsburgh, would be a promotion with the Coca-Cola Company. When Coca-Cola reneged on the five thousand dollar raise Paul had promised me, I began having second thoughts about being so adamant about staying with the parent company. Why not go where the money was?

In 1948 at the Soft Drink Convention in Atlantic City, I had dinner with my friend, Crawford Johnson, Jr., again.

"How is Pittsburgh?" he asked.

"It stinks."

"Stinks?"

"I'm the most unhappy guy you ever saw in your life."

He didn't say anything.

"Crawford," I said, "I'm trying to buy the Coca-Cola plant in Peace Dale, Rhode Island, and I need one hundred thousand dollars."

"Hmmmmm." He was thinking.

"I've got a little money," I said, "but very little. I think I can buy it for a hundred and fifty thousand, and if you'll loan me a hundred thousand, I'll appreciate it."

"All right," he said. "Get the dope and let me know."

That perked me up. When I returned to Pittsburgh, I called my old friend, Pig-Iron Brownlee, who was then in charge of selling company plants. I told him I wanted to buy Peace Dale.

"Peace Dale!" he said. "Oh, no, we're not gonna sell you Peace Dale. You're gonna stay right there in Pittsburgh. Harry

Kippe says you're doing a good job in Pittsburgh, and that's where you're gonna stay."

"Mr. Brownlee," I said, leveling with him, "I haven't gotten my raise."

"Don't be impatient."

"I'm not. It's been eleven months." This was in late November.

"That long?" he said. "Well, I'll talk to Harry about it."

I never heard anything more about it.

Mimi's condition was getting worse. She had trouble getting out of bed; she couldn't go anywhere any more. If she did go somewhere with me, like to the home of friends for an evening, we had to leave early. I knew we had to shake the dust of Pittsburgh off our feet!

One evening in February, I received a telephone call from Allen Johnson in Birmingham. Crawford had told him how unhappy I was in Pittsburgh, and they had been doing some thinking.

Allen said they still had not replaced their general manager, and he was calling me because Crawford was in the hospital. "We wonder, since you're so unhappy in Pittsburgh, if you'd like to come down here and talk about our job?"

"I'll be there in the morning," I said.

Allen laughed. "No, that's too soon," he said. "Crawford's in the hospital for a minor operation. Come down next Monday."

That was a week away. I said, "I'll be there."

It was customary that when a man ponders a new position, he keeps his boss abreast of things, but I did not call Harry Kippe, the Eastern Regional Manager. Harry and I did not get along. His ideas were contrary to mine, and I felt he did not have the loyalty to people that his predecessors had.

He came to Pittsburgh in 1948 and said to me, "You have just signed new contracts with the union."

"Yes," I said, "and they all have the approval of Joe Collins."

"Pittsburgh is not making money," he said, getting to the point he had driven to Pittsburgh to make. "I know you can't do anything about the union people, but you've got twelve other people in this organization that I want you to let go."

"What?" I couldn't believe my ears. He handed me a list of twelve names. All were in managerial positions and did not belong to the unions. Some of them had been with the Pittsburgh company twenty-five years. Not one name on the list had worked less than ten years for Pittsburgh.

"I can't do that, Harry," I said.

"Sure you can. You're not making money. You've got to do something."

"Then let's do something about these union goldbricks."

"You know we can't do that."

I argued with him until I was blue in the face, and finally he stopped the argument.

"You let them go," he said, and his voice was ominous, "or I'll send somebody out here who will—and you won't have a job."

I called the twelve people together the next day and let them go. Of all my Coca-Cola experiences, that was the saddest. I don't know what else could have been done, but I do know that firing good and faithful employees who have been with you that long is not the way to accomplish anything.

When I thought of that incident and coupled it with the fact that Pig-Iron Brownlee had told me I had to stay in Pittsburgh, my mind was made up.

I didn't care what the Johnsons offered me. I was going to Birmingham!

Not only was that a job I would like, with people I liked, in country I loved—it was also my escape.

On Sunday, I flew on Capital Airlines, of which Crawford Johnson was a director, to Birmingham and checked into a hotel. The next morning I went to the Coca-Cola plant. Crawford and Allen Johnson were there, and I met Crawford III and Cecil Parks, the Sales Manager. The company had not had a general manager in two years, and the office needed to be filled. Parks had been in charge of the loading crews and the office and a lot of other things that a Sales Manager shouldn't have to worry with. He had also been overseeing the garage operation.

Sometime that day I managed to get Cecil off to one side, and I said, "You've been handling this job. Why don't you take it instead of me?"

He said, "I don't want it. I have the job I want, but I will tell you this: If you don't take it, I'm going to quit. I've never had so much trouble in my life."

I knew then that Cecil would be my friend. I already knew he was a hard and capable worker.

On Tuesday, Crawford took me to lunch at the Mountain

Brook Club. We had a few scotches—Crawford had five or six, and I had two. Anymore and I would have been under the table. I never could drink much.

When we were seated at the table, Crawford said, "There are some things I want to talk to you about in private—some things I will want you to do if you accept this job.

"I know you well," he said. "I've known you a long time. You don't know Allen. You saw him at the school in Atlanta for two weeks, and that's about the extent of your relationship with him."

"Yes, that's right," I said.

"You've met my son, Crawford Three."

"Yes. He's a fine lad."

"Allen," Crawford said, "is a musician. He is not a business-man. When my father died in 1942, he said to me on his death-bed, 'Look after Allen.' He said, 'Somebody has to look after Allen because he does not understand business.' "

We were quiet for a few moments while he thought what to say next.

"I want you to look after Allen," he said. "If you take this job, Allen is your responsibility; you must get him off my shoulders. You must keep him abreast of things."

"All right. I understand."

"The second thing I want you to do," he said, "is for Crawford Three. He has finished college and has done his time in service. He is twenty-three years old. He has been in the business about three years, and you've been in the business twenty-nine years. I want you to teach him everything you know about the Cola-Cola business."

"All right. I'd like to do that."

"And the third thing I want you to do is run these seven plants we have in Alabama. I mean run them, build them into some-thing they haven't been before. You can do it because you're a good Coca-Cola man."

Just like that, he put all of his cards on the table. He didn't pull any punches. I felt he was leveling with me, and I liked that. I didn't believe I would have to pussyfoot around in Birmingham like I had been doing in Pittsburgh.

We had a pleasant lunch and went back to the plant. Crawford Junior, Crawford Three, Allen and I sat in the office, and Craw-ford Junior said to me, "Well, Sanders, have you had time to think about your answer to us? Are you interested in this job? You've seen all the operation and you know what we'll expect of you."

"Yes," I said, "I'm very interested in it."

"We'd like to have you."

"Are you going to pay me the twenty-five thousand you offered me in Atlanta two years ago?"

"Oh, no," Crawford said. "Sixteen thousand is the salary."

"Crawford, sixteen thousand is what I'm making in Pittsburgh."

"I know that," he said. "I've talked to Harry Kippe, and Harry will be glad to get rid of you, and I think you'll be glad to get rid of him."

Disappointment must have been written all over my face. But I thought of going back to Pittsburgh to stay, and I knew I would have accepted the job if he had offered ten thousand.

"I'll take it," I said. "I'm too unhappy where I am."

I don't know what Crawford's ploy was in making me come to work for sixteen thousand because the following year—1950—he raised me to the twenty-five thousand he had originally offered.

I telephoned Mimi that evening and told her we were going to take the Birmingham job, and I thought she would shout. As soon as I flew back to Pittsburgh, I turned in my notice to the Coca-Cola Company.

Soon thereafter, Dick Fowler, a vice president of the Coca-Cola Company, and Bob Kirksey arrived in Pittsburgh to replace me. Their great interest the day they arrived wasn't in seeing the plant but in securing rooms at the plush Pittsburgh Athletic Club. I spent an hour taking them to the club and checking them in.

We got to the plant shortly before I was to leave at noon; so I didn't have a lot of time to talk to them or to show them around. But I thought I would try to answer any questions they had. I said, "Dick, if there is anything I can tell you about Pittsburgh, I'll be glad to try."

"No problem," he said. "Bob and I can clean this thing up in about six weeks."

But in six weeks, they had the start of a six-month strike on their hands.

And I thought: I accomplished one thing in Pittsburgh—I didn't have a strike.

CHAPTER 14

The Pause That Refreshed Birmingham

THE PROBLEMS IN BIRMINGHAM were not unlike those in the other places I had worked—there were just more of them. In New Haven, Hartford, and Providence the operations were in their infancy when I began, and all we had to do was feed the people Coca-Cola. Rather, we had to teach them to like it.

The Birmingham operation was already a sprawling giant. But Birmingham was ideally located for a bottler of Coca-Cola. The summers were long and hot, the people rural and thirsty. Indeed, there was room to expand, plenty of room to build the business even larger in Birmingham.

My most immediate problem was akin to some of the problems I had in Pittsburgh. There my nemesis had been union people. In Birmingham, my immediate nemesis was two men.

Because the Birmingham operation had been without a general manager for more than two years, there were no set lines of authority. People did not know what to do. Two men who should have been holding everybody together were not doing so. Dave Stewart, whom everybody called "Pop," was in charge of the office. J. B. Vance was superintendent of the plant. Both men had been with the operation almost fifty years. They had begun with the elder Crawford Johnson.

Because of that, no one dared cross them. They ran the operation to suit themselves—and many of their ideas, sound in the beginning, were archaic in 1949.

I noted this first in the area of race relations. I had been working in the North for more than twenty years and had made little

150

distinction between black and white. Now I was back in the South and in Birmingham at that time, black and white did make a difference, believe me.

About half of the Birmingham employees were black. They were the laborers, the loaders and clean-up men, those who did the heavy duty. They dressed in Coca-Cola uniforms and had to buy their own. The company furnished the uniforms and deducted two dollars a week from their pay until the uniforms were paid for. If Pop Stewart didn't like a certain man, Negro or white, he would deduct five dollars from his pay. Five dollars dented a common laborer's 1949 paycheck to the point that he almost couldn't feed his family. I put a quick stop to such practices and saw to it that all employees were treated alike.

What the Birmingham operation needed was organizational structure.

The best and quickest way to begin was to call everybody together and get them organized. I scheduled Monday and Tuesday morning meetings for all department heads, and we got down to business.

When I told Pop about the meetings, he laughed, "I don't guess I'll come," he said. "Don't guess J. B. will, either. Not much you could teach two old dogs like us."

"I could teach you how I'm going to run things," I said as gently as I could.

Pop didn't like that. He was about sixty-two years old, and here was a forty-two-year-old whippersnapper telling him how he was going to organize. I suppose it did rub him the wrong way.

J. B. Vance was even more stubborn than Pop.

No matter what I said to J. B. he replied, "That's not my department. That's sales department." He was not willing to cooperate at all.

Even when I insisted that Pop and J. B. attend the meetings, they wouldn't come.

After about six months, I had to go out of town for a week. In deference to Pop's age and longevity, and with the thought that this might be a way to get him to attend the meetings, I asked him to preside at the meeting on Tuesday morning. He agreed to do so, rather eagerly, I thought, but I misread his eagerness. His desire was to show some authority again.

When I returned to Birmingham, I asked Crawford Three, who had attended the Tuesday meeting, how things went.

"Sanders," he said, "he tried to change everything you have put in."

"What happened?" I asked.

"We wouldn't let him."

I told Pop I didn't appreciate what he had tried to do, and I insisted again that he attend the meetings. He complained to Crawford Junior. Here was a man who worked for Crawford Senior, and who bounced Crawford Junior and Allen on his knee when they were lads; so he figured his complaint would be sufficient to silence me. He told Crawford Junior that my ideas were not sound and that I would ruin the company. He stabbed a finger at Crawford and said, "Your father would never stand for such as this."

Crawford called me in and asked me to sit down. Pop apparently thought I was about to get my come-uppance. Instead Crawford Junior said softly but firmly, "Dave," (he never called Stewart, Pop) "I want you to know that Sanders Rowland is general manager of this company, and what he says is what you will do."

That shocked Pop down to his bootstraps, and from that day on I never had another problem with him. He did his job very well.

In Birmingham, as in every other town I had been, the first thing I did was meet the people who worked for me, and the next thing was to ride the routes. I spent time with people in the office and in production: I walked through the plant daily to see how things were going and to get the employees used to seeing me come around. It was like casing the joint—and having the joint case me.

And then I rode the trucks. I rode with all my salesmen to familiarize myself with them and their routes. By the time I finished riding the trucks, I knew Birmingham fairly well.

Birmingham was a manufacturing town. U. S. Steel at that time employed thirty-two hundred people in a gigantic steel mill there. The Continental Gin Company was intriguing to me because it was owned by Bob and George Woodruff, as in Coca-Cola Woodruffs. The Continental Gin Company manufactured cotton gins.

The Continental Gin Company was also the only manufacturing plant in Birmingham that had Coca-Cola vending machines for its employees. That was because Bob Woodruff had requested they be put in.

The city was wide open for full vending service; and when I looked at all those industrial plants, I saw dollar marks.

But Pop Stewart didn't. He was against installing vending machines in industrial plants. He said our obligation was to the corner store because the corner store and the local drug store had made the Coca-Cola Company what it was. He reasoned that placing vending machines in industrial plants would take money away from the corner store.

His reasoning was wrong, of course, and I announced at the Monday meeting of department heads that we would call on every industrial plant in Birmingham to offer them full service. We would install the vending machines, keep them stocked, collect the money, and pay the commission to the plant, just as we had done in Providence.

On my get-acquainted rounds of the Birmingham plant, I asked individuals I met to outline their jobs for me. Not only did I want to know what they were doing, I wanted to know what they thought they should be doing.

One man I met was Robert L. Franklin. Everybody called him "Preacher" because his father was a Methodist bishop.

"Mr. Franklin. . . ." I said.

"Call me Preacher. Everybody does."

"All right, Preacher. Outline for me what you do."

"I am supervisor of our four warehouses," he said. The warehouses were located in Cullman, Brookside, Montevallo, and Leeds, and they bracketed Birmingham in the outlying regions. "Each warehouse has salesmen, and I supervise the salesmen, the stock, the routes, and the entire operation."

"Preacher," I said, "I'd like to visit your warehouses and meet your people and see the operations."

We went to Cullman first. It was about fifty miles due north of Birmingham. The manager was named Barrow. As we talked, Barrow swung his attention to Preacher.

"Preacher," he said, "I wonder if you would go down here and see this cigar store about the sign we were talking about. I'd appreciate it if you'd write up the sign. And then, this grocery store on down the street needs a cooler, and I haven't been down there to talk to him. If you could do that, it would help me."

Preacher made notes of both requests, and before we left
Cullman he made both calls, got permission to put up the sign,
and sold the cooler.

Captain John Lewis was manager of the warehouse in Montevallo. He had been confined to his bed more than ten years with
arthritis, but the Johnsons paid his salary every week and his
son-in-law, Pete Givan, ran the operation for him. That arrange-
ment was all right with me as long as the Johnsons wanted to do it
that way. Givan gave Preacher a list of things he wanted him to
do, and Preacher noted them carefully and said he would get to
them as soon as he could.

At the Brookside and Leeds warehouses, the story was the
same. Preacher, do this; Preacher, do that for me. And Preacher
wrote a couple more pages in his notebook and promised he'd do
them

When we returned to Birmingham about four in the afternoon, we went into my office. Preacher accepted the Coca-Cola I
gave him and sat down to talk.

"Preacher," I said, "I have decided that we don't need a supervisor of warehouses."

Preacher came bolt upright. "What?" Indignation spread
across his face. "I am going to take it, Brother, that you're firing
me." He called everyone Brother.

"No, I'm not firing you, but you're not going to be supervisor
of warehouses anymore. You're not a supervisor. You're an errand boy. You're doing the work that those warehouse managers
ought to be doing for themselves."

He said, "Brother, don't fire me. Betty's pregnant, and I've
got to have a job."

I had pulled his records jacket from the files and opened it up
to see how much we were paying him.

"You're making two-fifty a month," I said. "Now, I have another job for you. I want you to be our Industrial Sales Manager.
I want you to call on every industrial plant in Birmingham and
place vending machines in them. I will handle the warehouses
from now on, and we will pay you three hundred dollars a month
to do your new job."

He was beaming. "When do I start?"

"Let's start in the morning. I want to get this show on the
road."

"Fine," he said, then paused. "You know what the job is. You know what you want me to do. Will you make the first call with me and show me?"

"Yes," I said. "Let's start at the top. Let's start with U. S. Steel."

Suggesting U. S. Steel as a starter did not reflect any idea of mine to show off to Preacher by tackling the biggest first. There was a reason for the choice. Our daughter, Polly, had a dog, and in walking him down the block she had met a neighbor who had two dogs. The neighbor was Ed Lemay, public relations director for U. S. Steel in the South. I telephoned Lemay and told him what I had in mind and asked him who we should contact at U. S. Steel.

"Start with the President," he said. "His name is Bob Gregg."

Preacher and I went downtown to the Brown Marx Building and went into Bob Gregg's office without an appointment. He was gracious enough to see us.

I began making my pitch, telling him we wanted to place vending machines in his plant; and when I began to tell him how much more work refreshed workers would turn out, he stopped me.

"You're talking to the wrong man," he said. "Art Weibel is vice president in charge of the plants. He's the man you'll have to see."

At that point, I learned just how much brass Preacher had about him.

"Mr. Gregg," he said, "would you mind calling Mr. Weibel to see if he would see us?"

"Sure, I'll call him," Gregg said, and he phoned Weibel's office and told his secretary that we were on the way and to give us an appointment with Weibel.

Weibel was also the wrong man. "Oh, I don't do any purchasing," he said. "That's all handled by Lavette Teague, the purchasing agent. I don't interfere in that area."

"Brother Weibel," Preacher came through again, "would you call Mr. Teague and see if he would see us?"

Teague said he would see us, and we went straight to his office. He said we were finally in the right place, that he was the man we needed to talk to. So I launched into the biggest sales pitch I had ever made. I knew this would be a gigantic contract if we could land it. I told him about the pause that refreshes, how Coca-Cola would keep his workers fresh. Suddenly, he began giving me a rough time. He questioned every point I made, and without coming straight out and saying so he tried to make me believe I didn't know what I was talking about.

Five minutes into this conversation, Preacher came to his feet. He placed both hands palms down on Teague's desk, and in stentorian tones said point blank, "Brother Teague, quit giving Mr. Rowland a hard time."

I cringed. I could see both of us flying out into the street, thrown there by U. S. Steel thugs. But when I looked at Teague, there was a twinkle in his eye, a trace of a smile, I thought.

Very quickly I terminated the interview, and Preacher said, "Mr. Teague, I will be back to see you."

When we walked out on the street, I was mad as hell with Preacher. I said, "What in the world do you mean, saying what you did to Mr. Teague, and us trying to sell him?"

"Don't worry, Brother," he said. "My pappy married Mr. Teague and his wife, and Mr. Teague is on the board of stewards with me at the Methodist Church. I know Brother Teague real well—and we will sell him. Just leave that to me."

Now Preacher was a golfer. He held the Birmingham Country Club West Course record with a sixty-two, ten strokes under par. But primarily he was a customer's golfer. He would take one of our good customers out to the Country Club, get in a foursome playing against two other guys, and whatever score was needed for Preacher and the customer to win, that's the score Preacher shot. If he needed a ninety, he shot ninety. If he needed a sixty-seven, he shot sixty-seven. He could shoot any score he wanted to on the golf course.

About six weeks later, I was working at noon one Saturday— we had not instituted the five-day week then—when my telephone rang.

"Brother, this is Preacher."

"Yes, sir, Preacher, what can I do for you?"

"I'm fixing to play golf with Mr. Teague," Preacher said. "I've been playing golf with him every week since we called on him. Some weeks I've played with him twice."

"That's fine, Preacher," I said. "Get to the point."

"Brother Teague thinks I've gone to the pro shop to get some balls," he said, "but I came down to tell you that he is going to let us put in twelve machines on Monday."

"Congratulations," I said. "Good work."

On Monday morning we sent trucks carrying twelve vending machines to the U. S. Steel plant, and that was the start of a contract that eventually reached three hundred ten machines. We sold two hundred fifty thousand cases at U. S. Steel the first year. With Preacher spearheading our Industrial Division, we placed machines in enough plants to sell five hundred thousand cases— twelve million Coca-Colas!—that year through industrial vending machines alone.

By the end of that year, the Industrial Sales Department had ten trucks of its own, and five were used exclusively to deliver Coca-Cola to U. S. Steel.

We bought many new trucks and vending machines by the hundreds. Five trucks did the job at U. S. Steel, which had six miles of steel mills at Fairfield, a suburb on the southwest side of Birmingham. But we had to work the trucks around the clock to keep up with the vending machines. U. S. Steel worked twenty-four hours a day; and in order to keep the employees served with enough Coca-Colas, we had to keep crews on the job twenty-four hours.

When I bought the new trucks for the Industrial Sales Department, I also bought some Volkswagens. A classmate of mine at Georgia Tech, Roy Bridges, had the Volkswagen dealership in Birmingham. Bridges had sold me on how economical Volkswagens were, and when he demonstrated a VW van that would be good for our mechanics, I contracted to buy from him. We got them for two hundred dollars less than Fords and Chevrolets, and we were very happy with the deal and satisfied with the performances of the vans. I purchased ten vans and figured I had saved our Company two thousand dollars.

Some of the mechanics who serviced the vending machines at U. S. Steel drove Volkswagens.

Soon after this purchase, my telephone rang in the office. Art Weibel was on the other end, and he was hot. Weibel succeeded Bob Gregg as President of U. S. Steel.

"Sanders, this is Art Weibel," he said.

"Yes, sir, Art, how are you today?"

He didn't say he was good, bad, or indifferent. He snapped, "Is this your truck down here?"

"Which one?"

"This Volkswagen truck? Is it one of yours?"

"Yes, sir, it's ours."

"Then," he said slowly and clearly, "I want you to come down here and get every damned cooler out of this plant."

"What?"

"Don't argue with me," he said. "Just do it. Now!"

"I don't understand," I said.

"We are competing with the Germans on steel," he said. "American steel is used in American trucks. German steel is used in German trucks. Volkswagen makes German trucks."

I quickly saw what he was driving at—and I knew what I had to do.

"Wait a minute, Art," I said. "I've made a mistake. I made it unwittingly, and I apologize for it. We won't have a single Volkswagen truck left tonight. I'll get rid of all of them."

"If you do that," he said, "I'll keep your machines in the plant."

Let me tell you, the sun didn't set on Volkswagen Coca-Cola trucks in Birmingham that evening. I got rid of them that afternoon and put in orders for Fords and Chevrolets to replace them.

A year or so after we placed all those vending machines in U. S. Steel, the Coca-Cola Company in Atlanta began running national contests to reward salesmen who sold the most coolers in a month.

I had promoted Preacher to vice president in charge of full service sales and stores, and he was doing a bang-up job. His enthusiasm permeated his department, and his people were really on the ball. Preacher himself kept the chain store heads loose. He played golf with them and maintained steady contact and helped his department tremendously with cooler sales.

Coca-Cola had tremendous competition from Pepsi Cola, Royal Crown Cola, and 7-Up, and all those companies emphasized cooler sales, too. We were all selling the same coolers. They were just painted differently and had different names on them.

It was because of this competition that Coca-Cola started a national contest to spur sales. Charley Adams was in charge of the contest, and he announced in December one year that a six-months contest would be run beginning in January. The Salesman who sold the most coolers in each of those six months would be given a new Chevrolet, a two-thousand dollar automobile.

The grand prize—for the salesman who sold the most during

the entire six months—would be a twenty-eight hundred dollar electric kitchen.

We had fifty-five salesmen at that time, and all were eligible to win those prizes. All of us agreed that we should encourage our salesmen to try to win automobiles.

When we held sales meeting, either Preacher, or Crawford Three, or Cecil Parks, or I would give an "altar call." We gave the salesmen a rousing pep talk. We thought it would help if we got the wives in on it also; so we scheduled a meeting for all salesmen and their wives. We had a Chevrolet car there so the salesmen could see it; we had pictures of the electric kitchen, the grand prize; and in addition we brought some fur neck pieces from a local furrier and announced that we would give one to the wife of each salesman who won a car in the national contest. The wives really got behind their husbands when they saw those furs.

The night we announced the furs, I gave the altar call. I said, "How many of you salesmen or your wives fell out of bed last night?" Nobody raised a hand.

"Okay," I said. "Now, I have been to your house—to each of your houses—and I have jacked your beds up on sixty-foot poles in your front yards. I have placed a sixty-foot ladder against your bed for you to crawl into bed on, but as soon as you get in bed I'm going to take the ladder away."

"Remember, now, I don't want any of you to fall out of bed." I let them think about that a moment.

"Do any of you think you will sleep tonight?" No one responded.

"Most of you would be afraid to go to bed like that, wouldn't you?" Some nodded. "Well, I tell you that only because I want you to be afraid of what is happening with the cooler sales in your territory. Competition is getting some sales that you should have, and you are not conscious of it. You are not cognizant of the fact that other salesmen are stealing from you, but they are. They're making money you should be making."

I said a lot of other things to them that night, and when I finished I was wringing wet. Three salesmen came to me after that talk and said, "Mr. Rowland, I'm going to win one of those cars."

And all three of them did. Birmingham salesmen won three of the six Chevrolets the Coca-Cola Company gave away during the next six months. And one of them won the Westinghouse kitchen.

One of our salesmen, Ludford Eagan, who won a Chevrolet and the kitchen, sold one hundred two coolers during the month of May. That was such an astounding number that Charley Adams sent two men from the Atlanta office to verify every sale Ludford had made. This made me so angry, to think that Coca-Cola would question our honesty, that I protested directly to Bob Woodruff.

Ludford played by the rules. He arranged for sales in January, February, March, and April, and had actually sold the coolers in May. There was nothing wrong with this. Everybody did it that way. They lined up sales for a month or two, then delivered and collected in one month to get a better shot at a Chevrolet. Ludford had almost two hundred customers, and some were very good customers. He sold Bill Durrow, the mayor of Leeds, Alabama, sixteen coolers for his city's parks and swimming pool. And he had some other customers who bought more than one.

Preacher really had cooler sales going in Birmingham.

CHAPTER 15

The Johnson Dynasty

OVER MANY YEARS there had been animosity between the Johnson family of Birmingham and the Coca-Cola Company of Atlanta, and the business of checking to see if Ludford Eagan had honestly sold one hundred two coolers in a month only fanned the flames a little brighter.

On the other hand, I had logged twenty-eight years and eleven months working for the Coca-Cola Company, and I knew that Coca-Cola had a tremendous lot of good men in it. There was so much expertise in the Coca-Cola Company that no Coca-Cola bottler anywhere should leave his problems unsolved.

In Birmingham we had problems in production which needed immediate attention. On my own, I called Ed Sutter, an engineering graduate of Georgia Tech who worked with me in New England. I asked him to come to Birmingham and help me solve our production problems.

When he came he saw an immediate solution. We needed to palletize the plant, he said. Ours was a three-level plant which is hard to palletize, but he showed us how.

Sutter showed us how to take the cases off the conveyor, put forty-eight cases on a pallet, and move the pallet to the trucks with a forklift.

This, of course, eliminated positions, cut down on the payroll, and streamlined the operation. One forklift could do the job of several people. In our shop, we eliminated forty-four laborers by palletizing.

I knew that we had to put more efficiency into production. When I presented Sutter's palletizing plan to the Johnsons, they accepted it immediately. There was opposition within the plant;

161

most of it came from J. B. Vance, the superintendent. He didn't like most of our "new-fangled" ideas, he said. He was of the old school, and that's where his ideas came from.

We had a bottling machine capable of bottling three hundred bottles a minute; but Vance ran it at rated speed, bottling two hundred ten a minute. His theory was that it would last longer running at that speed and that people didn't have to rush "and work themselves to death" to keep up with the machine.

I had been in Tom Moore's plant in Minneapolis, which had a similar bottling machine, and I watched it run three hundred bottles a minute with no strain at all.

Vance was paying overtime to keep the machine bottling enough drinks to supply our customers. I talked to him about increasing the machine's production to cut the overtime, and he balked.

"No," he said, "I won't do that. I won't wear out my machine."

"Okay, J. D.," I said, "I'm going to take you to Minneapolis. There's something up there I want to show you."

I knew I could never talk him into running the machine at capacity, but perhaps if he saw another plant doing it he would change his mind.

"How are we going to Minneapolis?" he asked.

"We're going to fly."

He shook his head. "I've never been in an airplane," he said.

"I want you to go," I said.

"Atlanta's the only place I've ever been," he said. "No, I don't believe I'll go."

"You're going," I said. "We're going up there and spend a couple of days."

He got the message, and we flew to Minneapolis. He was amazed at Tom Moore's machine running full bore, turning out three hundred bottles a minute. But he never said a word. Moore actually had two of the machines bottling six hundred bottles a minute.

"See what they're doing here?" I asked.

"Yeah," he said, "I see."

"Does it appear to be hurting the machines?"

"I don't know. It might be."

I had him talk at length with Moore's production foreman, and

I could tell he was thinking. His wheels were really rolling.

On the way back home, we went through Chicago, and my old boss from Providence, A. M. Day, was working there. I telephoned him, and he invited us out to dinner. We went to a good night club with a great floor show, and Vance was mightily impressed. Before he got back to Birmingham I believe he was convinced there were other good ways to live than the way he had been existing in Birmingham.

Anyway, he changed. He immediately stepped his machine up to capacity and began turning out three hundred bottles a minute.

I had to spend a little money on him to swing him around to a way of making more money for the company.

He worked girls on his accumulating table. In Providence we had the same production as in Birmingham; and where we worked two men on the Providence accumulating table, Vance worked four women. They loved him because he made it so easy on them.

I convinced him that two girls would be sufficient. When he cut back to two, they handled the job easily.

He also had other extra help here and there, and I helped him tighten up his operation which immediately began to show black ink in the books. It was a simple matter of separating wheat from chaff.

A young man from Montgomery had invented an automatic palletizer and sold it to the Litton Company which marketed it. When I palletized our plant, I went all the way and put in automatic palletizers so that in our operation no one had to handle the cases. They came off the machine onto the pallet, and everything was done automatically.

We affected other savings here and there. Syrup was delivered from Atlanta in stainless steel drums. When the drums were drained, enough syrup was left in each one to fill a dozen bottles of Coca-Cola. I bought a small stainless steel pump that could draw the last drop of syrup from every barrel, and that accounted for the saving of several hundred cases a month.

When we finished streamlining the production department, our savings were impressive.

Then I switched my attention to improving the sales department. Preacher Franklin was then vice president in charge of sales. He was a great idea man, and he and I often got together and brain-stormed to see what we could come up with to improve business.

We were stressing cooler sales and were thinking about Wednesdays. Most businesses in Birmingham closed on Wednesday afternoon in the 1950s, and Wednesday was our lightest day. So we began thinking of how we might sell more coolers on Wednesday, even at the expense of selling Coca-Colas. We weren't selling many drinks on that day, anyway.

We came up with the idea of a Wednesday blitz. We gave all the route salesmen a month's notice. We told them that beginning on Wednesday a month hence we would no longer load Coca-Cola on the trucks on Wednesday. There were eight bays in each truck. We ordered each truck to load eight coolers and for all salesmen to concentrate on selling coolers.

We had fifty-five or sixty salesmen at that time, and we offered extra incentive to sell as many coolers as they could—and on that first Wednesday we sold more than six hundred coolers in the Birmingham area.

That was unheard of. We had notified the Vendo company, which made our coolers, of our intentions. Vendo had a representative on hand to watch the blitz. It was such a smashing success that the Vendo rep had Preacher go to Miami and Jacksonville and several other cities on a tour to sell the "blitzing" idea to other Coca-Cola companies.

While I was straightening out the Birmingham operation and putting it on sound footing, I heard from some "old friends" in an indirect way. I had come to Birmingham April 1, 1949, and that November or December, I heard that the Teamsters were going to try to organize the Birmingham plant. I am sure some of the Teamsters in Pittsburgh got in touch with Teamsters in Birmingham and said, "If you haven't organized the Birmingham Coca-Cola plant, run over there and organize it. Sanders Rowland is general manager and he's a soft touch.

Manipulations began. One of our salesmen who hadn't been employed long, maybe six months, began inviting salesmen to a nearby bar where he would stand for drinks and talk union. He was taking two or three guys a day, figuring such small advances would not be noticed. He was a union plant, but he was smart; he had been a major in the Army during the war. One of our salesmen, Hard Rock Murphy, told me about it.

Murphy had been invited by the major and had gone to the bar. He had been told that a meeting was scheduled for the following Monday. Unfortunately, Murphy had told the major that he wasn't interested and figured he would not be welcome at the meeting.

Before Monday, another anti-union salesman, Harold White, told me, "I'm going to the meeting. I'll give you a complete report." I didn't feel at all bad about slipping an undercover agent into the meeting.

I told Hard Rock Murphy to go on to the meeting, and he did. He gave the organizers such a hard time they asked him to leave, and when he left, the union men figured they had uprooted and cast out the company's undercover man. White remained silent and later reported to me everything that went on.

White said the union men were at something of a loss in explaining why the Coca-Cola salesmen should organize. We already paid them more than any other route people earned in Birmingham, more than the bread or milk men, more than any other soft drink salesmen. We paid salary and commission, and our people made more money than anybody else on a truck in Birmingham.

I spent a lot of my time talking to salesmen about why they didn't need a union, and finally the union petitioned for a National Labor Relations Board election. The major represented the union at the election. He sat at the table and checked the votes, I am sure he was surprised when Harold White turned up as the Company's representative to check the ballots against the major.

Sixty-six salesmen voted and the company beat the union, forty-six votes to twenty.

We had three other elections in the next few months. The Retail Wholesale Department Store Union forced an election in our plant; then a metal union forced one; and finally the Teamsters came back for another whack after a year—and the company beat the union every time.

In that second Teamsters election, we beat them by one hundred two votes to twenty. That took care of the unions in Birmingham; we never had any more elections called.

We beat the unions with common sense—and caring for people. When I talked to employees before a union vote, I didn't run the unions down. I simply said, "Now, I work for the Johnsons here, and I work for you. If you have a problem, you bring it to me. I'm the guy who will take your problem to the Johnsons, and they can correct it. We don't need a union to do that."

The employees knew that what I told them made sense. The Johnsons had always paid good wages and taken care of their employees. They never let a sick employee go without pay, and they never terminated a man because of extended illness; like Captain John Lewis, the manager of the Montevallo warehouse, who had been bedridden with arthritis for ten years and was still drawing full salary.

Another thing the Johnsons did was see to it that their young employees who wanted to further their education got a chance to do so. There were a lot of colleges around Birmingham, and a lot of young people working for us because the Coca-Cola business then was a physical business. You had to have strong young men to throw those cases of Coca Cola around. Any employee who wanted to go to college could do so at Coca-Cola expense. The Johnsons would pay tuition, books, and supplies, and the only requirement was that the student pass his college work.

The unions found they couldn't fight relations like that.

The Johnsons, indeed, were fine people—but Crawford Junior had a trait that his close friends learned about quickly, or they suffered the consequences. When he was drinking, he never remembered what he said.

We were in Washington in the early 1950s and Crawford and Mimi and I went to dinner in the Sheraton Hotel where our convention was being held.

We had a few drinks, and I relaxed and crossed my leg over my knee. A part of my leg was exposed above the ankle-length socks I wore.

"Sanders," Crawford said suddenly, "you're wearing the wrong socks."

"I am?"

"You should never wear ankle socks. A man in your position should always wear knee-length socks. It looks terrible when you can see skin above a man's socks."

"And look at your tie," he said. "You don't wear a checkered tie with Harris tweed."

He lectured me about fashion, about what ties to wear with certain suits; and he belabored the fact that I had cuffs on my trousers, and cuffs were no longer in real style.

He had a few more drinks and finally said, "Look at you, You're nauseating." Well, by that time, I thought perhaps I was, though I thought his description a little strong.

"You're our General Manager," he said, "and you are executive vice president of our company. I want to be proud of you. But I can't when you walk into a store and buy anything straight off the rack.

"Yes, sir, that's what I do," I said. "I buy my clothes off the rack."

I was listening, and so was Mimi. Crawford Junior had been to The Lawrenceville School and to Yale. He was a rich man who traveled in dress-conscious circles. We figured he knew what he was talking about.

"I hope you're listening to me," he said, "because there's an outfit in New York named Gray and Lampall that I want you to visit the next time you're there. They're tailors, and they make my suits. Ask for Mr. Duffy. Have him make you four suits, and I will pay for them. You let him select the material, design the suits, and tailor them. Just tell him I sent you and he is to dress you, and he can send the bill to me."

"Well, thanks," I said, "that's mighty fine of you."

"That's all I can do for you tonight," he said.

A few weeks later I went to New York for ten days and discovered that Gray and Lampall was near the Coca-Cola offices on Madison Avenue. When I found some time I went in and asked for Mr. Duffy. He was a short little Irishman who absolutely beamed when I told him Crawford Johnson, Jr. had sent me. I told him exactly what Crawford had me to say.

Duffy went out and brought back a bolt of cloth. "How do you like it?" he asked.

"How do you like it?" I asked. "Mr. Johnson told me to let you select the color and the cut and everything."

"Fine," he said. He measured me and told me to come back in a few days for a fitting.

When I came back I saw that the suit was going to be beautiful.

On impulse, I asked how much the suit would cost. "Three hundred and sixty dollars," Duffy said, and I was glad I wasn't paying for it.

Two more fittings were required, and Duffy asked me once if I knew Paul Austin, Lee Talley, and Mr. Woodruff. I said, "Yes, I know them all," and he said, "They're fine gentlemen. They're all customers of mine."

I don't know why I told him I only wanted one suit, rather than the four that Crawford told me to ask for. I suppose I wanted to make sure I liked it.

The suit was the finest I had ever had in my life, even better than the one Pig-Iron Brownlee had tailored for me years before in Boston. The suit fit like a glove, its color complemented me, and Mimi loved it.

A few days later, Crawford Junior walked stiffly into my office. "What's this?" he asked, flashing a bill from Gray and Lampall for the suit. "Why are you sending me the bill for your suit?"

"You told me to," I said. "Remember the dinner we had at the Sheraton in Washington and you crawled on me about my dress. You told me to go to Mr. Duffy at Gray and Lampall in New York and have four suits tailored. I only had one."

"I don't remember a word about it," he said.

"Crawford, that's three hundred and sixty dollars for this suit," I said. "I can't afford that much for a suit."

"I know how much it is," he said. "That's what I pay for mine. I have paid more if I wanted cashmere or something special."

"Well, it's the finest suit I ever had," I said, "but you told me you were going to pay for it."

"Oh, Sanders," he scolded, "you got to remember I was drinking."

I paid for the suit. I knew I couldn't afford more suits of that price, but I found an Italian tailor in Birmingham who said he could copy my suit. So he made a couple of suits for two hundred dollars each that were the same cut as that New York suit. He copied the suits exactly, and I was so pleased with his work that I wore his suits for years.

Crawford was my friend. He only let me down like that a couple of times. Each time it was when he was drinking, or had something unusual on his mind.

When Crawford saw how much our profit escalated after we sold the vending machines to U. S. Steel, he promised me a five-thousand dollar raise. "We're having a director's meeting," he said, "and I'm going to put it through this afternoon."

I should have known better. He had been to lunch and had a few drinks.

Later in the afternoon, after waiting for him to call me, I called him. "Could I see you a minute?" I asked.

"Oh sure, come on in."

I went into his office. "How did the directors' meeting go?" I asked.

"Everything went just fine."

"Then I want to thank you again for my raise."

"We didn't give you a raise," he said, looking puzzled.

"You said you were going to get me a five thousand dollar raise."

He frowned deeper. "When did I say that?"

"You said it today," I said. "You said because we turned such a good profit in the U. S. Steel contract that you would get me a five-thousand dollar raise, and you didn't do it."

"Nope," he said, "we didn't do it."

"That upsets the hell out of me," I said, and I walked out. I walked out of the building, went to the Downtown Club and started drinking. Mimi found me later, or I went home, I don't remember which.

But I was going to turn in my resignation the next morning. I was really mad.

However, when I got to the office next morning, there was a note on my desk in Crawford's handwriting. He apologized to me and asked me to give him a little time and he would work it out.

He did, too. In a month or so, I got the raise.

Crawford Junior's brother, Allen, was a different cut altogether. He loved music and was not a businessman. I don't think his major interest lay in business. That's just where he made his living.

One of the first people Preacher Franklin and I contacted in 1949 about a new account was Eddie Glennon, general manager of the Birmingham Barons baseball club of the Southern Association. We got an exclusive contract with Glennon, put a five hundred dollar sign on the outfield fence of the ballpark, and sold thirty thousand cases of Coca-Cola in the park that summer.

The second year we bought the sign on the fence and a box of seats, six or eight seats for every home game. We made them available to our employees, and to the salesmen to take customers to the games.

Allen Johnson loved baseball and he, of course, had priority on the tickets, being a Johnson. He took two friends to a game one evening, got there in the third inning, and found someone in his seats. The ushers didn't remove the people quickly enough to suit Allen, who then went looking for Eddie Glennon. He found him in the press box with several friends and proceeded to curse him roundly.

The next day Eddie Glennon telephoned me and told me in no uncertain terms to remove all Coca-Colas from the ball park and to get our sign off the fence. Nothing I could say would change his mind; so we removed the Coca-Cola from the Birmingham ball park, and as long as Glennon was there, we did not get back in.

I reported to Crawford Junior on the incident, and he went to see Allen. But Allen was adamant.

"Allen," Crawford said, "we sold them thirty thousand cases last year. That's thirty thousand."

"We were in business before we sold them thirty thousand cases," Allen said, "and we'll still be in business without them. To hell with Eddie Glennon."

That was that.

Allen's temper almost cost us another contract. He drove to work one morning and found a Baggett Transportation Company truck blocking a side street. The driver was unloading, and when Allen lay down on his horn, the driver came over. "I'm sorry," he said, "but I'm in the middle of unloading. As soon as I finish, I'll move the truck."

Allen made his way to the office on another street and came in storming mad. "Do we do any business with Baggett?" he asked. "Do they haul any of our stuff?"

"No," I said, "but they're an awful good customer. We've got four coolers over there and probably sell them a hundred cases a week."

"I didn't ask that," Allen snapped. "I asked if we do business with them."

"No, sir," I said, "we don't do any business with them."

Allen wrote a stinging letter to Bill Sellers, who owned Baggett Transportation. He blasted the hell out of Sellers.

Sellers called me and invited me to remove the Coca-Cola from his plant. I took Preacher and hustled over there. When he showed us Allen's letter, I said, "Well, Bill, you know Allen."

"Yes," he said, "I know Allen. I'm not really going to throw Coca-Cola out of here, but I thought I'd get your attention and show you this letter."

There seems to be no question about it: Allen would have been better off in the music business.

CHAPTER 16

Mimi and the Kids

BIRMINGHAM WAS GOOD for the Rowland family. Mimi had a nervous breakdown under all the pressure we had in Pittsburgh. When I came to Birmingham on April 1 of 1949, she stayed in Pittsburgh another six weeks until Henry and Polly were out of school.

Mimi's condition concerned me deeply, and I talked to Crawford Junior about it. "Take her to see John Hillhouse," he said. "He can straighten her out."

Hillhouse had given me the required physical exam when I came to Birmingham; so I called his office and made an appointment for Mimi. I drove her to his office the day of her exam. I had told him Mimi feared she had cancer.

Before her examination, he told her, "Now, Mrs. Rowland, I am going to take x-rays and make tests and find out exactly what's wrong with you. I want you to come back next Monday, and we'll talk about what's wrong with you."

She turned to me. "Sanders, will you bring me?"

"Yes, I'll bring you," I said.

But Dr. Hillhouse said, "I didn't ask Sanders to bring you. I asked you to come down here. Sanders has a job and he needs to be working. He can't take off from work any time you want to be chauffered around town."

She said, "I haven't driven a car in several months."

"But you do have a second car?" he asked. When she said yes, a station wagon, he said, "You get in that car and you drive down to my office. If for any reason you think you can't drive down here, then you call me and I'll come and get you. But I want you to drive down here by yourself, and I want to talk to you by your-self."

I thought Dr. Hillhouse was being a bit hard on her, and she thought so, too. But she couldn't help but like him, he was so honest. So she got in her station wagon the following Monday and drove to his office.

The doctor had her problem diagnosed. "Mrs. Rowland," he said, "I have studied your x-rays and all the tests, and you do not have cancer. The only thing wrong with you is you are forty pounds overweight. I am going to give you a diet, and I want you to follow it closely and come here every week to be weighed. You'll be feeling better soon."

Mimi followed Dr. Hillhouse's diet religiously, and in eight or ten weeks she lost the forty pounds. She felt much better and never again had a problem like the breakdown in Pittsburgh.

We used John Hillhouse as our family doctor, and he was ter-rific. Once when Henry was sick all night, I called John early the next morning and asked him to stop by our house and look at Henry. He lived nearby.

Henry was upstairs in his room, and John examined him there. Then John and I walked downstairs, and I asked, "What's wrong with Henry, John?"

"I'll be damned if I know," he said. "But I gave him a couple of pills, and I'll stop by this afternoon and give him a couple more. We'll see."

Henry got over whatever ailed him in a day or two, and John Hillhouse remained our doctor. We all thought the world of him.

Henry was well-grounded in his education. He had attended the outstanding Moses Brown School in Providence and the ex-clusive Shadyside Academy in Pittsburgh, a fine boys school where a lot of steel executives sent their sons. In Birmingham we put him in public high school. In 1953 he was graduated with honors.

He went on to Georgia Tech where he earned an engineering degree and then studied at Harvard Business School.

At the end of Henry's second year at Georgia Tech, he was chosen for a student swap with a technical institute in Stuttgart, Germany. For a year he went to school for six weeks and had six weeks off during which he traveled around Europe. It was expensive, but he learned so much from it. Mimi and Polly and I went over and spent six weeks with him and had a delightful time visiting not only Henry but several European Coca-Cola bottlers who had come to Providence and learned the business from me.

When Henry finished Harvard Business School, he went to work for Pan-American Airways. Charlie Tripp, son of Juan Tripp, chairman of the Board of Pan-Am, was a roommate of Henry's at Harvard. They were good friends. Henry spent the summer between his two years at Harvard traveling Afghanistan, Turkey, and Africa with a Pam-Am official looking for hotel sites for Continental Hotel Corporation. And when Henry finished the Harvard Business School, he went to work for a classmate of mine from Georgia Tech, Hazard (Bus) Reeves, who had perfected talking pictures and invented various things. Through sharp business acumen, he had become the wealthiest man who ever was graduated by Georgia Tech.

Henry worked for him three months in Brooklyn and decided he did not like the work. He quit and went back to Pan-American Airways. Henry and Charlie Tripp were sent to Melbourne, Australia, to build a hotel. Someone had recommended a location, and Henry and Charlie closed for the land and raised eighty percent of the capital in Australia. Pan-Am put up the other twenty percent, and the hotel was built.

Mimi and I visited Henry in Australia, and I spent some time with the Coca-Cola bottlers there and learned how Cokes are bottled Down Under.

In 1957 Henry married Susan DeSantis of Boston, whose father was a successful real estate broker. Susie was the perfect wife and mother. She bore triplets in 1963. She and Henry at that time had sons three and two years old, and suddenly they were the parents of five children under three years of age.

The triplets were born in Birmingham. One of the men I played gin rummy with was an obstetrician named Julian Hardy. I liked him and liked the way he handled his patients. Henry and Susie had Dr. Hardy deliver the triplets. Hardy had never delivered triplets. He found out about six weeks before birth there were triplets when he found three heads on an x-ray. Susie was so big we suspected twins; her mother was a twin.

The triplets were the first born in Birmingham in twenty-two years. There were two boys and a girl born in nine minutes, perfectly normal and healthy. Susie took them home from the hospital in five days.

Harding sent Henry a bill for two hundred fifty-two dollars. He marked the bill: "Baby One, two hundred fifty dollars; Baby Two, one dollar; Baby Three, one dollar."

Henry and Susie have six children. The older sons are Frank and Fred. The triplets are Andrew, Bruce, and Sara. The youngest is a girl, Eve, born six years after the triplets.

The year Henry entered Harvard Business School, his sister Polly entered the University of Alabama. It was known as the country club among colleges. In her first year she took courses like cooking and home appliances, sewing, synchronized swimming, golf, and English. She really went to the university to get a MRS. degree.

In her third year, she got a summer job in Yellowstone National Park, and there she met a young man whom she married. The marriage was unfortunate. Her husband became a forester and after six years of marriage and two children, aged six and four, he walked out on her and never came back.

She divorced him and later married Dr. Robert Elliott, a Ph.D. in organic chemistry. He has been a cancer researcher with the Southern Research Institute in Birmingham for more than twenty years. He and Polly have a good and happy marriage. Her children, Marian and Sandy, are fine young people of whom Mimi and I are extremely proud. Robert adopted Marian and Sandy, and he and Polly have a daughter of their own, Elizabeth.

Children are my weakness. I have enjoyed my grandchildren, all nine of them, as much as any grandfather ever did.

When Susie bore the triplets, she and Henry had five babies. It would have been impossible for them to tend five kids that young. Mimi and I hired a practical nurse named Lonnie Carlisle, a black woman who had no family and no real home, and Lonnie moved in with Henry's family. She slept in the room with those three babies for two years. She tended to them as if they were her own. Susie had her hands full tending to Frank and Fred.

When the triplets were three and a half years old, Lonnie quit. When she announced her decision to Henry and Susie, Susie said, "Lonnie, what's wrong? Why are you going to quit?"

"These children need some neglect," Lonnie said. "Andrew won't take a bite till I feed him; Sara won't dress herself; and Bruce won't go to the bathroom by himself. They need some neglect."

Lonnie had always bathed the children and dressed them one at a time. When she left, Susie put all three in the tub together. One day she left them for a moment and dashed into the hall to get a towel. As she reached for the towel, Sara came dripping to the door crying.

"Sara," said Susie, "Whatever is wrong?"

She squalled even louder. "Why don't I have a dickie like Andrew and Bruce?" she wailed.

We all lived within five minutes of each other in Birmingham, Mimi and I in our house, Henry and Susie and their family in one direction from us, and Polly and her two children in the other direction.

On Saturdays, before the triplets came, I picked up the other four grandchildren and spent the morning with them. I took them to the zoo, to the Coca-Cola plant, the airport, the railroad station to watch the trains come in, and anywhere I could entertain them. At noon I bought fried chicken or hamburgers. Sometimes we took a bucket of chicken home, and Mimi and I enjoyed the kids while we ate on the patio.

When Henry's triplets became big enough to go, I had seven in the car with me—and we had great times.

Once when I had the four out, little Marian, Polly's daughter, was about five. She sat on the arm rest of the car beside me. The next day was my birthday and Polly invited me to come over for my birthday supper.

Suddenly Marian said, "Papa, Mama's got you a birthday present."

"That's fine," I said. "What is it?"

"Oh, Papa, Mama wouldn't want me to tell you."

"I'd sure like to know," I said. Everybody knows a five-year-old can't keep a secret; so I kept after her, enjoying the exchange.

"Marian, give me a hint. Tell me something."

"Papa, it starts with A."

"Starts with A?," I said. "It can't be an automobile—I've got one. Is it an apple?"

"Oh, no."

"You tell me what it is and I won't tell Mama."

"Papa, it's *a* tie."

Sure enough, the next night at Polly's, I got a tie for my birthday.

Those were wonderful years when the grandchildren were small.

CHAPTER 17

Black Birmingham

WHEN I RODE THE ROUTES with the salesmen at the beginning of my stay in Birmingham, Hard Rock Murphy had a route that intrigued me.

Of his sixty customers, fifty-seven were black. Their businesses were of a variety—bowling alleys, cafes, variety stores, corner hot dog stands. The other three customers were Armenian and Greek, and their businesses were located in the black section of Birmingham.

This, of course, was before integration—actually five years before the Supreme Court decision outlawing segregation—and in Birmingham whites were supreme.

When Murphy called on a customer, he didn't let the customer tell him what he wanted—he told the customer. "I'll bring in five cases," he told the customer, and at the next stop, he said, "You need two cases," and no one questioned his figures. They paid for the number of cases Hard Rock told them they needed. Not any of his customers was ever entirely out of Coca-Cola when Murphy made his stops, and I took this to mean that he knew what he was doing. He didn't let his customers run out.

But he didn't get a lot of cooperation or glad-handing along the route, either. I sensed a deep-seated sullen resentment in several of his customers.

I had been away from the South for twenty years. In most of the places I worked in New England, we employed blacks on an equal basis with whites, and I had left the South at such a young age that I really did not realize until I returned to Birmingham just how disadvantaged black people were in the South. In many instances, they weren't even treated as human beings.

178

Each morning fifteen or twenty black men stood outside a big gate that led into the back yard of the plant, and the manager of the loading dock would go to the gate and hire as many as he thought he would need that day. He paid twenty-five cents an hour, and if one of those standing out there got to work a full five-day week, he only made ten dollars. That was the poorest kind of pay, and really the poorest kind of conditions for those men who stood in the rain and sometimes in the snow waiting for work.

After I studied that situation of couple of weeks, I called in the loading dock manager and told him, "Now, we're going to do away with all this casual help. And we're going to hire better people. We're going to pay forty cents an hour for that work, and that in itself should bring us a better class of worker." Forty cents for forty hours amounted to sixteen dollars a week. For common labor in 1949 that wasn't bad.

I had talked this over with the Johnsons. I was general manager of their company, but I knew that any drastic changes I wanted to make would stand a better chance if the Johnsons knew about them in advance. Too, I didn't like to do anything without their knowledge. They did own the business.

The loading dock manager agreed with me and was happy to hire steady hands for his dock. This not only eliminated the standing at the gate, it also helped our bookkeeping department because it no longer had to keep up with all of that casual help.

By the time I rode with Hard Rock Murphy, I knew I was considered something of a Negro-lover, but that was all right. I had been called worse things—and, by golly, right was right. I intended to be on the right side of human relations.

Hard Rock went into a Negro cafe on his route, an immaculate place painted white, with white tablecloths on the tables. The food looked and smelled delicious. Two black women in white uniforms operated the cafe, and Hard Rock told them he was going to put up a sign on one of the bare walls. He didn't say what kind of sign it was, or he didn't say "may I?" or "please." He just said he was going to put it up, and he did. The sign was a beautiful one. It cost us five dollars from the Coca-Cola Company, and it had a piece of roast beef and a bottle of Coca-Cola on it. It told how good Coca-Cola went with food.

I watched Hard Rock work, but I also watched the two women. They resented what he did, but neither said anything. The next day I drove alone back to that cafe and, just as I suspected, the sign was not on the wall. I apologized to the woman who was there. "I am sorry," I said, "because our salesman put up that sign without asking your permission."

She was surprised at the apology.

"I would appreciate it," I said, "if you would give me the sign back. It cost five dollars, and I would like to put it up where it can do some good if you don't want it.

"Why we have signs like that," I said, "is to sell more Coca-Cola and more food—and they work. That's been proved over and over in thousands of places."

Her wheels were rolling, especially when I mentioned selling more food. Before I left she agreed to let me put the sign back up, but I did it with her permission.

She didn't comment on the way Hard Rock treated her. He walked all over his customers, and not any of them talked back to him; but they resented his attitude all the same.

Back at the plant, I called the sales manager in and told him what I had done and what I had observed.

"Nothing wrong with that," he said matter-of-factly. "You gotta handle 'em like that."

About once a week the three Johnsons—Crawford Junior, Crawford Three, and Allen—and I got together to talk things over, and the next time we met I told them what I had observed.

I said, "I've thought about this for almost a week, and we've got to do something about the situation before it affects business. What I want to do is put on a Negro salesman."

"Oh, no," Crawford Junior said, "you can't do that. You've been up in Yankeeland too long."

"It would be the best thing to do," I argued.

"No, you're not going to do that," Crawford said flatly. "How could we have a Negro salesman in the locker room? He'd have to take a shower with the other salesmen and mix and mingle with them in the locker room and—no, sir, we can't do that, and that's final. If we put on a Negro salesman, every white salesman we've got will quit.

"Well, we've got a problem developing down in black town. I saw it," I said.

"Then you'll just have to train the salesman better," Crawford said. "But you don't need a Negro salesman."

I had been completely rebuffed, and I went my way; but I kept thinking of ways to lick the problem.

Not long after that, I attended a Coca-Cola meeting in Atlanta. There I spent time with a friend, Doc Bowman, the Coca-Cola bottler in Jackson, Mississippi. He was a medical doctor, but he had given up his practice when he got the Coca-Cola franchise. I knew he ran a good business and had no prejudices; so I told him what I had encountered.

"Well, now," he said, "I'll tell you how to overcome that."

"You tell me, Doc; I'd like to know."

"I had the same problem," he said, "so I hired a Negro Special Representative—that's what I call him. He calls on Negro schools and Negro churches, and he calls on Negro customers. I furnish him a car, and he puts up advertising. I'll tell you, he more than earns his keep. It was about the smartest move I ever made, I guess."

There was my answer. Doc Bowman was a good bottler. He did a good job and ran a good plant. Everybody knew him, and everybody knew how outspoken he was. If he didn't like a guy, he'd catch him in a meeting and absolutely castrate him. But he was respected for his business acumen.

The next time the Johnsons and I got together, I told them what Doc had told me. "He's got a least a part of the solution to my problem of a Negro salesman," I said. "I would like to hire a special Negro representative like Doc has."

"How would he be different from a salesman?" Crawford Junior wanted to know.

"He won't be in the sales department," I said. "He won't be in the locker room, and none of the white salesmen will have to associate with him. He'll be on his own; he'll put up signs and call on black customers—and I'll guarantee you he will more than pay his salary."

"All right," Crawford said, "do that," and the others nodded their affirmation.

In the Atlanta office there was a black man named Moss Kendricks, a really sharp guy. He traveled around a lot, representing Coca-Cola at various black functions across the country, and he knew how to get along with people. He was book smart, too; he had a college degree, but more than that, he had the common sense to make it work for him.

I wanted to talk to Moss Kendricks about my Special Negro Representative; so I telephoned him, and he came to Birmingham to see me. That was part of his job. I told him what I wanted

to do and that I wanted to pattern the job after the one that Doc
Bowman had. Moss was familiar with what Doc was doing.

"Okay," he said, "I understand what you're trying to do.
First thing you need to do is get three good prospects. I mean
top-flight men. You've got a dealer here named Bob Stanley . . ."

"I know Bob," I said. "I've been in his place." Stanley ran a
bowling alley with six lanes, a big restaurant, and a dance hall on
Fourth Avenue. His place covered half a block in the Negro district on Fourth Avenue, and he was thought of highly by everyone.

"You talk to Bob," Moss said. "He's a leader in the Negro
community, and he can come up with the names of a couple of
good men."

"Then," he said, "you talk to the president of Miles College."
That was a Negro college in Birmingham. "I'll call him and tell
him you're coming," Moss said. "He can give you some good
names, too." He used my telephone and made an appointment
for me with the college president.

"When you get your names and narrow them down to three,"
he said, "I'll come back and interview them for you."

I called on Bob Stanley and the president of Miles College and
came up with the names of three good men—Paul Douglas, Jesse
Lewis, and Walter Moon. I talked to them and liked all of them. I
would have hired all three if I thought I could get away with it,
but I told them that Moss Kendricks would be over on a certain
day to interview them. I told them what the job would entail and
that it would pay two hundred dollars a month and ten cents a
mile for the use of their personal cars.

Moss came for the interview, and when he had talked at length
with the three, he said to me, "You've got two real good men
here in Paul Douglas and Jesse Lewis. Moon is good, but I
wouldn't rate him with the other two. You won't make a mistake
whichever you hire."

Since Bob Stanley had recommended Jesse Lewis, and Bob
Stanley was our best black customer, I gave the job to Lewis.

We had records of all sales to individual customers. I had someone go through our records and do some checking and discovered
that of eighty-five hundred customers in Birmingham, six hundred sixty were black. I had Jesse Lewis go through a good training course. Then I gave him the Negro account sheets and told

him, "Here are our black customers. I want you to work with
them, put up advertising, sell coolers, and increase their stock
and their sales as much as you can. And I will want you to help
our salesmen who call on black customers."

Jesse was smart. He was also a college graduate. He didn't
smoke; he didn't drink; his father was a minister; and he was
married to a good-looking wife, a fine woman. He had a lot of
things going for him.

The first year he worked for us—1950—our total sales increased five percent, but sales among our black customers increased twenty-six percent. When I showed these figures to the
Johnsons, they were pleased. I believe they were convinced that I
had indeed known what I was talking about.

If one of the salesmen invited Jesse to attend one of our regular
sales meetings, it was all right with the others if he came. Jesse
was always being approached by one of the salesmen, who had
black customers, who would say, "Jesse, I want you to help me
sell a cooler to so-and-so," and Jesse would help. Soon, Jesse was
a regular attendee at our weekly sales meetings.

In short, Jesse was a whiz. He was more than that. He was a
man going in the right direction, and he knew exactly where he
wanted to go.

Jesse worked out just fine. He was a likable fellow who fit well
into our organization.

After he had been with us three years, he asked me, "Do you
remember Walter Moon, who applied for the job I got?"

"Yes, I remember Walter."

"He needs a job. He was a classmate of mine, and I would like
to help him out. You know the Red Diamond Coffee people and
the man at Holsum Bread."

"Yes, I know them."

"Would you call Mr. McGaw at Holsum and Mr. Donovan at
Red Diamond and tell them what I've done for you?"

"Why do you want me to do that?"

"I would like to hire Walter Moon and train him to do what
I've been doing for you," he said. "Then he could do the same
for Holsum Bread and the coffee company."

I saw what he was driving at, so I called both men and told
them what Jesse wanted me to. "I think he's got a man," I said,
"who'll spend his full time with you doing what Jesse does for

us. He wants to hire the guy himself, and he will be responsible for your work. Then you pay him, and he'll pay the fellow he hires."

They agreed to the plan, and Jesse formed Jesse J. Lewis and Associates and put Walter Moon to work for him. They discovered that Moon could not do the job for both companies; so he stayed on the coffee job, and Jesse hired another man to take the Holsum bread route.

Jesse didn't stop there. He continued to hire people and put them to work on other jobs. He branched into an advertising agency and public relations firm. He had an office and a secretary and six men working for him at various jobs. He worked as an employment agency.

In his fourth year in all this, Jesse asked if I would lend him four thousand dollars.

"What do you want that much money for, Jesse?" I asked.

"I want to buy a lot on Fourth Avenue," he said. "There's a lot down there I can get for four thousand dollars right near Bob Stanley's place, and I hope to build a building on it, or something."

"All right," I said. "I'll lend you the money."

"I'll pay you back a thousand dollars a year," he promised.

We drew up papers and signed them and Jesse bought the lot. Before he had repaid the four thousand, he was offered twenty-two thousand dollars for the lot. He asked me what he should do.

"Sell it," I said. "With that kind of profit, you can find another lot somewhere and build your building and have money left over."

All this time, he continued to work for Coca-Cola, and he still did as good a job for us as he had done at first.

He came into my office not long after he sold the lot. "Mr. Rowland," he said, "I can buy the *Birmingham Times*. What do you think of that? The Times was a weekly Negro newspaper.

"It's not a very good paper," he said, "but it has a circulation of three thousand, and the man who publishes it is a drunkard. I really think I could do something with it, but I want to know what you think of me going into the newspaper business."

I thought Jesse could make a go out of anything he tackled. "You've got two sons, haven't you?" I asked.

"Yes sir," he said. "Both in college."

"Well, couldn't that be something for one of your sons to do?"

"Yes, sir, it could be."

So Jesse bought the paper. He borrowed the money and bought a press and hired a man at four hundred dollars a month to set type and run the press. When he discovered there wasn't enough work on the newspaper to keep that man busy, he started doing job printing, and made a success of that.

Over the years, a lot of things that Jesse touched turned to success. He put one of his sons to work running the newspaper and put the other to running Jesse J. Lewis and Associates.

In 1970 Jesse Lewis became the first black member of Governor George Wallace's cabinet in Alabama, and when the governor's wife, Lurlene, died, the governor sent an Alabama State Highway Patrolman to Birmingham to drive Jesse to Montgomery for the funeral.

George Wallace was known as a racist, and he had stood in the schoolhouse door to prevent integration of Alabama schools; but he and Jesse Lewis were fast friends as well as governmental associates. Jesse was the first black since reconstruction days to hold such a post in the Alabama government.

When George Wallace ceased to be governor for a term, Jesse Lewis accepted the position of president of Lawson State College at a salary of fifty thousand dollars a year. He continued on the payroll of the Coca-Cola Company of Birmingham at five hundred dollars a month, and goodness knows what else he was doing. Whatever it was, it was all legal and for the good of his family and his people. Jesse was one of those rare men who truly became a credit both to his race and to the state. Through his role as a bonafide leader in the black community, he helped ease racial tensions in Alabama. He helped make the transition more orderly from segregation to integration.

We lived through stormy days in Alabama—and Jesse Lewis was a Trojan all the way.

When desegregation came in 1954, we added four black salesmen to the Birmingham sales force and became the first bottler in the South to have Negro salesmen.

CHAPTER 18

A Drink of
Another Brand

DURING THE YEARS I WORKED in Birmingham, Coca-Cola faced much stiffer competition than it had in Providence, Hartford, New Haven, Boston, or even Pittsburgh. Much of this competition can be credited directly to the Coca-Cola Company itself.

Al Steele was a vice president of Coca-Cola. Someone told me that he is the only man Mr. Woodruff ever gave a contract to. He gave Al Steele a five-year contract, and at the end of the five years—I don't know why—he would not renew the contract. Steele left the Coca-Cola Company and soon resurfaced as president of the Pepsi Cola Company. I give Al Steele credit for putting Pepsi where it is today.

Al Steele was a smart man. He knew when to capitalize on something. For instance, the Coca-Cola Company had thirty-two traveling laboratories going around the country checking the quality of the Coca-Cola that each bottler put on the market. Coca-Cola had to meet certain standards.

Woodruff would never think of talking about or advertising the quality of Coca-Cola; quality, he thought, was something that people understood and accepted. "People," he said, "know that Coca-Cola is a quality drink. We don't have to remind them of that."

But Al Steele had to remind people of the quality of Pepsi. He bought one traveling lab, had it photographed on the road by an advertising agency, and put ads in *Good Housekeeping, The Ladies Home Journal,* and a number of other magazines, stressing the quality of Pepsi Cola and boasting that Pepsi kept constant check on the quality of its beverage with the traveling lab.

Al Steele knew he had to have good men to sell Pepsi Cola, and having worked five years for Coca-Cola he knew that Coca-Cola had the good men but was not the best-paying company in the country. So he went after quality people within the Coca-Cola Company.

He hired eight of my men from Providence and several more that I had trained in New England. He offered me a job with Pepsi in Detroit, but I turned it down because we were happy and satisfied where I was.

He knew how to hire people. Seven hundred-fifty dollars a month seemed to be a favorite Coca-Cola salary for executive people in those years. When Al Steele wanted one to fill a certain position at Pepsi, he simply offered fifteen hundred a month and got his man.

I trained a sixteen-year-old lad named Al Olsen in Providence. He was a studious fellow who by the time I went to Birmingham had earned three degrees and was superintendent of the Providence plant. He telephoned me in Birmingham.

"Mr. Rowland, I've just had a call from Mr. Steele," he said, "and he would like for me to be a vice president of the Pepsi Cola Company."

"I see."

"He wants an answer now, and I wanted to see what you thought of it."

"Alvin, what are you making now?" I asked.

"Seven-fifty a month," he said. "The same that I was making when you left here two years ago."

"How much has Mr. Steele offered you?"

"Fifteen hundred a month," he said, "and I still have my mother-in-law living with me, and I have two children, and . . . ."

"Alvin," I cut him off. "Take the job."

"What?"

"Take the job with Mr. Steele. He's a good man."

That's all I could say and be totally honest.

Steele hired Bob Hailey, another of my men in New England, and made him a vice president. He made Curly LaFleur vice president, too. Curly had been a route salesman and plant manager in Woonsocket, Rhode Island. Al Steele moved in and doubled his salary to lure him to Pepsi.

Dick Freeman, the Coca-Cola bottler in New Orleans, told me of a Pepsi Cola meeting in a New Orleans hotel once when twenty-two of the forty key Pepsi people there were ex-Coca-Cola. He said Al Steele came in about thirty minutes late, and his first remark was, "All right, you sons of bitches, you're not in the Coca-Cola business. Quit talking about Coke; we're going to talk about Pepsi."

Al Steele was a terrific guy. He was one of the smartest men in the beverage business. He eventually married Joan Crawford, the movie star.

Steele had been a circus barker and later was vice president of D'Arcy Advertising Agency. That's where Woodruff found him, and when Woodruff brought him to Coca-Cola, he was a dynamo.

Once when I was vice president of Coca-Cola plants in Rhode Island, I attended a Coca-Cola meeting in Chicago at which Al Steele presided. We all arrived on Sunday. On Monday morning we went to Coca-Cola's beautiful offices on LaSalle Street and gathered in the huge conference room. It would accommodate fifty or sixty people, and there were about fifty of us. We met at nine o'clock and waited for Steele and his entourage to arrive. When they didn't show up in a few minutes, Cliff Hodson, president of company-owned plants, asked his secretary to call Steele's suite in the Ambassador East and see if he had left.

She returned in a minute to say, "Mr. Steele said to tell you that he expects all of you at the Ambassador East. He has everything set up in the penthouse.

We took cabs to his hotel and went up to the penthouse where he had a bar open at nine-thirty in the morning. When we all had a drink, Steele put on his dog-and-pony show.

When the promotion and marketing department turned an idea into a workable promotion, it was tried out in one of the company-owned plants where Coca-Cola released it to the franchised bottlers. I was one of the guinea pigs in Providence on some things they tried out. Some of the ideas were terrific, and some were bombs that fizzled before they reached the mass market. We always went whole hog into whatever Al Steele wanted us to do.

Anyway, there was Steele in his penthouse entertaining fifty Coca-Cola guys, and Coca-Cola footed a terrific bill that day. The bartender stayed on duty all day. Steele had a "gofer," a young man who stood by and did nothing but what Steele bade him do. We didn't go down to the dining room for lunch; we ordered ala carte, and lunch was served in the penthouse.

Al Steele was a flamboyant individual, and I enjoyed him. I loved him and I would have gone to work for him in a minute, but we didn't want to move again.

He saved my bacon at a meeting in New York just after the end of World War II. Woodruff ran a strategy session to launch Coca-Cola into the post-war era. Everyone expected a boom, and we wanted to be sure we covered all bases.

Woodruff asked four men at that meeting what Coca-Cola needed most at that time. I was the second man he asked, and I gave him an honest answer, "We need a larger bottle."

He jumped right down my throat. He could do that. He said the six and one-half ounce bottle was the perfect drink and Coca-Cola had perfected it and would stay with it.

Suddenly Al Steele said, "Bob, Sanders is right."

"What?" Woodruff demanded.

"He's right, Bob. We need a larger bottle."

We hashed it around and enough feeling came out of that meeting to warrant a larger container for Coca-Cola.

Al Steele is the only man I knew who would argue with Woodruff. He could get away with it. Or maybe that's why his contract wasn't renewed.

After he left Coca-Cola, he caused the company a lot of trouble, and by trouble I mean nothing more than competition. He was as fair as they come, but he was sharp. He capitalized on every gimmick—like the traveling lab.

In Birmingham, when Steele took over at Pepsi, the competition came on strong. Jimmy Lee, the Buffalo Rock bottler, got the Pepsi Cola franchise. At the time he started with it, Pepsi had about two percent of the business in Birmingham. Royal Crown had ten or eleven percent, and we had the rest.

Jimmy did a terrific job. One thing that helped him was that he could take off his hat and have a meeting of the board of directors. He owned forty-nine percent of the stock, and his family owned considerably more. He knew what he was doing, and when he linked up with Al Steele, the fur flew in Birmingham.

At Steele's behest, I am sure, Jimmy Lee came out with a ten-ounce one-way bottle. No returns. The bottle was disposable, a throwaway. I had talked to the Johnsons about getting the throwaway bottle, but Allen wouldn't hear of it. He was energy conscious and thought one-way bottles was a tremendous waste of raw materials.

So Jimmy Lee had it two years before we were forced to get it, and in those years his two percent of the Birmingham market increased to twenty-two percent. Even then, Allen Johnson was determined that Coca-Cola would not adopt the one-way bottle. But when I took the figures to Crawford Junior and Three and Bob Jones and the rest of the directors, they saw very quickly what was happening and overruled Allen. Only then did we come out with a disposable bottle.

We still had the market cornered in the cooler business. The coolers at that time cost anywhere from four hundred to six hundred dollars, and we were moving them fast. Each of our salesmen worked his route with a cooler demonstration truck every now and then. We in the front office made it a habit to go along because coolers seemed to go faster when one of us was present. Maybe it created an image with a store-owner that Coca-Cola really cared, at least cared enough to send one of the executives to see him.

We competed against each other. I went out once and the salesman I was with sold eighteen coolers. Crawford Three went next time, and his man sold twenty. Then Preacher's man moved twenty-two, and Cecil Parks' got twenty-five. Finally I went back and moved twenty-eight. We had real competition among ourselves, and we were saturating Birmingham with coolers. We sold them to the dealers, who could pay them off quickly with the cooler sales they made.

Jimmy Lee had the same type coolers, but Pepsi coolers didn't sell. He placed one here and one there, but while he was placing one, we moved twenty-five.

Jimmy went into a service station one day and tried to sell the owner a cooler, but the owner was stubborn. He wouldn't buy. Finally, in exasperation, Jimmy threw up his hands. "Would you take it," he asked, "if I gave it to you?"

"Sure," the owner said. "I'd take it under those conditions."

So Jimmy gave him the cooler, and when he got back to his office he did some figuring and discovered that all the man had to sell was eighty cases a month and Jimmy's profit from the eighty cases would pay for the machine in a few months.

So when Pepsi machines began showing up beside our Coca-Cola machines, we began to wonder how Jimmy was selling so many. We sent a man to find out, and he reported back that Jimmy was not selling them; he was giving them away.

And his ploy worked. He had various flavors—Pepsi, orange, grape, ginger ale, and all we had was Coca-Cola.

Jimmy Lee forced us into flavors.

At the same time we went into the flavor business, we also had to start stocking some of our machines with canned drinks. That was forced by U.S. Steel.

Art Weibel called me to the steel office in Birmingham one day and said he heard that Coca-Cola was sent overseas in cans during World War II. I told him yes, that some of it was canned, but not much. In fact, we in Providence had built a new plant in New Bedford, Massachusetts, that was completed at the beginning of the war. It became a canning plant for Coca-Cola during the war.

"Then I want you to put your Coca-Cola in cans," he said. "We make steelplate. You're selling us six million bottles a year. Why can't that be six million cans?"

"I don't know," I said. "I'll check with Atlanta and see if we can get some cans."

Crawford Junior and I went to Atlanta and talked to Woodruff, but he would not let us have any cans. I had to go back to Art Wiebel and tell him that we could not fill his request."

"That's too bad," he said. "Canada Dry has drinks in cans."

"Yes," I said. "They do." They were in those early cans that had crowns on them.

"You put some cans of Coca-Cola in here," he said, "or you figure out a way to put some cans of Canada Dry in here—or I'll throw you out of the plant." He was that way, hard as nails.

The Canada Dry plant in Birmingham was a small operation run by two brothers-in-law, Jerry Cocharto and Jimmy Valdone. I called Jerry and asked if he would sell me some Canada Dry in cans.

He laughed. "I've talked to Art Weibel," he said. "You want them for the steel plant, don't you?"

I said yes. I couldn't lie to him.

"In that case," he said, "we can't sell you any cans."

"Well, if that's. . . ."

"But," he cut in, "we'll sell you our plant."

I was squarely over the barrel. "What do you want for it?" I asked.

"I'll come over," he said.

Soon Jerry Cocharto and Jimmy Valdone came to my office, and in a few minutes they set a price. I went to the Johnsons and told them we were going to lose the U. S. Steel contract if we didn't get cans of something—so we bought the Canada Dry plant. Soon we were furnishing canned drinks to U.S. Steel.

Jimmy Lee wound up making a fortune with canned Pepsis. He canned them for distributors all over the South, and his business grew to enormous proportions. At one time he had more than eighty transport trucks running day and night, delivering Pepsi Cola all over the South.

CHAPTER 19

Retired, But Not Finished

ONE OF THE THINGS Crawford Junior asked me to do when I came to Birmingham in 1949 was teach his son, Crawford Three, everything I knew about the Coca-Cola business. The youngster was such a fine man that I attempted to do that with pleasure. He never gave me the slightest bit of trouble. He was willing to try anything and do anything I suggested. He was the most cooperative young man I ever met.

He and I made trips together. Once when we went to Atlanta for a Coca-Cola meeting, I took Mimi, and he took a young lady named Virginia Goodall of Birmingham. We stayed in the Biltmore Hotel, Crawford and I sleeping in one room, and Mimi and Miss Goodall in another. Crawford and Miss Goodall became engaged that weekend and were later married. In nineteen months they had two sets of twin girls who are now four fine ladies.

Through the years, Allen made no effort to get along with Crawford Three. If Crawford suggested something to me, Allen got me aside and said, "Don't do that. I don't think it's a good idea." Some of Crawford's ideas were good and some weren't, just the same as mine, or anyone's.

Finally, Crawford Junior retired in early 1970, and the board made Allen chairman of the board and Crawford Three president of the company. I was still to be executive vice president and general manager. Allen stipulated with the board's approval that since I would be running the plant as I had for more than twenty years, I would not have to report to Crawford Three.

Since Allen still didn't have all that much interest in operating

193

the company, he moved his office out of the company building and into an office building not far from his home. He simply did not want to be in the same building with his nephew if he thought Crawford Three might carry any authority. Allen fixed up his and his secretary's new office and had a small reception area. He was satisfied out there away from the hustle and bustle of Coca-Cola company life.

The Johnson brothers, Crawford Junior and Allen, had a strange relationship. I never did completely figure them out.

I observed an open door policy in my office. If I didn't have a closed-door conference going on in the office, my door was open and anyone who wished could come in. My office was on the second floor.

One morning Allen and Crawford Junior came in together. They came up the steps and had to pass my office on the way to their's, and they always spoke, "Good morning, Sanders," "Hello, Sanders."

But this morning, neither spoke. When they were past my door, Crawford suddenly wheeled around, stepped into my office, and commanded, "Come in my office."

I went into Crawford's office, and he bade me sit in the chair I usually occupied. Allen also sat down.

"Brother," Crawford said to Allen, "tell Sanders what you said last night."

Allen began to talk, and I could not piece together heads or tails of what he was saying. In a minute Crawford broke in. "Wait a minute," he said. "That's not what you said last night."

"That's exactly what I said last night, Brother," Allen said.

"Really?" said Crawford. "Well, I'll be damned."

They got up and kissed each other and walked out arm in arm and left me sitting there. To this day, I don't know what they were talking about.

I was often called on to referee their fights, and it put me in an uncomfortable position. Allen was not as loyal to me as Crawford Junior was, but I tried to be fair to both of them since they were both my employers.

When Allen moved his office out of the plant, I went to Crawford Three and said, "Three, you just tell me what you want me to do. This is not going to work the way they set it up. You can't be president and me be executive vice president and me not report to you. That's just not going to work, and besides, I don't mind in the least reporting to you. You're the president of this company now."

"Sanders, I don't know. . . ."

"Three," I said firmly, "I have trained you for twenty years to be president of this company, and I'm proud that the day has come. I want you to be a real president."

And he was. He and I never had a cross word nor a problem between us.

I love Crawford Three. If he had been a son, I couldn't think more of him. I would do anything for him.

That was my retirement year. The company had a policy of mandatory retirement at age sixty-five, and my sixty-fifth birthday fell on December third that year, 1970. I retired at the end of the year.

I looked back over almost twenty-two years with the Birmingham operation and saw many things to be proud of. We had built the firm into a sprawling giant, and its tentacles were about to reach into other areas, Augusta, Georgia; Chattanooga, Tennessee; Spartanburg, South Carolina; Jasper, Alabama. All of those companies would soon merge with the Birmingham company under Crawford Three's direction.

Under my direction as general manager, the Birmingham company had made the best possible use of vending machines. We had introduced new bottle sizes and new Coca-Cola products. King-sized Coke had been introduced in Birmingham in 1957. Coca-Cola in cans came in 1960. And in 1962 we came out with the sixteen-ounce bottle of Coca-Cola.

When I retired, I didn't quit work. I left the Coca-Cola plant but found other things to do. My retirement was effective on December 31, 1971, and I immediately went to work temporarily for George Wallace. The governor of Alabama asked me to join a Cost Control Study, a committee of fifty men appointed to study the State of Alabama, looking for ways by which the state could be more efficiently operated.

The committee consisted of a chairman and vice chairman and six teams of eight men each. I was appointed leader of one of the six teams. I was sponsored by the Coca-Cola Bottlers of Alabama, who paid my expenses by the day. I worked that job from January first to May first.

We were based in Montgomery, and my team and I lived in the same hotel for those five months. We were a hundred miles from

Birmingham, a two-hour drive, but I didn't even think of commuting. I went home on Friday afternoon and returned to Montgomery Sunday evening.

I got together with my team every evening to go over what we had learned that day, and on Monday mornings all team captains came together with the chairman, the vice chairman, and Governor Wallace and his paid consultants, and we gave progress reports on the work we had done the preceding week.

I had met George Wallace but did not know him well until that period of early 1972. He grew to be a fantastic person in my eyes before the end of that time.

I had been assigned to study two departments in the state government, the Department of Labor and the Department of Commerce. I sent my team members into various phases of each department, digging and probing and looking for excesses in anything.

One of my men was an engineer, originally from New Jersey, who was working in Montevallo making wheels for boxcars, a tremendous job. I assigned him to study the Alcoholic Beverage Control. During the time we were making the study, the head of the ABC Board requested more space. He had two hundred thousand square feet of floor space in his warehouse in Montgomery, and he said, "I frankly don't have space for all this whiskey."

I sent this young engineer to look over the situation. He reported that he believed the existing space was sufficient, but the stock needed to be better organized. I told him to organize it. The ABC head put enough manpower with this engineer to do the job and a week later the Alcoholic Beverage Control had a third too much space in that warehouse. My engineer reworked the inventory, rearranged the storage, and wound up with plenty of space for expansion.

We found much duplication in the Commerce and Labor departments. It appeared to me that all too often people from the Commerce Department were working on the same tasks in Alabama industry that people from the Labor Department were working on. So after careful study of the situation, I came to a conclusion and reported same to Gov. Wallace on Monday morning.

"Governor Wallace," I said, "I think we ought to combine the Commerce and Labor departments. There is too much duplication between the departments, and if we combined them we could save a lot of money.

I saw a twinkle rise in the governor's eyes. "Sanders," he said, "there are many hundreds of thousands of laborers in Alabama, and we are not going to do without either the Department of Commerce or the Department of Labor—and you can forget that right now."

"Yes, sir," I said. "I've already forgotten what I was talking about."

Everybody laughed, and in the governor's eyes I am not sure that I saw laborers. I believe I saw voters.

In one area, we made a vast improvement. I kept trying to find things we could streamline, just the same as I had streamlined the operations in every Coca-Cola Company I had run but Pittsburgh.

In the State of Alabama were sixty-three men who gave driving tests and issued driver's licenses. They served all the counties and each had a state automobile. Some of them worked in more counties than one or two. Their cars were the same as those of the Alabama state troopers—big, heavy, supercharged dragons that would do a hundred fifty miles an hour without pushing the pedal to the metal. Their cars were equipped with sirens, flashing blue lights, and all sorts of electronic things. Now and then the state had to replace all those examiners' cars, and we recommended that they be replaced with smaller, more efficient automobiles than the gigantic gas-guzzlers then in use. After all, these men were not highway patrolmen who spent their time running down speeders. They usually just drove the cars back and forth to work and left them parked all day.

By purchasing small, four-cylinder cars for the license examiners, the state could save more than a quarter of a million dollars a year. That was one of our suggestions that was adopted.

By the end of April our committee of fifty gave Governor Wallace more than sixty-six million dollars worth of saving suggestions. We disbanded the first of May and later that month the governor was shot. When he finally got back around to the business we had presented him, he was in a wheel chair and it was 1973. But he and the Alabama state government accepted and instituted forty-four million dollars of our suggestions.

When Fred Dickson became president of the Coca-Cola Company, U.S.A., in the early 1960s, he appointed a Presidential Advisory Council of twenty-three Coca-Cola men from all over the country to feed him expertise. Two from Alabama were appointed: Sanders Rowland of Birmingham and Charlie Brightwell of Montgomery. Later, Crawford Three was added. We met quarterly all over the country—Vermont, San Francisco, Dallas, Houston, Los Angeles—exchanging ideas and arguing developments.

Luke Smith succeeded Dickson as president and continued the Presidential advisory Council. The next president, Don Keough, did not continue the council, and it died. But I think its contributions helped the Coca-Cola Company. And for me, my presence on the council reacquainted me with a lot of old friends in the bottling business.

Before I retired, at Mimi's request we bought an Airstream house trailer. It was the subject of several good jokes around the Coca-Cola Company. Crawford Johnson, III, would tell his friends that I had an Airstream, and he would laugh and say, "Can you imagine Sandy pushing the doorbells of his friends around the country and saying, 'Where can I plug it in?' "

That was hard even for me to imagine. Mimi loved the trailer, but it wasn't my cup of tea. Oh, I enjoyed the vacation trips we took in it, but even though it was the Cadillac of house trailers, it was still a bit cramped to suit me. We pulled it to Maine to visit Mimi's brother and to Wisconsin to visit our son, Henry, and his family.

Suddenly, here I was at loose ends. I no longer had a job to occupy my time. I had worked fifty-one and a half years, and suddenly I had nothing to do.

I was miserable. I woke up one day and looked in the mirror and said to myself, "Sanders, what in the world are you gonna do today? You went to the library yesterday and got two books, and you can't get interested in them; you don't need to go to the post office, or the bank; you had your hair cut last week; you've played so much gin rummy you're almost sick of it."

I sat down and really thought about my situation, and the only answer I could reach was this: "Sanders, you need a job."

But where could I find some work to do. I searched my brain and kept coming back to Coca-Cola.

I dialed the Coca-Cola Company in Atlanta and asked to speak to Luke Smith, the president. I had known Luke for years. He was manager of the New England Coca-Cola Bottling Company in Concord, New Hampshire, when I was manager in Providence.

"Luke, I'm bored to death," I said. "I need a job. I hit a dead wall this week and just can't think of a thing I'd like to do except work. How about giving me a job? Let me do something for the Coca-Cola Company."

"Come over and see me Monday, Sandy," he said, "and we'll talk about it."

He was very nice on the phone. I knew he would find something for me to do, if I could hold out till Monday. This was Thursday.

I drove to Atlanta on Sunday and went to see Luke Monday morning. As I thought, he had a job for me.

"You can be a big help to me, Sandy," he said. "I'd like you to handle some things for me. The first thing you can do is study the Fountain Department."

Fountain had a president of its own, but he worked under Luke Smith. I took it that Luke was not too happy with the way the Fountain Department was going.

"I want you to attend two meetings," he said, "and critique them for me." The first was a five-day meeting on the West Coast, and the second was at Greenbriar in West Virginia. He sent me to both places in the company plane.

At the meetings I renewed a lot of acquaintances, met a lot of nice people, and critiqued all the sessions for Luke Smith. I reported directly to him, and I hope my work helped him in straightening out the Fountain Department. A lot of the information I passed to Luke came from individuals and not out of the meetings. The business sessions were held in the mornings, and the afternoons were free for golf or swimming or whatever. I sat around the pool a lot and talked to other Coca-Cola people, and one afternoon I met a fountain representative who was an intensely frustrated man. It turned out that he had to answer through nine layers of supervision in his department: nine levels of supervision above him, each one instructing the other. No wonder there were problems in the fountain department!

Luke quickly eliminated three of those layers, and said, "There are still too many, and I may work on them some more."

But I didn't get a chance to help him further. There was another task he wanted me to tackle.

CHAPTER 20

Land of the Sky

"THEY'RE HAVING PROBLEMS in Asheville," said Tony Butterworth, Coca-Cola's vice president in charge of the Southeastern region. "The president of the Asheville company has had a heart attack, and they need somebody to fill in for two months until they get a new president."

That didn't sound ominous. The two months were to begin August 21, 1974.

Tony's next words put the situation in better perspective. "It may be a pretty big job," he said. "It will certainly be full-time, but we would like you to go up there and see if you can get the company back on it's feet."

I had been a consultant for two years and had handled some fairly tough assignments, but nothing like what I stepped into in Asheville.

Of all the jobs I held, only Pittsburgh was tougher—but nothing could be tougher than Pittsburgh.

Asheville is one of the garden spots of the world, sitting on a high plateau between the Blue Ridge and the Great Smoky Mountains. Asheville is a beautiful little city in an exceptionally breathtaking area known as the "Land of the Sky."

"If you would like me to go, I'll go," I told Tony Butterworth. "I'm in good health. I feel just like I did when I was twenty-one. If you think I can straighten Asheville out, I'll be happy to try."

Lee Ellis, who had pioneered Asheville with the Coca-Cola Company, had been a long-time friend of mine. He was a doer, and he had a reputation of running a good Coca-Cola plant. I knew he had set up the Asheville company on sound footing and had run it properly while he was living. But Lee had been gone for some time, and I had had no contact with Asheville.

Lee's widow, Nan, was still around, but at ninety-four she was not too active in the company. A ninety-four-year-old woman can't be too much of a help or a hindrance, I thought.

Little did I know!

I met Lee Ellis first in 1936 on the Coca-Cola Company's fiftieth anniversary convention and became acquainted there. Then in 1947 I came down from Providence to visit Asheville. We stayed at the Grove Park Inn, one of the world's fine hostelries. We played golf at the Country Club of Asheville and at Biltmore Forest Country Club, an exclusive club that bordered the Biltmore Estate, George Vanderbilt's fantastic French chateau and gardens on the outskirts of Asheville. I was extremely impressed with Asheville. The more I thought about the opportunity, the more I liked the idea of moving to Asheville.

Besides, I had been idle for a while, and I needed something to do.

Paul Warlick was president of the Asheville company. He was the one who had a heart attack. He was incapacitated and in his absence the company was going to pot.

I was interviewed for the Asheville position by Kip Warlick, the president's son and director of the company, and by Bob Weiler, a vice president of Wachovia Bank and Trust Company and the bank's representative on the Coca-Cola Company's Board of Directors. I gave Weiler a figure I would work for, and he called me the next day and said he had cleared my employment for two months at the specified figure. He also said he wanted me to call Dr. Nicholas Beadles of Athens, Georgia, a director and stockholder in the Asheville company. Nick and his sister owned a sixth of the company's stock.

I telephoned Dr. Beadles, and he began to tell me what he wanted me to do. I said to him, "Dr. Beadles, I have not had time to look the situation over personally, and I don't know whether the things you've told me ought to be done or not. I've made notes and when I get there if I think they should be done, I'll do them."

He didn't like it a bit that I didn't say "Yes, sir."

Kip Warlick was running things. He was twenty-eight and had a master's degree in something and was a nice young man.

But he began countermanding my orders. I called the auditors and told them I wanted the company's cash statements, and when I didn't get them in a week I called to ask why. I was told that Kip had called and said not to send the statements to me. I had to straighten Kip out.

The first week I was in Asheville I terminated four of Kip's friends, whom he had hired. They were on the payroll but were doing nothing. Kip told me off for that.

I had not been on the job long when I realized it would require much more than two months to get the operation shipshape again.

Bills were unpaid. I didn't know if we had enough money to meet the payroll. Worst of all, the company, at the insistence of the Warlicks—Paul and Kip—was building a new plant southwest of Asheville. The company had paid $128,000 for a beautiful piece of land, and $65,500 to grade it. Four hundred thousand dollars worth of steel had been erected, and $98,000 worth of siding put up and a roof put on.

And there was no water or sewer available!

The plant was on a paved county road, and water and sewer lines ran along the road—but they were for residential use only. They were in no way large enough to serve a Coca-Cola plant's needs. Coca-Cola needs a lot of water for a bottling operation since Coke is eighty-nine percent water. Too, the rinse water from the cleaning machine goes into the sewer.

When I discovered we did not have adequate water and sewer at the new site, I called a meeting of the directors and presented them with a six-page letter that detailed why we could never use the new plant; why it never should have been built; and that we should sell it. I estimated that it was twenty-five miles from the center of distribution, a statistic that Coca-Cola later confirmed, and the extra fifty miles a day that each truck would have to run was staggering. No previous studies had been made on the center of distribution.

The lot was a nice, wooded, country lot, but it was not suitable for our purposes.

The directors agreed, and we put the property up for sale. They also gave me a one-year contract at $75,000 to straighten things out.

The following June, of 1975, I told the directors I could not clean up the mess in a year. "We still have machinery coming in for the new plant," I said. "I have returned all of it that can be returned, and I'm trying to sell the rest. The building hasn't been sold, and frankly I need another year." They extended my contract.

A year and a half were required to sell the building, and in the meantime I disposed of most of the machinery. The Westinghouse Corporation bought the building and now employs six hundred people in a manufacturing operation. The building suited Westinghouse fine, and sewer lines were adequate since they were only used for toilets. Westinghouse does not use water in its operation.

At the start, I had to address myself to the most important problem—money. I came to work in late August, and in November we ran out of money. We had none in the bank. I went to Wachovia to float a loan. Coca-Cola in Asheville had been a customer on Wachovia's since the start. Lee Ellis, the founder, had been on Wachovia's board of directors.

I gathered up all the papers and statements to show why I needed money and went to our Coca-Cola director, Bob Weiler, at the bank. I told him I wanted to borrow a million seven hundred thousand dollars to pay the bills and make the payroll. He was the trust officer and was not authorized to make loans. He introduced me to a vice president in the commercial department and when I told him I needed to borrow some money, he asked, "How much do you need?"

"I need a million and seven hundred thousand," I said.

"Why do you need so much?" he asked.

"I must pay our bills and meet the payroll," I said. "Some of the contractors haven't been paid, and we owe for machinery that's coming in almost every day for the new plant. We're in bad shape financially, but I have to have some money in order to start our recovery. That's why I'm in Asheville. I was sent by the Coca-Cola Company in Atlanta."

"I am aware of that," he said. "Do you have a statement?"

I did. I had a pathetic September statement. He looked it over.

"We loaned Paul Warlick five hundred thousand in January," he said.

"Yes, it shows on the statement," I said. "We owe you five hundred thousand dollars."

"He hasn't paid any of that back," the officer said. "I'm sorry, but we can't lend you any more money—and we would really appreciate it if you would pay the five hundred thousand back."

"You mean you're not going to lend us the money?" I asked. I couldn't believe my ears.

"That's exactly right," he said.

When I left his office I was ill—physically ill. I had never borrowed money. In Birmingham when I needed money, Crawford Junior would get it. He was a director of First National Bank, on the executive committee. He would call the president of the bank and say, "Sanders is coming down to get fifty thousand dollars," and I would go get the money.

Before that, with the Coca-Cola Company, I would call the president of company-owned plants and say, for example, "I need a hundred thousand dollars."

He would always ask, "What do you need it for?"

When I told him, he said he would send a check. We paid three percent interest to the Coca-Cola Company. I never had experience borrowing money.

I returned to Bob Weiler's office and said, "Your friend won't lend me any money. What are we going to do?"

He said, "Have you met any other bankers in Asheville?"

I said, "Yes, a man named Sidney Hughes. I remember his name because he gave me a good cigar. He's vice president of First Citizens Bank and Trust Company. He said to me that he knew we banked at Wachovia but he said if I ever needed another bank to call him."

Weiler handed me the phone.

Sidney Hughes said to come on over. His bank was across the street from Wachovia, and when I entered his office he greeted me warmly.

I didn't beat around the bush. I said, "Mr. Hughes, I'd like to borrow two million, two hundred thousand dollars."

"All right," he said, "I'll lend it to you."

Just like that. He didn't even hesitate.

"There will be some conditions," he said.

"Yes, sir," I said. "I expect that."

"We want all of your banking business," he said. "We want to be your bank, and nobody else. We want all your accounts."

"That's no problem at all," I said. "I will transfer them tomorrow."

He gave me the money on the spot. I asked him for a check for five hundred thousand dollars and took it across the street to Wachovia and gave it to the loan officer who refused my loan. I used the rest to pay bills.

We repaid the money quickly and two years later borrowed three million from First Citizens to build another plant.

After my second year I told the board we needed a new plant. I had the Coca-Cola Company send experts in to determine the center of distribution and since the Asheville operation was so far-flung, covering all of Western North Carolina, the experts thought we should have two plants, one in Asheville and one over the mountains to the east. So much of our operation was in the piedmont that it was prohibitive to haul Coca-Colas from Asheville to those distant places.

We found sixty acres of land in Morganton, sixty miles east of Asheville, bought the property for three thousand an acre, borrowed three million from First Citizens, and built the plant in Morganton.

Two years were required for me to get the Asheville company into sound and profitable condition.

But the job was not easy.

I had a problem in Asheville that I had not faced elsewhere, not even in Pittsburgh.

The problem was ninety-four years old. It was Nan Ellis.

I realize that age gives a person advantages, but she carried them to the extreme.

Our first run-in came just after the board elected me president of the company. I had occupied her late husband's spacious office which had a terrazzo floor. Sound bounced off that floor, richocheted off the walls, and came around again, and perhaps my hearing wasn't what it once was, but when we gathered around the conference table in my office, I couldn't hear anything anyone said. Carrying on a normal conversation was an effort. I found myself straining to catch every word.

So I had the floor covered with a rug—a big rug.

One day I heard a knock at the door, and the door flew open. An elderly woman walked in. I had never seen Nan Ellis, but I knew this was she.

I stood and said, "Mrs. Ellis, come in." I went around the desk to help her to a chair.

But she didn't give me chance. She took one look at that rug and said "What have you done to my husband's beautiful floor?"

"Why, Mrs. Ellis, I. . ."

"You have no right!" she said. "You had no right to put that ugly rug on my husband's beautiful floor!"

"Well, that floor makes an acoustical problem in here," I said, "and I am president of this company; so I had the terrazzo covered."

"Well, you can just uncover it!" she screamed. "I understand that the board of directors made you the president; and if this is the way you're going to run this company, then they have made a terrible mistake!"

And she stormed out.

She never did sit in the chair I offered her. She just wheeled around and walked out.

The first week I was in Asheville, I met one of our employees named Joe Davis. He introduced himself.

"Mr. Rowland," he said, "I'm Joe Davis. I pick up the mail. I'm a special deputy sheriff, and I handle security for the plant."

I liked that. In a nutshell he told me what he did.

"I understand you and the missus have a trailer parked at Swannanoa," he said, and I nodded. We were living in the Airstream in Tanglewood Park in Swannanoa, a community about ten miles east of the Coca-Cola office. "Do you want me to bring the mail out there on Saturday and Sunday?" he asked.

"No, Mr. Davis," I said. "I don't want the mail on Saturday and Sunday."

"I had to take it to Mr. Warlick every Saturday and Sunday."

"Well, you don't have to bring it to me. I'll read it on Monday morning when I get to the office."

"Do you mean I don't have to go to the Post Office on Saturday and Sunday?"

"That's exactly what I mean, Mr. Davis. Those are your days off."

I made a friend for life right there.

Joe Davis had a heart attack not long after I came to Asheville. As soon as he was on his feet again, even though he couldn't drive, he continued to bring the mail. Luther Worley was a good employee, and I assigned Luther to drive Joe after the mail, and together they ran other errands.

When Nan Ellis needed something done at her home, she

called Lloyd Smith, the plant superintendent, and insisted that
he come and help her. It didn't matter what he was doing at that
moment, she expected him to drop it and come. She would also
call up the garage and insist that a mechanic, sometimes two,
come to her home and work on her lawn mower.

She interfered with the business of the company, and until
then no one would back Lloyd Smith, who wanted to stop these
shenanigans. I gave the matter a lot of thought, and came to a
conclusion. I called Luther Worley in.

"Luther, you know Mrs. Ellis."

"Yes, sir."

"You've driven her places now and then?"

"Yes, sir."

"Okay, here's what I want you to do: When you finish your
mail run and other errands in the mornings, I want you to call
Mrs. Ellis and ask if there is anything you can do for her that day.
If so, do it. Take her to lunch, to the hairdresser, to the doctor, or
wherever she wants to go. If she needs something else done, do it
for her. Do you understand what I'm asking of you?"

"Yes, sir."

"Good. I want you to take care of Nan Ellis."

That solved her problem. Luther was a good man, and he and
Mrs. Ellis got along beautifully.

One day as I made my rounds of the plant, it occurred to me
that we had no black employees in the office. I mentioned this at
a director's meeting. One of our directors, a vice president of Wachovia, mentioned that a nice, qualified black girl had applied at
Wachovia but had not been hired because there were no openings.
He suggested we hire her to work in the office.

He put the young lady in touch with me, and I hired her. She
was a fine person and a good worker. She caught on quickly and
soon was doing her share of the work.

Soon after that, Nan Ellis came in. She was of the old school, I
suppose, because when she saw the black girl working, she became livid.

"Get out of here," she screamed. "You can't work here.
There's no place for you here."

She upset the girl so badly the girl fled. She ran out of the
office and went home.

When I found out what happened, I went to the young wom-

an's home and told her that she still had a job, and that Mrs. Ellis
had nothing to do with employees, and I apologized to her. She
consented to return to work.

Then I confronted Nan Ellis and told her the young woman
was going to continue to work for us, and I ordered her not to
interfere again. Mrs. Ellis was a stockholder, nothing more.

She flew up at me again. "Nigger lover!" she shouted, shaking
her cane at me. "You spent time up North, didn't you?"

"Yes, ma'am, about twenty years," I said.

"I knew it!" she said. "No wonder you're a nigger lover."

She didn't faze me. Talk like that rolled off my back like water
off a duck's down.

She created several other scenes, not only in the Coca-Cola
plant but about town, also. She would come into the plant, go
upstairs to the offices and raise Cain with anyone she wanted to.

These times, I suppose, were on her bad days. For the most
part, we got along all right. I decided to win her over with kind-
ness. I would compliment her on her hair, or on her dress, and
she would beam. Once I complimented her on a beautiful aqua-
colored dress. "That's my wife's favorite color," I said, "and a
beautiful dress. When you get through with that dress, would
you give it to my wife?" She pranced around the office and gig-
gled and said, "Can she wear a ten?"

I understood her. She was ninety-four and in her advancing
years she had become a little crotchety. Well, for the most part,
people can bear a person like that if they really understand.

She didn't approve of the way I ran the company. She didn't
approve of the people I hired.

To be the Asheville zone manager in 1975, I hired a retired
army general named Frank Blazey. He was in the office one day
when she came in.

She looked at him. "Who is this guy?" she asked me.

"Mrs. Ellis, this is General Blazey, our Asheville zone manager. He served three tours in Vietnam."

"A retired general," she snapped. "You shouldn't be working
here. Can't you find something more important to do?"

As I did with everyone else, I explained to him that she was
Nan Ellis and she was a little cranky. He understood.

One of my goals in Asheville was to find an outstanding young
man to become president of the company, someone who could

run it after I got it on its feet, and someone who could help Coca-Cola realize the potential of the area.

Kip Warlick was the logical candidate. He was Paul Warlick's son and Nan Ellis's grandnephew. She had said she would leave him her shares of stock in the company.

Kip Warlick wasn't the man I was looking for. I thought he was a fine young man. I had met him once before at a meeting, and he had impressed me. But after I had been here a few months, I realized he was not the man this company needed for its president.

I sent him to Atlanta to a six-months school for S.O.B.'s. That's what Coca-Cola called the school. S.O.B. stood for "Sons of Bosses." The school put young men through the paces and taught them as much as possible about Coca-Cola operations.

Toward the end of the six months, when I was up to my neck in problems, Kip began coming home on weekends full of ideas contrary to what I was trying to do. His ideas did not fit the financial status of the company. He wanted to expand immediately and didn't like it when I wouldn't let him go out and hire a group of people.

I gave a lot of thought to the problem of Kip and concluded that I couldn't put up with his coming into my office all the time and telling me how crazy I was for trying to do this and that. So I went to Atlanta and had a long session with Kip and fired him. He took it like a man. He went to Anderson, South Carolina, where his family controlled the Coca-Cola Company and became president there.

We were moving toward financial stability by the end of my second year in Asheville. Profits were nothing to shout about but were beginning to be respectable. The company was not going to go broke.

I was seventy-one years old, and my contract was about to end. I knew I could not leave Asheville without having a successor lined up. So I intensified my search, and I went before the board and asked for a new five-year contract.

A couple of the directors jumped on that with both feet. Why do you want five years? You'll be seventy-six in five years! You've done the job we've hired you to do. Why do you want five more years?

"Gentlemen," I said, "there is only one reason. I need to train somebody to take my place, and I can't do it in one year. Maybe I could do it in three years, but I want five years because I'll be sure in five years of the man I train."

They were all very thoughtful.

"I've trained some awfully good men," I said, hammering the point home. "I have trained two vice presidents of the Pepsi Cola Company and one vice president of Coca-Cola. I trained the president of the New England Coca-Cola Bottling Company, the president of Birmingham, and I have trained many, many plant managers.

"It takes time to train a man properly," I said. "I will work five more years here without asking for any more money. I'm satisfied with what you're paying me."

I got the five-year contract, and that's when I began looking very seriously for a successor.

Eddie Nash had been with the Coca-Cola Bottling Company of Asheville for more than forty years. He was a director, and I had made him a vice president soon after I came and put him in charge of half of the territory. He was a good man and was doing a good job.

He had a son named Tom who impressed me very much. Tom was head of the fountain department of the Coca-Cola Company in Charlotte. He had done a fine job everywhere he had been during his fourteen years with the Coca-Cola Company.

He had a lot of other things going for him. He was a native of Asheville. He attended Mars Hill College, twenty miles north of Asheville, and he knew this territory and the people in it. He worked here in the summers when he was going to school—and he wanted to get back to Asheville.

I hired Tom in 1978. Tom had what I was looking for: determination, ability, personality, brains, and common sense. He was smart. I discovered that after he worked for me awhile. I saw that he could handle responsibility and keep a clear head. He had all the other attributes of a good leader, and I knew he was the man I wanted to succeed me.

Tom came with us after I had been in Asheville for four years, and I knew it wouldn't take five years to train him for the presidency. He caught on too quickly to need that much time.

At my behest, the board of directors elected Tom executive vice president and chief operating officer, on June 29, 1978, and I felt free to train him then. Tom set up a five-year plan under which he would double the company profits. He actually accomplished that in four, and I knew it was time to recommend him for the presidency.

Before he attained that office, however, there were two trips to Atlanta I had to make.

I sat alone in my office one afternoon looking at a picture of Bob Woodruff hanging on the wall. My mind wandered back to 1931 when I got the picture. I was manager of the New Haven company, and I went home to Atlanta for Christmas. Every time I went to Atlanta in those years, I went by to see Mr. Woodruff; and he always took thirty or forty minutes to talk to me. Not only did he know his personnel, he continued to learn all he could about them.

When I went in to see him that Christmas, I told his secretary I had been made manager of the New Haven operation. I didn't tell her the "operation" consisted of one plant employee, four salesmen, and me. I told her, "I want a picture of Mr. Woodruff to hang in my office. Do you think he would give me one?"

"Oh, I think he will do that for you," she said. "He has just had some new ones made. Let me show them to you."

She withdrew three pictures from the drawer of her desk. "He will show you all three," she said, "and this is the one you should pick. It's the one he likes."

I thanked her and went in. When, in the course of our conversation, I asked for a picture, just as his secretary had said, he drew out three pictures and said, "Which one do you like?"

I pointed to the one she told me to. "This one," I said. "This is the one I like."

"That," he said, smiling, "is my favorite, too," and he autographed it and gave it to me.

As I looked at that picture hanging on the wall of my Asheville office in 1978, the thought occurred to me that Tom Nash should meet Mr. Woodruff.

I made an appointment and took Tom to Atlanta and introduced him to Mr. Woodruff. As I used to, we visited with him about thirty minutes. He told Tom how he had come into the Coca-Cola business, how bad the business had been at the time, and how he had turned the company around.

All the while we were there, Mr. Woodruff kept saying to me,

"Sanders, what can I do for you?" And it occurred to me that I had never asked him for a thing in my life except the picture that hung on my wall.

Somewhere along the way, I should have asked him to help me get a franchise. Tom said later, "You're the craziest guy in the world, Sanders. Mr. Woodruff appeared to be genuinely fond of you, and I believe he really wanted to do something for you."

I'm sure he would have. I knew him sixty years, and I treasured my friendship with him.

Later we were having dinner with Tom's old boss, Knox Tabb of Charlotte. Tom and his wife, Brenda, and Mimi and I took Knox and his wife to the Downtown City Club in Asheville, and in the course of our conversation Tom mentioned something about meeting Mr. Woodruff.

"Mr. Woodruff?" Knox said. "Bob Woodruff? How in hell did you meet him? I've never seen the man."

I remembered Mr. Woodruff's private parking garage in the building on North Avenue in Atlanta. I remembered the private elevator to Mr. Woodruff's private quarters that he built on top of the three-story building. I remembered his personal barber chair, the massage table, the rest area in his suite of offices. It was almost sixty years ago that I ran the cleanup detail in the building and designated the old Negro man, Tom Freeman, to personally clean Mr. Woodruff's office and quarters.

I remember a picture on the wall of Mr. Woodruff's office. It was the picture of an owl sitting on the limb of a tree. The words below the picture read: "A wise old owl lived in an oak; the more he saw the less he spoke; Oh soldier, imitate that birdie."

I couldn't help laughing aloud when I looked at Knox Tabb.

I didn't laugh at him.

I laughed for old time's sake. I laughed for Mr. Woodruff. And I laughed for Tom Nash.

The second trip I had to make to Atlanta was in 1982 when I broached the Asheville board of directors about electing Tom Nash president and chief executive officer.

I ran into some opposition on that one. Not about electing Tom president; there was little opposition to that. But some of the directors felt we should elect him president and elect a member of the Warlick family chairman of the board.

I could see the same situation developing there that we had in Birmingham when Crawford Three was named president and his uncle Allen chairman of the board. So I resisted the board and insisted that Tom be given full power as president and chief executive officer to run the company without opposition.

A couple of members of the board apparently were having an influence on the board's bank director, then Dick Guthrie, a vice president of Wachovia. Since I had already discussed the matter with and had the full agreement of the front office of the Coca-Cola Company in Atlanta, I felt that Dick should accompany me to Atlanta and talk with some of the company officials. I telephoned Donald R. Keough, president of Coca-Cola, and asked if he could have Marvin Griffin, executive vice president, meet with Dick Guthrie and me the next morning about the presidential situation in Asheville.

The meeting was set for ten a.m., and Dick and I flew to Atlanta early the next morning. We were met at the airport and taken to the Coca-Cola Company in a limousine.

Dick, Marvin, Don, and I sat in Don's office, talking about why Tom Nash should be given full control in Asheville when Roberto Goizueta, the chairman of the board at Coca-Cola, came in.

Don Keough introduced Goizueta to Dick and me, and I said, "I'm delighted to meet you. I've been looking forward to it."

Goizueta laughed. "Sanders, this is not the first time we've met," he said. "I met you at the Capitol City Club several years ago with Paul Austin."

"Is that right?" I was surprised.

"You were having lunch with Ovid Davis, and we came over and spoke to you, and Paul introduced me to you. I told you I had been looking forward to meeting you because you had trained the man who hired me, Monte Thomas."

If there had been a hole in the floor, I would have fallen through it. Here was the chairman of the board of the Coca-Cola company remembering me, and I couldn't remember a thing about meeting him because at that time his name didn't mean anything. I was deeply embarrassed.

Roberto turned to Keough and asked, "What's the occasion of Sanders being here?"

"Sanders brought his director, Mr. Guthrie, up here to talk to us about the Asheville situation," Keough said. "Sanders has gotten Asheville straightened out and wants to give Tom Nash the presidency and the executive power to run the company."

"Yes, I've heard about that," Roberto said, "and it's a fine job you've done, Sanders."

That made me feel a little better.

"I believe we have convinced Mr. Guthrie of what we want in Asheville." Keough said.

"If that's what Sanders wants," Goizueta said, "that's what we want."

Smart? Oh, yes. I've seen Roberto Goizueta several times since, and he still speaks with an attractive Spanish accent. He is a good-looking devil, a graduate of Yale, a chemist. He knows both formulas for Coca-Cola, the Classic and the new. He is a heck of a nice guy.

When Nan Ellis heard that Tom had been elected president, she charged into my office as livid as any woman I have ever seen. She was spitting sparks.

I had gone around the desk to meet her as she came in, and she lit into me, saying things I wouldn't want to repeat, and she waved that cane as if she were going to hit me with it. I grabbed the cane, and when I did, she kicked me in the shin. So I sat her down.

"Nan," I said, "you are just terrible today. You shouldn't let your temper get the best of you like this. You kicked me and I don't appreciate it."

Her nurse, Barbara Callahan, was with her and saw everything that happened.

I was so fed up with her I wrote her a letter the following week. It read:

Dear Mrs. Ellis:

Since I have been the President and Chief Executive Officer of the Coca-Cola Bottling Company of Asheville and since I first met you over seven years ago, I have tried to the best of my ability to be nice to you and do whatever I could to make your life more pleasant and comfortable.

For several years I have furnished you with a company car and a company employee by the name of Luther Worley who has been at your disposal five days a week after he has picked up the mail and run the errands that were necessary for him to run here at the plant. He has been taking you to the hairdresser, the doctor, and to lunch, and has been riding you wherever you wanted to go. I did this for you because you are the widow of the founder of this company who was a friend of mine and a real gentleman.

You have told me on several occasions that you own this company, which is not true. You are one of the stockholders and I do not feel that I am being fair to other stockholders to give you the preferential treatment that I have given you since I have been here.

Last week when you came into my office and abused me verbally and kicked me in the shins in the presence of a witness, Mrs. Barbara Callahan, and accused me of some things which I am not guilty of, I am convinced that I have been too good to you and therefore, as of today, we are no longer furnishing you Luther Worley and the car for you to use at your convenience.

At your convenience and at your pleasure, you have been coming to the Coca-Cola Bottling Company at 345 Biltmore Avenue, and when you come down here I have asked that you come to see me. I didn't want you interfering with other people who have work to do. You have not heeded my request to come to see me and have been visiting other people and interfering with their work. As of today, I would appreciate it if you would not come to the Coca-Cola Bottling Company and I do not want to see you any more. I do not want you to be contacting any of our employees while they are at work, and if necessary I will obtain a court order to keep you out of this plant during working hours. I hope this won't be necessary but if I find you not adhering to my wishes that you stay out of the plant, I will certainly get the court order.

You have threatened me physically on several occasions and when you kicked me in the shin last week, this leaves me to believe that you might inflict bodily harm on me with your cane, which you have waved over my head on several occasions. Because of your previous actions, I don't think it is safe for me to be around you.

Yours very truly,
Sanders Rowland

She telephoned me.

"Sandy, this is Nan Ellis."

"Nan, how are you today?"

"I got your letter, and I want to tell you that I appreciate your letting me have Luther Worley and the car to run my errands and to take care of me."

"That's all right, Nan."

"Now, I want to tell you that I did not kick you," she said. "I crossed my legs and inadvertently creased your trousers."

"Nan," I said, "you kicked the hell out of me."

"I didn't kick you."

"You know you did, and everything I said in the letter stands. I cannot have you coming into this plant any more."

She then had her attorney call my attorney and demand an apology from me for accusing her of kicking me, and she wanted me to rescind my letter.

My attorney, Bobby Robinson, told her's that he had talked to me and I would neither apologize nor rescind the letter. He made it clear that the letter stood, and if she came back in the plant I would get a court order and keep her out.

Thus ended the Nan Ellis matter. She never came back to the plant.

Anyway, Tom Nash was then president, and Nan Ellis became his problem, not mine.

Right off the bat, Tom made two mistakes, and he made them by listening to me. I gave him some bum advice. He hired two men on my advice, one a financial "expert" who managed to put the company in grievous financial condition before Tom could let him go, and the other was my son, Henry.

Henry was in Wisconsin working as an engineer in a nuclear plant. He had six children, and Susie, his wife, didn't like his being around radioactive material like he had to be.

I thought I could do his family a favor. Henry had always wanted to be in the Coca-Cola business, but I have never let him come in, primarily because I had always worked for someone else and had never owned anything. Had I owned a Coca-Cola company, I would have had Henry in the business years ago.

We were about to open the Morganton plant, and I talked Tom Nash into hiring Henry to be manager at Morganton. I remembered all those men who had asked me to hire their sons, and many of them had become excellent Coca-Cola people. I figured it was now my turn.

So Tom hired Henry, and it was soon apparent that their genes didn't flow the same way. Tom liked to speak and be heard, and

Henry didn't listen too well. He wanted to press home his ideas.

After about a year and a half, Tom cut Henry loose, and Henry now does something he always wanted to do: He owns his own business. He makes porcelain lamp bases, mostly for the Ethan Allen Corporation. Susie is a good designer, and they make a good team. They have a business in Morganton that they can really build into something.

In retrospect, hiring Tom Nash may have been the best thing I ever did as a Coca-Cola man. Of all the young men I have trained, Tom Nash and Crawford Johnson Three are the smartest. They are excellent businessmen and smart bottlers. I have had trouble with Tom a few times, but we have always been able to work it out. He will go far in the Coca-Cola world.

He bought the Coca-Cola company in Greenville, South Carolina, bought the Anderson company from Kip Warlick, and now controls most of the territory in Western North Carolina and upper South Carolina.

By 1991 he and George Renfro, whom he hired after he became the Asheville president, will own the Asheville company lock, stock, and barrel.

After Tom became president of the Asheville company in 1982, I stayed on as consultant. The last task he asked me to do—and the last job I did for Coca-Cola—was to locate some land. The Southeastern Container Corporation, a co-op of bottlers that makes plastic bottles, wanted to build a plant in the North Carolina-South Carolina area.

Bishopville, South Carolina, is the site of a canning co-op of about forty Coca-Cola bottlers. That's were Coca-Cola is canned and shipped out to bottlers all over the South. It appeared for a while that the plastics plant would be located there, but Tom Nash told me if I could find about ten acres for three thousand dollars an acre around Asheville the plant would be built here.

In Asheville, land is hard to come by at that price, but I went to see Dave Conroy, vice president of the American Enka Company, which had a huge plant west of Asheville. I told him the possibility of the plastics plant coming to Asheville if sufficient land could be found at the right price, and there was also the possibility that American Enka could sell materials to the plant. So American Enka sold the co-op twenty acres west of Asheville for three thousand dollars an acre, and the plastic bottle plant was built there. Tom is vice president of the container corporation which manufactures plastic bottles for about thirty-five bottlers.

That job was the last thing I did for Coca-Cola in a career that spanned more than sixty years.

CHAPTER 21

Sound Business
Principles

LOOKING BACK OVER THE YEARS, I realize my long suit was not in selling Coca-Cola, but in selling people on themselves. As a company president or manager most of my working life, it has been a usually pleasant task to direct people, and I have not done that without some hard and fast rules to go by.

When I became manager of the New Haven Coca-Cola Company, I had the good fortune of working under good men who taught me sound business practices; but more than that, they taught me fairness. That is also Tom Nash's greatest trait. He is imminently fair.

I moved on through Hartford and to the bigger job in Providence, Rhode Island. Not ever having been formally trained, I knew I was making mistakes, especially in handling personnel. In Providence when the company began to grow so fast, I knew I needed to do some studying about management and personnel.

The Providence Chamber of Commerce sponsored a course for ten evenings in which businessmen were taught theories of management. This was in 1937 just after we moved into our new plant. The course was two hours each night for ten nights and was taught by a professor from Rhode Island School of Design.

He outlined four principles that I have employed in all my working years since, and I don't believe any principles I've ever heard make more sense. Also, I could see, after listening to him lecture, how I had made some of the mistakes I made in the area of personnel.

The first principle was "Get All The Facts." The professor

emphasized that he said to get *all* the facts, not just to get the facts. Never make judgments before having all the facts in hand. If you do, more than likely you'll have to change horses in midstream somewhere along the way.

After you get all the facts, then you should "Decide What You're Going To Do." This, too, must be well thought out. Hasty decisions can lead to grief. But weighing all the facts will help you make correct decisions.

The third principle is to "Take Action." Don't wait around and hope the problem will work itself out. If you have all the facts in hand, and you have decided what to do; do it.

Never stop there. Never let the initial action be your last act in solving a problem. "Follow Up To See If What You Did Was Right." That's the fourth principle. If you didn't do it right, then do it again and again until you get it right. Following this fourth principle will also help you not to make the same mistake twice.

Before I attended these lectures and established the four principles soundly in mind, I made some needless mistakes with personnel.

Early in my twelve years in Providence, I saw one of my young route salesmen coming in at two o'clock in the afternoon. He parked his truck and left it. Knowing that he couldn't be finished with his route, I approached him and in a rather gruff tone asked, "Sonny, what in hell are you doing here at two o'clock."

He looked at me sadly and said, "My father just died."

I felt like a fool. I had acted before getting any facts, let alone all of them.

Another incident occurred in New Haven. It began to snow one afternoon and I was out in town. I came upon one of our trucks parked on the side of the road with the route salesman putting chains on the truck. The snow had not yet created a hazard to driving.

I stopped to reprimand the salesman. "Get that truck on back to the shop," I told him. "The snow isn't deep enough yet for chains."

"City ordinance requires the chains when it begins to snow," he said. "I don't want to get a ticket."

I acted before I got all the facts.

After taking the course in Providence, I knew I should have asked the young man who came in early, "Sonny, are you all right?" and I should have asked the man in New Haven, "Do you really think you need chains?" Either question would have brought me the facts.

But I was young, in my twenties, and like so many others of that age, I was inclined to make snap judgments.

I learned not to judge by appearance, which is the inclination of a lot of young people placed in executive positions.

I once hired a good-looking young man. He appeared to be an extremely intelligent person, and when an opening came for a sales manager in a branch plant, I gave him the job. He needed a car, and since he didn't have one of his own, I bought him a new company car.

One morning he came in without his car, and when I asked where it was, he replied, "Somebody stole it."

I immediately put the police on the track of the stolen car, and they found the car wrapped around a tree. My sales manager had gotten drunk, wrecked the car, and lied about it.

The manager who does not have all the facts about his employees tends to make misjudgments. I had an assistant foreman in Providence who had a family. He was a hard-working man, and that was about all I knew about him. When we opened a small plant in New Bedford, I assigned him as superintendent of the plant. He did not object; though he did not appear to be too happy, even when I told him how much more money he would be making for his family.

Three months later, he got sick. I went to see him at his home and asked what was wrong with him.

"Mr. Rowland," he said, "I don't know why, but I just can't do that job you've given me. Please, if you can, put me back in Providence as assistant foreman."

I did, and he became better immediately and became the fine, competent worker he had always been. He did not know mathematics, and he could not schedule the production of people. He could never figure how to get so many ounces out of a gallon, and that was driving him crazy.

I quit making snap judgments and began to spend more time with my people to get to know them, to know their capabilities and limitations better, and I learned the rudiments of management.

The most important thing in advertising, which is a tremendous part of successful business, is judging people: judging what they will buy, or what will make them buy.

No one knows everything about advertising. Sometimes I think no one knows anything about it.

When radio was in its infancy and people were beginning to think it might be a tremendous advertising medium, the Coca-Cola Company was one of the first to use it for advertising. We sponsored a music program featuring Frank Black and his orchestra.

Frank Webber of D'Arcy Advertising Company visited me to discuss advertising and told me of having called on August Busch, the major domo of Anheuser Busch Brewing Company in Saint Louis, Missouri.

"Radio is becoming very popular, Mr. Busch," Webber told him. "We think you should begin advertising Budweiser on the radio."

"All right," Busch said. "What do you suggest?"

"We would suggest a nice music program."

"That sounds fine. When do you think it should be on the radio?"

"Sunday afternoon would be a good time," Webber said. "People are relaxed after Sunday dinner, and we believe great numbers of Americans will spend Sunday afternoons listening to music on the radio."

"What time on Sunday do you suggest?" Busch asked.

"Four o'clock would be a good time."

"Oh, no," Busch said, "not four o'clock. Everyone is still playing polo at that hour."

Maybe Busch's perspective was a bit narrow there, but his advertising agency's wasn't—and that is what makes advertising agencies worth their weight in gold to big business.

I learned a good lesson in advertising in 1936 when I managed the Providence plant. Felix Coste was vice president in charge of advertising for Coca-Cola. He called a special meeting of all New England bottlers that summer, and thirty-seven of us gathered in Springfield, Massachusetts, on the appointed day.

"Gentlemen," Coste said, "Coca-Cola is going to start a radio advertising program on our new six-bottle cartons. We're going to have a morning program and advertise to housewives." We had cartons for some time, metal cartons, but they had just been improved so they wouldn't chaff the bottles. In the new cartons, every bottle was in an individual compartment.

"I have called you gentlemen here," Coste said, "to ask your opinion on the kind of radio program we want to sponsor. I want you to listen to two thirty-minute transcriptions. One is a new program called 'Don McNeill and the Breakfast Club,' which has never been on the air. We think it's going to be a good one. The second one is Morton Downey singing."

He played the Breakfast Club transcription. McNeill was great, and he had a girl singer who was terrific. We really liked her. Then he played the Morton Downey program.

When he asked for a vote, one voted for Morton Downey, and the other thirty-six voted for Don McNeill.

"Gentlemen," Costa said, "you have confirmed what we thought. We're going to sponsor Morton Downey."

Being as outspoken as I was, I said, "Felix, what the hell do you mean? Thirty-six of us voted for Don McNeill and you're going to sponsor Morton Downey?"

"Yes," he said. "Don McNeill appeals to men, as you may have noticed by your vote. He had a girl singer and good music and you liked it."

"We certainly did."

His voice grew soft. "Morton Downey sings with balls in his throat," he said. "The housewives will love him."

Coca-Cola sponsored Morton Downey—and he sold the hell out of cartoned Cokes. Women loved him.

Big recordings called transcriptions were sent to the radio stations we sponsored the programs on. The transcriptions were recordings of his programs. In Providence we sponsored the program five mornings a week.

One day Downey's transcription didn't come in the mail, and the station had to use something else in that time slot. Our switchboard was flooded with so many calls we couldn't handle all of them. "Where's Morton?" "What happened to Morton?" "Why isn't Morton on?" "Have you taken Morton off?"

He was terrific. He sold millions of cartons of Coca-Cola.

I have always been a workaholic, and if I had sixty-five more years to devote to Coca-Cola, I'm sure I would be the same. That is my nature, but I don't recommend it for everyone else.

Mimi has always said that we have had a very full and eventful life. She had never tasted Coca-Cola until the day she met me. She said it was not exactly her cup of tea, but it was not long before it became her bread and butter.

It has been a real challenge for Mimi to live and work with me because of my work habits. A couple with more opposite ideas could not be found outside of Ripley's Believe-It-Or-Not, and that may be what made us click. Remember that the first law of physics is that "opposites attract."

Old Pig-Iron Bill Brownlee, who introduced us, said he had never seen two people with as determined and square jaws as we had.

But our life has been a real adventure. I wouldn't have traded with anyone, and I don't think Mimi would have, either.